T0211166

Expert Oracle Indexing and Access Paths

Maximum Performance for Your Database

Second Edition

Darl Kuhn
Sam R. Alapati
Bill Padfield

Apress®

Expert Oracle Indexing and Access Paths

Darl Kuhn
Morrison, Colorado, USA

Sam R. Alapati
Flower Mound, Texas, USA

Bill Padfield
Aurora, Colorado, USA

ISBN-13 (pbk): 978-1-4842-1983-6
DOI 10.1007/978-1-4842-1984-3

ISBN-13 (electronic): 978-1-4842-1984-3

Library of Congress Control Number: 2016953748

Managing Director: Welmoed Spahr
Lead Editor: Jonathan Gennick
Development Editor: Laura Berendson
Technical Reviewer: Michelle Malcher
Editorial Board: Steve Anglin, Pramila Balan, Laura Berendson, Aaron Black, Louise Corrigan,
    Jonathan Gennick, Robert Hutchinson, Celestin Suresh John, Nikhil Karkal, James Markham,
    Susan McDermott, Matthew Moodie, Natalie Pao, Gwenan Spearing
Coordinating Editor: Jill Balzano
Copy Editor: Kim Burton-Weisman
Compositor: SPi Global
Indexer: SPi Global
Artist: SPi Global

Distributed to the book trade worldwide by Springer Science+Business Media New York, 233 Spring Street, 6th Floor, New York, NY 10013. Phone 1-800-SPRINGER, fax (201) 348-4505, e-mail orders-ny@springer-sbm.com, or visit www.springer.com. Apress Media, LLC is a California LLC and the sole member (owner) is Springer Science + Business Media Finance Inc (SSBM Finance Inc). SSBM Finance Inc is a Delaware corporation.

For information on translations, please e-mail rights@apress.com, or visit www.apress.com.

Apress and friends of ED books may be purchased in bulk for academic, corporate, or promotional use. eBook versions and licenses are also available for most titles. For more information, reference our Special Bulk Sales–eBook Licensing web page at www.apress.com/bulk-sales.

Any source code or other supplementary material referenced by the author in this text is available to readers at www.apress.com. For detailed information about how to locate your book's source code, go to www.apress.com/source-code/.

Printed on acid-free paper

To Deni Luelle Rossiter Staheli, she inspired greatness

—Darl Kuhn

With love to Oyuna, Evan, and my family

—Bill Padfield

Contents at a Glance

Contents

About the Authors

Darl Kuhn is a DBA/developer working for Oracle. He also teaches Oracle classes at Regis University in Denver, Colorado. He is an active member of the Rocky Mountain Oracle Users Group. Darl enjoys sharing knowledge, which has led to several book projects over the years.

Sam R. Alapati is a principal administrator at Sabre Holding in Southlake, Texas. He has written several Oracle and WebLogic Server books. Sam is passionate about data and databases, and he enjoyed writing his part of this book.

Bill Padfield is an Oracle Certified Professional. He works for a large telecommunications company in Denver, Colorado, as a senior database administrator. Bill helps administer and manage a large data warehouse environment consisting of more than 90 databases. He has been an Oracle database administrator for more than 19 years and he has worked in the IT industry since 1985. Bill also teaches graduate database courses at Regis University.

About the Technical Reviewer

Michelle Malcher (@malcherm) is a well-known volunteer leader in security and database communities. She is currently on the board of directors for the FUEL Palo Alto Network User Group and has served on the board of directors for the Independent Oracle User Group (IOUG). As an Oracle ACE director, she has had the opportunity to present around the world at user group conferences. She continues to participate on the conference committee for the IOUG. Her technical expertise on topics from database to cybersecurity, as well as her senior-level contributions as a speaker and author, have aided many corporations across architecture and risk assessment, purchasing and installation, and ongoing systems oversight. These corporations include Wells Fargo & Company, where Michelle is currently team lead for Enterprise Database Security.

Acknowledgments

Thanks to Jonathan Gennick, Jill Balzano, and the Apress staff; it takes a quality team to produce a quality book. Thanks also to Michelle Malcher who made numerous suggestions and modifications to improve the quality of this book. Also thanks to the many people I've learned from over the years: Dave Jennings, Scott Schulze, Andy Brown, Mark Lutze, Nitin Mittal, Venkatesh Ranganathan, Valerie Eipper, Mike Tanaka, Simon Ip, Laurie Bourgeois, Scott Grover, John Finocchiaro, Kevin O'Grady, Jack Chung, Akshay Trivedi, Suresh Raju, Mosharof Hossain, Brent Davis, Evangelia "Valia" Antonatou, Peter Compel, Petr Fojtik, Tim Spangler, Jan Pewner, Michael Rohrbacher, Mingyan Fan, Ashwin Rao, Chandupavan Panditi, Naveen Shankaranarayana, Dustin Garvey, Sampanna Salunke, Rahul Khandelwal, Siraj Sherriff, Gaurav Mehta, Janet Bacon, Naomi Kuhn, Peter Schow, Todd Sherman, Patrick David, Carson Vowles, Aaron Isom, Tim Gorman, Tom Kyte, Jaden Jackson, Brad Stucki, Scott Lovell, Terri Cannon, and Jim Stark.

—Darl Kuhn

I wish to acknowledge the great help provided by Jill Balzano, the coordinating editor, in seeing this book through all the stages without a problem. I appreciate Jill's patience and good cheer, to say nothing about her efficiency in keeping track of all the changes in a book co-written by three authors.

As with all of my other books, I wish to thank the great help and support (and love) from my family: Valerie, Nina, and Nicholas, as well as Shannon, Keith, Shawn, and Dale. I wish to acknowledge the great debt to my other family as well: my mother, Swarna Kumari; my brothers, Hari and Siva Sankara Prasad; my sisters-in-law, Aruna and Vanaja; and my nieces and nephews, Ashwin, Teja, Appu, and Soumya.

—Sam R. Alapati

As always, thanks to Apress for the opportunity to contribute to their great library of publications. Thanks to Jonathan Gennick and Jill Balzano for their input, support, and patience. Thanks to my great co-authors, Darl and Sam.

Doing this helps me reflect on all the help I've had in my career. This includes, but is not limited to the following individuals. To some of my managers over the years—thanks to Bob Ranney, Beth Bowen, Larry Wyzgala, John Zlamal, Linda Scheldrup, Amy Neff, Maureen Frazzini, Billie Ortega, and Chad Bower. Thanks to my current team, which includes Dave Carter, Sandy Hass, Atul Shirke, Kevin Tomimatsu, John Townley, Paul Watkins, Sunkarsh Guduthur, Rajendra Mishra, Ulagammal Kaliyappan, and Gopinath Kanagal.

Over the years, I've learned an awful lot from countless people. Some of the people that have helped me along the way include Mark Nold, Mick McMahon, Sandra Montijo, Roby Sherman, Adric Norris, Brent Wagner, Tony Arlt, Jerry Sanderson, Mike Hammontre, Pat Cain, Gary Whiting, Ron Fullmer, Becky Enter, John Weber, Dianna Belangee, Randy Rezac, John Chatto, Pankaj Guleria, Avanish Gupta, Scott Bunker, Paul Mayes, Rick Barry, Sue Wagner, Glenn Balanoff, Linda Lee Burau, Deborah Lieou-McCall, Kristi Sargent, George Huner, Pad Kail, Curtis Gay, Ross Bartholomay, Carol Rosenow, Sheryl Gross, John Piel, Kim Lake, Rob Grote, Zane Warton, Pat Wuller, Wil Minor, Jim Barclay, Jason Hermstad, Shari Plantz-Masters, Denise Duncan, Bob Mason, Rob Coates, Debbie Chartier, Blair Christensen, Meera Ganesan, Kedar Panda, Kirsten Franz, Valarie Martinez, Mallick Robyeat, Liping Zhang, Satish Pasupathy, John Lungerhausen, Richard Rawles, Cindy Powell, Mary Ann Wooten, Deb Kingsley, Paula Obering, and Deb Sutton.

—Bill Padfield

CHAPTER 1

■ ■ ■

Introduction to Oracle Indexes

An index is a combination of a value and an associated location that allows you to quickly locate an object. If you think about it for a couple of seconds, you probably often use index structures to navigate throughout the day, such as:

- Browsing a catalog menu to efficiently find a desired item

- Accessing a bookmark to retrieve a web page

- Glancing at the calendar to determine a date

Similar to the way you use indexes in everyday life, a database index primarily exists to enable fast access to one or more rows of information stored in a database. In Oracle, an index stores a table column value along with the table row's physical address (ROWID). Each ROWID contains details on the location of a table row (e.g., the data file number, block number, and row location).

With the column value and ROWID stored in the index, Oracle can efficiently retrieve table data with a minimum of disk reads. In this way, indexes function like a shortcut to the table data.

■ **Note**　In addition to improving performance, Oracle uses indexes to help enforce enabled primary key and unique key constraints. Also, Oracle can better manage certain table-locking scenarios when indexes are placed on foreign key columns.

Although it's possible to build a database application devoid of indexes, without them you're almost guaranteeing poor performance. Indexes allow for excellent scalability, even with very large data sets. So if indexes are so important to database performance, why not place them on all tables and column combinations? The answer is short: indexes are not free. They consume disk space and system resources. As column values are modified, any corresponding indexes must also be updated. In this way, indexes use storage, I/O, CPU, and memory resources. A poor choice of indexes leads to wasted disk usage and excessive consumption of system resources. This results in a decrease in database performance.

For these reasons, when you design and build an Oracle database application, expert consideration must be given to your indexing strategy. As an application architect, you must understand the physical properties of an index, what types of indexes are available, and strategies for choosing which table and column combinations to index. A correct indexing methodology is central to achieving maximum performance for your database.

Electronic supplementary material　The online version of this chapter (doi:10.1007/978-1-4842-1984-3_1) contains supplementary material, which is available to authorized users.

This chapter introduces you to Oracle indexing concepts. It begins with a few to-the-point examples of implementing an index. Then it explains index types available within Oracle and provides guidelines and recommendations for choosing which columns to index. If you're new to indexes or require a refresher, start here.

Index Basics

Database indexes are typically created to facilitate better query performance. To understand how an index works, we're going to walk through the following basic scenarios:

- Performance without an index

- Implementing an index to improve performance

- Accessing only the index to return a query result set

- Demonstrating when an index is ignored

Let's first investigate how Oracle retrieves data when no index is in place.

Performance Without an Index

To set up this example, suppose you create a table to hold customer information, like so:

```
create table cust
(cust_id    number
,last_name  varchar2(30)
,first_name varchar2(30));
```

Your first customer is inserted into the database, as follows:

```
insert into cust (cust_id, last_name, first_name) values(1, 'STARK','JIM');
```

The performance of this query is initially very fast:

```
select cust_id, last_name, first_name
from cust
where last_name = 'STARK';
```

```
   CUST_ID LAST_NAME  FIRST_NAME
---------- ---------- ----------
         1 STARK      JIM
```

However, your business grows quickly; after a short time, thousands of customers are created. Let's simulate this growth by inserting thousands of random string values into the CUST table:

```
insert into cust
select level + 1
  ,dbms_random.string('U',dbms_random.value(3,15)) rand_last_name
  ,dbms_random.string('U',dbms_random.value(3,15)) rand_first_name
from dual
connect by level < 100000;
```

Here's a sample of what the data looks like in this table:

```
select * from cust;

  CUST_ID LAST_NAME             FIRST_NAME
---------- --------------------  -----------
        1 STARK                 JIM
        2 BAGAQWTD              WWQLVECQ
        3 FSNVCPCBH             STBXLV
... <lots of rows here>
   100000 DHFKB                 STNFDSI
```

Now you run daily reports against the CUST table and notice that performance has progressively decreased when issuing queries like the following:

```
select cust_id, last_name, first_name
from cust
where last_name = 'STARK';
```

When there was minimal data in the table, the prior query returned in subseconds. Now, with thousands of rows and growing, the prior query is taking longer and longer. What's going on here?

When a SQL SELECT statement executes, the Oracle query optimizer quickly calculates a step-by-step *execution plan* detailing how it will retrieve column values specified in the query. In calculating the plan, the optimizer determines which tables and indexes will be used to retrieve data.

When no index exists, the table itself is the only access path available to satisfy the results of the query. In this scenario, Oracle has no choice but to inspect every row within every used block in the table (this is known as a *full table scan*) to see if there are rows with the last name of STARK. As more data is inserted into this table, the query takes longer. The *cost* of this query (as a measure of CPU, memory, and I/O resources consumed) is proportional to the number of table blocks accessed.

When generating an execution plan, the query optimizer relies on table and index statistics to generate an optimal execution plan. *Statistics* in this sense means information about the table and associated indexes, such as number of rows, number of blocks, number of distinct values, and so on.

To illustrate an execution plan in action, first generate fresh statistics for the table:

```
exec dbms_stats.gather_table_stats( user, 'CUST' );
```

Next, generate an execution plan for the query:

```
explain plan for
select cust_id, last_name, first_name
from cust
where last_name = 'STARK';

select * from table(dbms_xplan.display(null,null,'BASIC +COST'));
```

The following execution plan output shows the cost associated with the full table scan of the table:

```
-------------------------------------------------
| Id  | Operation         | Name | Cost (%CPU)|
-------------------------------------------------
|   0 | SELECT STATEMENT  |      |    88   (2)|
|   1 |  TABLE ACCESS FULL| CUST |    88   (2)|
-------------------------------------------------
```

This process of Oracle performing a full table scan is shown in Figure 1-1. Keep in mind this depiction of using an index is at a high level and that Oracle is performing many more steps than what is shown in the diagram. Listed next is a description of the process steps:

1. The user submits a query.

2. The query is passed to an Oracle server process.

3. The optimizer is invoked. It creates an execution plan, which determines that a full table scan of the CUST table is required.

4. Since there is no index in place, every row of the table must be inspected to determine if it should be returned to the user, even though there is only one row in the table that will eventually be returned.

5. The table row is returned to the Oracle server process.

6. The Oracle server process returns the result set to the user.

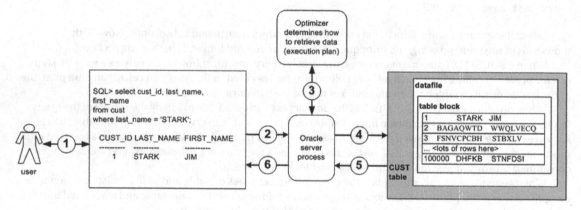

Figure 1-1. *Oracle inspects every row in table but only returns one row to user*

The only way to make this query run faster is to buy better hardware... or to use a performance-enhancing feature such as an index.

Implementing an Index to Improve Performance

You can peek ahead in this chapter to determine that an index on columns that appear in the WHERE clause of a SQL query might improve performance, and then decide to create an index on the CUST table's LAST_NAME column, like so:

```
create index cust_idx1
on cust(last_name);
```

The prior statement creates a B-tree index. This is the default index type in Oracle. After creating the index, let's now see what the execution plan looks like with the index in place:

```
explain plan for
select cust_id, last_name, first_name
from cust
where last_name = 'STARK';

select * from table(dbms_xplan.display(null,null,'BASIC +COST'));
```

Here is the corresponding execution plan output indicating that only the index is accessed first to determine which table ROWIDs should be used to look up data in the table:

```
--------------------------------------------------------------------
| Id  | Operation                          | Name     | Cost (%CPU)|
--------------------------------------------------------------------
|   0 | SELECT STATEMENT                   |          |    3   (0)|
|   1 |  TABLE ACCESS BY INDEX ROWID BATCHED| CUST     |    3   (0)|
|   2 |   INDEX RANGE SCAN                 | CUST_IDX1 |    1   (0)|
--------------------------------------------------------------------
```

Wow, notice that the cost of the query has dramatically dropped and that the newly created index is being used to assist in the retrieval of data.

To conceptualize how the index improves performance, recall that an index stores two types of information: the value of the table column(s) and the corresponding ROWID. The ROWID uniquely identifies a row (for heap-organized tables) within a database and contains its physical location (data file, block, and row position within the block). Once the index is created and subsequent queries execute, the query optimizer considers whether the index will reduce the amount of resources (cost) required to return the results of the query.

This process of Oracle using an index to retrieve data is depicted in Figure 1-2. Listed next is a description of the process steps:

1. The user submits a query.

2. The query is passed to an Oracle server process.

3. The optimizer is invoked. It creates an execution plan that includes accessing the index.

4. The index is accessed to retrieve the ROWID of the table row of interest.

5. Using the ROWID, the row is located within a data file and block.

6. The table row is returned to the Oracle server process.

7. The Oracle server process returns the result set to the user.

Keep in mind that as Oracle processes a query, there's a lot more that happens than is shown in Figure 1-2; but for a simple introduction to index usage, this diagram will suffice.

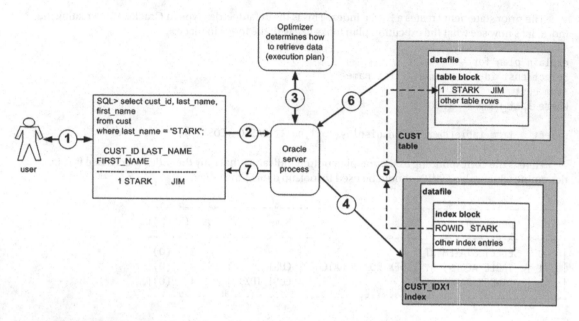

Figure 1-2. *Oracle using an index and a table to efficiently retrieve data*

In the prior example, suppose there are thousands of records in the CUST table but only one record in the table with the last name of STARK. The query optimizer can inspect the index, and within a few disk reads, locate the exact location (via the ROWID) of the one block and row that contains the record of interest. This results in very fast performance. In this case, it wouldn't matter if there were millions and millions more records in the table; as long as the value contained in the index is fairly unique, Oracle is able to return the required rows with a minimal amount of disk reads.

■ **Tip**   The higher the degree of uniqueness, the more efficient a B-tree index becomes. In database jargon, a very selective (unique) column value compared to the total number of rows in a table is said to have *high cardinality*. Conversely, *low cardinality* refers to few unique values compared to the total rows for the table.

Accessing Only the Index

In certain scenarios, Oracle can return a result set by accessing only an index without having to access the table that contains the data (this may sound counterintuitive at first). A simple example will illustrate this point. Suppose instead of selecting all column values out of the CUST table, you only select the LAST_NAME column.

```
select last_name
from cust
where last_name = 'STARK';
```

In this scenario, since the index contains all of the column values in the SELECT clause (LAST_NAME), Oracle is able to satisfy the results of the query by accessing only the index. Oracle doesn't have to read the table structure at all. When the SELECT clause columns are all contained with an index, this is known as a *covering index*. We'll next generate an execution plan for this scenario to drive home this point:

```
explain plan for
select last_name
from cust
where last_name = 'STARK';

select * from table(dbms_xplan.display(null,null,'BASIC +COST'));
```

Here is the corresponding execution plan output, which indicates that only the index is accessed to return the result set of the query:

```
----------------------------------------------------
| Id | Operation      | Name      | Cost (%CPU)|
----------------------------------------------------
|  0 | SELECT STATEMENT |          |    1   (0)|
|  1 |  INDEX RANGE SCAN| CUST_IDX1 |    1   (0)|
----------------------------------------------------
```

This process is shown in Figure 1-3. Keep in mind that this depiction of using an index is at a high level and that Oracle is performing many more steps than what is shown. Listed next is a description of the process steps:

1. The user submits a query.

2. The query is passed to an Oracle server process.

3. The optimizer is invoked. It creates an execution plan.

4. The index is accessed to retrieve the LAST_NAME column value.

5. The column value from the index is returned to the Oracle server process.

6. The Oracle server process returns the result set to the user.

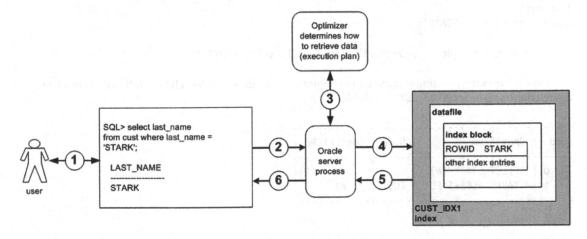

Figure 1-3. Oracle accessing only an index to satisfy the results of a query

Covering indexes are particularly efficient because only the index blocks need to be read. You can think of a covering index as a thinner version of its corresponding table. In this scenario, it's often faster to satisfy the results of the query using the relatively small index structure to retrieve the data (as opposed to using the larger table).

Oracle Ignoring an Index

Sometimes DBAs and developers wonder why the query optimizer sometimes chooses not to use an index. The short answer is that in some situations, using the index results in a higher cost than not using the index

A simple example will demonstrate this point. Consider if the value in the LAST_NAME column wasn't very unique. Suppose that thousands of records exist in the CUST table with the same value of STARK for the LAST_NAME. If the query optimizer did use the index, it would have to read from the index thousands of times, retrieve the ROWIDs, and then also read from the table thousands of times. In this situation, it's faster to bypass the index and instead scan every block in the table. For this reason, sometimes the optimizer calculates that the index isn't beneficial to performance and ignores it.

The following example shows the optimizer using a full table scan even though an index is available. First, the table is truncated and then it is populated with several thousand records with the same value for the LAST_NAME:

```
truncate table cust;

insert into cust
select level
  ,'STARK'
  ,'JIM'
from dual
connect by level <= 100000;
```

Next, statistics are generated and an execution plan is displayed:

```
exec dbms_stats.gather_table_stats( user, 'CUST' );

explain plan for
select cust_id, last_name, first_name
from cust
where last_name = 'STARK';

select * from table(dbms_xplan.display(null,null,'BASIC +COST'));
```

Here is the corresponding execution plan output showing the optimizer chose a full table scan, even though there's an index (CUST_IDX1) available:

```
---------------------------------------------------
| Id  | Operation         | Name | Cost (%CPU)|
---------------------------------------------------
|   0 | SELECT STATEMENT  |      |    87   (2)|
|   1 |  TABLE ACCESS FULL| CUST |    87   (2)|
---------------------------------------------------
```

This process is shown in Figure 1-4. Keep in mind that this depiction of using an index is at a high level and that Oracle is performing many more steps than what is shown. Listed next is a description of the process steps:

1. The user submits a query.

2. The query is passed to an Oracle server process.

3. The optimizer is invoked. It creates an execution plan.

4. A full table scan is performed on CUST table.

5. The table rows are returned to the Oracle server process.

6. The Oracle server process returns the result set to the user.

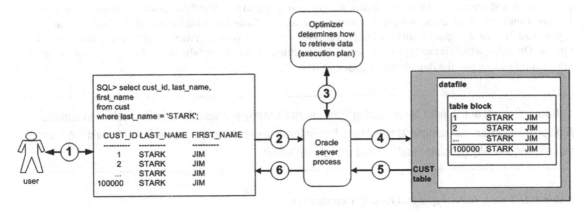

Figure 1-4. *Oracle performing a full table scan even when an index is available*

In this situation, the Oracle optimizer determined it was more cost effective to fully scan the table and not use an index.

Index Basics Wrap-up

Before reading on, let's review the concepts introduced up to this point in the chapter:

- Indexes are optional database objects defined on a table and one or more columns.

- Indexes are primarily used to improve query performance, but are also used to enforce primary/unique keys and help prevent certain table-locking scenarios.

- Indexes consume resources (disk, CPU, memory). Too many indexes on a table significantly slows down the performance of INSERT, UPDATE, and DELETE statements.

- The B-tree index is the default index type in Oracle.

- Without an index in place, Oracle must inspect every row in the table (full table scan) to determine if the row is a candidate to be returned to a query.

- A fairly unique column value compared to all other rows in a table (high cardinality) results in a very efficient B-tree index. In this situation, excellent performance is achieved even when tables contain millions of rows.

- In some situations, Oracle can retrieve data for a query by only accessing the index (covering index); the table doesn't have to be accessed.

- In some scenarios, the query optimizer chooses not to use an index. In other words, the query optimizer calculates that the cost of a full table scan is less than the cost when using an index.

An understanding of the prior index fundamentals provide a solid foundation for the rest of the concepts introduced in this chapter and book. Let's now turn our attention to determining which type of index to use.

Determining Which Type of Index to Use

Oracle provides a wide range of index types and features. The correct use of indexes results in a well-performing and scalable database application. Conversely, if you incorrectly or unwisely implement a feature, there may be detrimental performance implications. Table 1-1 summarizes the various Oracle index types available. At first glance, this is a long list and may be somewhat overwhelming to somebody new to Oracle. Deciding which index type to use isn't as daunting as it might initially seem. For most applications, you should simply use the default B-tree index type.

■ **Note**　Several of the index types listed in Table 1-1 are actually just variations on the basic B-tree index. A reverse key index, for example, is merely a B-tree index optimized for evenly spreading I/O when the index value is sequentially generated and inserted with similar values.

Table 1-1. *Oracle Index Types and Feature Descriptions*

Index Type	Usage
B-tree	Default, balanced tree index; good for high-cardinality (high degree of distinct values) columns. Use a normal B-tree index unless you have a concrete reason to use a different index type or feature.
Index-organized table (IOT)	Efficient when most of the column values are included in the primary key. You access the index as if it were a table. The data is stored in a B-tree-like structure.
Unique	A form of B-tree index used to enforce uniqueness in column values. Often used with primary key and unique key constraints, but can be created independently of constraints.
Reverse key	A form of B-tree index useful to balance I/O in an index that has many sequential inserts. It has the disadvantage of not being able to perform range scans.
Key compressed	Good for concatenated indexes where the leading column is often repeated; compresses leaf block entries. This feature applies to a B-tree or an IOT index.
Descending	A form of B-tree index used with indexes where corresponding column values are sorted in a descending order (the default order is ascending). You can't specify descending for a reverse key index. Oracle ignores descending if the index type is bitmap.
Bitmap	Excellent in data warehouse environments with low-cardinality columns and SQL statements using many AND or OR operators in the WHERE clause. Bitmap indexes aren't appropriate for online transaction processing (OLTP) databases where rows are frequently updated. You can't create a unique bitmap index.

(continued)

Table 1-1. (*continued*)

Index Type	Usage
Bitmap join	Useful in data warehouse environments for queries that utilize star schema structures that join fact and dimension tables.
Function-based	Good for columns that have SQL functions applied to them. This can be used with either a B-tree or a bitmap index.
Indexed virtual column	An index defined on a virtual column (of a table). Useful for columns that have SQL functions applied to them. A viable alternative to using a function-based index.
Virtual	Allows you to create an index with no physical segment or extents via the NOSEGMENT clause of CREATE INDEX. Useful in tuning SQL without consuming resources required to build the physical index. Any index type can be created as virtual.
Invisible	The index is not visible to the query optimizer. However, the structure of the index is maintained as table data is modified. Useful for testing an index before making it visible to the application. Any index type can be created as invisible.
Global partitioned	A global index across all partitions in a partitioned table or regular table. This can be a B-tree index type and can't be a bitmap index type.
Local partitioned	A local index based on individual partitions in a partitioned table. This can be either a B-tree or bitmap index type.
Domain	Specific for an application or cartridge.
B-tree cluster	Used with clustered tables.
Hash cluster	Used with hash clusters.

The B-tree index and other index types are briefly introduced in the following subsections. Where appropriate, we'll indicate where a particular index type is fully discussed in subsequent chapters in this book.

B-tree Indexes

We should point out that B-tree indexes are the entire focus of Chapter 2. We introduce them in this section so that you can compare them with other index types. As mentioned, the default index type in Oracle is a B-tree index. This index type is very efficient for high-cardinality column values. For most applications, this index type is appropriate.

Without specifying any options, a B-tree is created with the CREATE INDEX statement. All that you need to provide is the index name, table name, and column(s); for example:

```
create index cust_idx2 on cust(first_name);
```

Unless you have verifiable performance reasons to use a different index type, use a B-tree. Too often, DBAs or developers read about a new indexing feature and assume that the vendor's exaggeration of a feature matches the actual realized benefits. Always validate your reasons for choosing to implement a new index type or feature.

There are several subtypes of B-tree indexes.

- Index-organized table
- Unique
- Reverse key

- Key compressed

- Descending

These B-tree subtypes are briefly introduced in the next several subsections.

Index-Organized Table

An index-organized table (IOT) stores the entire contents of the table's row in a B-tree index structure. An IOT provides fast access for queries that have exact matches and/or range searches on the primary key.

Even though an IOT is implemented as a B-tree index structure, it is created via the CREATE TABLE... ORGANIZATION INDEX statement. Here is an example:

```
create table prod_sku
(prod_sku_id number
,sku         varchar2(256),
constraint prod_sku_pk primary key(prod_sku_id, sku)
) organization index;
```

■ **Note**   See Chapter 4 for implementation details regarding an index-organized table.

Unique Indexes

When creating a B-tree index, you can define it to be a unique index. In this regard, it acts like a unique key constraint. When inserting into the corresponding table, the unique index guarantees that any non-null values inserted into the table are distinct. For this reason, unique indexes are commonly used in conjunction with primary key and unique key constraints (see Chapter 2 for complete details).

A unique index is specified via the CREATE UNIQUE INDEX statement, like so:

```
create unique index cust_uidx1
on cust(last_name, first_name);
```

■ **Note**   See Chapter 2 for a complete discussion on the advantages and disadvantages of creating a unique index vs. allowing Oracle to automatically create the index when defining a primary key or unique key constraint.

Reverse Key Indexes

Reverse key indexes are useful to balance I/O in an index that has many sequential inserts in a table with a column managed by a sequence. These indexes perform better in scenarios where you need a way to evenly distribute index data that would otherwise have similar values clustered together. Thus, when using a reverse key index, you avoid having I/O concentrated in one physical disk location within the index during large inserts of sequential values. This type of index is discussed further in Chapter 5.

A reverse key index is specified with the REVERSE clause, like so:

```
create index cust_ridx1
on cust(cust_id) reverse;
```

Reverse key indexes may be appropriate in Real Application Clusters (RAC) environments where the ID column is populated from a sequence. In RAC environments, performance can suffer if each instance is using sequence numbers close in value while doing inserts. This results in contention as each instance attempts to access the same blocks. Specifying a reverse key index spreads out the IO and reduces contention for the same blocks. The disadvantage of reverse key indexes is that it can't be used for range scans.

Key Compressed Indexes

A key compressed index is useful in reducing the storage and I/O requirements of concatenated indexes where the leading column is often repeated. Use the COMPRESS N clause to create a compressed index, as shown here:

```
create index cust_cidx_1
on cust(last_name, first_name) compress 2;
```

■ **Note**   You can't create a key compressed index on a bitmap index.

Descending Indexes

By default, Oracle stores B-tree indexes in ascending order. For example, if you have an index on a column with a number data type, the smallest numbers appear first in the index (the leftmost leaf node) and the highest numbers are stored in the rightmost leaf nodes.

You can instruct Oracle to reverse this order to descending by specifying the DESC keyword with a column. This creates a descending index, as shown in the following:

```
create index cust_didx1
on cust(cust_id desc);
```

Descending indexes are useful for queries that sort some columns in ascending order and other columns in descending order.

Specialized Index Types

Sometimes a B-tree index isn't enough to provide the desired performance improvement. The following are indexes that should be used under specialized circumstances:

- Bitmap
- Bitmap join
- Function-based

- Indexed virtual column

- Virtual

- Invisible

- Global partitioned

- Local partitioned

- Domain

- B-tree cluster

- Hash cluster

Each of these types of indexes is briefly introduced in the following subsections. Many of these index types are discussed in full detail later in this book.

Bitmap Index

Bitmap indexes are commonly used in data warehouse environments. These indexes are recommended for columns with a relatively low number of distinct values (low cardinality). Bitmap indexes are also efficient for SQL statements that use multiple AND or OR join operators in the WHERE clause (which is typical in a data warehouse environment).

You should not use bitmap indexes in OLTP databases with high INSERT/UPDATE/DELETE activities. This is because the structure of the bitmap index results in many locked rows during singular DML operations (which results in locking problems for high-transaction OLTP systems).

A bitmap index is created using the BITMAP keyword. For completeness, the following shows the table creation script upon which the bitmap index is built.

```
create table f_sales(
 sales_amt number
,d_date_id number
,d_product_id number
,d_customer_id number);

create bitmap index f_sales_fk1
on f_sales(d_date_id);
```

■ **Note**   Bitmap indexes and bitmap join indexes are available only with the Oracle Enterprise Edition of the database.

Bitmap Join

A bitmap join index stores the results of a join between two tables in an index. These indexes are beneficial because they avoid joining tables to retrieve results. Bitmap join indexes are appropriate in situations where you're joining two tables using the foreign key column(s) in one table that relate to primary key column(s) in another table.

Bitmap join indexes are usually suitable for data warehouse environments that have tables periodically batch loaded but then are not updated. When updating tables that have bitmap join indexes, this potentially results in several rows being locked. Therefore, this type of index is not suitable for an OLTP database. A bitmap join index is specified with the BITMAP keyword and a join condition must be provided. The following is an example (for completeness, we also show the join table creation statement):

```
create table d_customers
(d_customer_id number primary key
,cust_name varchar2(30));

create bitmap index f_sales_bmj_idx1
on f_sales(d_customers.cust_name)
from f_sales, d_customers
where f_sales.d_customer_id = d_customers.d_customer_id;
```

■ **Note** Bitmap and bitmap join indexes are the focus of Chapter 3.

Function-Based Indexes

Function-based indexes are created with SQL functions or expressions in their definitions. Function-based indexes allow index lookups on columns referenced by SQL functions in the WHERE clause of a query. Here's an example of creating a function-based index:

```
create index cust_fidx1
on cust(upper(last_name));
```

These types of indexes are necessary because Oracle won't use a normal B-tree index when a query references a column with a SQL function applied to it.

■ **Note** Function-based indexes can be either B-tree, unique, or bitmap.

Indexed Virtual Column

An alternative to a function-based index is to add a virtual column to a table and then create an index on that virtual column. You'll have to test and determine whether a function-based index or an index on a virtual column better suits your performance requirements.

Listed next is a brief example. Suppose that you have an INV table created with a virtual column, like so:

```
create table inv(
 inv_id number
,inv_count number
,inv_status generated always as (
  case when inv_count <= 100 then 'GETTING LOW'
       when inv_count > 100 then 'OKAY'
  end)
);
```

Now you can create a regular index on the virtual column, as follows:

```
create index inv_idx1
on inv(inv_status);
```

■ **Note**   Virtual columns are only available in Oracle Database 11*g* and higher.

Virtual Index

You can instruct Oracle to create an index that will never be used and won't have any extents allocated to it via the NOSEGMENT clause, as follows:

```
create index cust_idx1
on cust(first_name) nosegment;
```

Even though this index is not physically instantiated, you can instruct Oracle to determine if the index might be used by the optimizer via the _USE_NOSEGMENT_INDEXES initialization parameter; for example:

```
SQL> alter session set "_use_nosegment_indexes"=true;
```

When would this be useful? Let's suppose you have a very large index that you want to create without allocating space. To determine if the index would be used by the optimizer, you can create an index with NOSEGMENT, which allows you to test that scenario. If you determine that the index would be useful, you can drop the index and re-create it without the NOSEGMENT clause.

Invisible Index

An invisible index means that the optimizer doesn't use the index when retrieving data for a query. However, the index structure is still maintained as the underlying table has records inserted, updated, or deleted. This feature is used when you want to test the viability of an index without impacting existing application code. Use the INVISIBLE keyword to create an invisible index.

```
create index cust_iidx1
on cust(last_name) invisible;
```

■ **Note**   Invisible indexes are only available in Oracle Database 11g and higher.

Global and Local Partitioned Indexes

A partitioned index is one where you have one logical index, but physically the index is implemented in several different segments. This allows for good performance even with very large databases. A partitioned index can be either global or local.

■ **Note** Partitioning is an extra-cost option available only with the Oracle Enterprise Edition of the database.

A global partitioned index is an index that uses a partitioning strategy that is not mapped to the underlying table's segments. You can build a global partitioned index on a regular table or a partitioned table. Global partitioned indexes are implemented as type B-tree and can be defined as unique. Use the GLOBAL PARTITION clause to create an index that is globally partitioned. This example creates a global partitioned index by a range:

```
create index f_sales_gidx1 on f_sales(sales_amt)
global partition by range(sales_amt)
(partition pg1 values less than (25)
,partition pg2 values less than (50)
,partition pg3 values less than (maxvalue));
```

A local partitioned index must be built on a partitioned table. This index type follows the same partitioning strategy as its underlying table. A given partition of a local partitioned index only contains values from its corresponding partition of the table. A local partitioned index can be either B-tree or bitmap. Use the LOCAL keyword to create this type of index. For completeness, the following is the creation of a partitioned table upon which the local partitioned index is built:

```
create table f_sales(
 sales_amt number
,d_date_id number
,d_product_id number
,d_customer_id number)
partition by range(sales_amt)(
 partition p1 values less than (100)
,partition p2 values less than (1000)
,partition p3 values less than (maxvalue));

create index f_sales_idx2
on f_sales(d_date_id, sales_amt) local;
```

■ **Note** Partitioned indexes are the focus of Chapter 6.

Domain, B-tree Cluster, and Hash Cluster Indexes

An application domain index is custom to a specific application. This accommodates indexes on custom data types, documents, images, video, and spatial data.

A B-tree cluster index is an index defined on a cluster table key. The B-tree cluster index associates a cluster key with a database block address. This index type is used with table clusters. A hash cluster is similarly used with cluster tables; the difference is that a hash cluster uses a hash function instead of the index key.

■ **Note**   Domain indexes, B-tree cluster indexes, and hash clusters are not covered extensively in this book. If you need more information regarding these index types, see Oracle's SQL Reference Guide at `http://otn.oracle.com`.

Determining Which Columns to Index

Now let's turn our attention to figuring out which columns should be indexed. For starters, we recommend that, for most applications, you create indexes in the following situations:

- *Define a primary key constraint for each table.* This results in an index automatically being created on the columns specified in the primary key.

- *Create unique key constraints on columns that are required to be unique and are different from the primary key columns.* Each unique key constraint results in an index automatically being created on the columns specified in the constraint.

- *Manually create indexes on foreign key columns.* This is done for better performance and to avoid certain locking issues (see Chapter 2 for complete details).

Each of these bulleted items is detailed in the following subsections.

■ **Tip**   See Chapter 9 for obtaining indexing advice from the SQL Tuning Advisor.

Indexes on Primary Key and Unique Key Columns

In most situations, you should create a primary key constraint for every table. If there is not already an index defined on the primary key columns, then Oracle automatically creates a B-tree index for you.

Similarly, for any unique key constraints you define on a table, if there is not already an index defined on the unique key columns, Oracle creates an appropriate B-tree index. Here's a simple example:

```
create table cust
(cust_id    number primary key
,last_name  varchar2(30)
,first_name varchar2(30)
,ssn        varchar2(16) unique);
```

Chapter 2 provides complete details on primary key and unique key constraints, and explains how they relate to indexes.

Indexes on Foreign Key Columns

Oracle doesn't automatically create indexes on foreign key columns. Oftentimes, it is desirable to create B-tree indexes on foreign key columns. One reason is that foreign key columns are often referenced in WHERE clauses and therefore performance can be improved with these queries.

Another reason to index foreign keys is to reduce table-locking issues. Namely, if no index exists on the foreign key column, when deleting from a child table, the parent table becomes locked. This unnecessarily locks rows and reduces concurrency.

Here's a simple example of creating a table that has a foreign key and then manually creating an index:

```
create table address
(address_id number primary key
,cust_id number references cust(cust_id)
,address varchar2(1000)
);

create index address_fk1 on address(cust_id);
```

Other Suitable Columns

When choosing an index, keep in mind this basic rule: the indexing strategy should be based on the columns that you use when querying the table. You can create more than one index on a table and have an index contain multiple columns. You will make better decisions if you first consider what types of queries you execute on a table. If you've identified a poorly performing SQL query, also consider creating indexes for the following columns:

- Create indexes on columns used often as predicates in the WHERE clause; when multiple columns from a table are used in the WHERE clause, consider using a concatenated (multicolumn) index.

- Create a covering index on columns used in the SELECT clause.

- Consider creating indexes on columns used in the ORDER BY, GROUP BY, UNION, or DISTINCT clauses.

Oracle allows you to create an index that contains more than one column. Multicolumn indexes are known as *concatenated indexes* (sometimes referred to as *composite indexes*). These indexes are especially effective when you often use multiple columns in the WHERE clause when accessing a table. Concatenated indexes are oftentimes more efficient in this situation than creating separate single-column indexes.

Columns included in the SELECT and WHERE clauses are also potential candidates for indexes. Recall that a covering index is one that includes all columns returned by the query. In this situation, Oracle can use the index structure itself (and not the table) to satisfy the results of the query. Also, if the column values are selective enough, Oracle can use an index on columns referenced in the WHERE clause to improve query performance.

Also consider creating indexes on columns used in the ORDER BY, GROUP BY, UNION, or DISTINCT clauses. This may result in more efficient queries that frequently use these SQL constructs.

It's okay to have multiple indexes per table. However, the more indexes you place on a table, the slower DML statements will run (as Oracle has more and more indexes to maintain when the table column values change). Don't fall into the trap of randomly adding indexes to a table until you stumble upon the right combination of indexed columns. Rather, verify the performance of an index before you create it in a production environment. (See Chapter 7 for details on validating performance benefits.)

> ■ **Note**   Oracle allows a column to appear in multiple indexes on the same table. A footnote to this: prior to 12*c*, Oracle did not allow multiple indexes in one table on the exact same combination of columns. Starting with 12*c*, you can define multiple indexes on the same set of columns. However, you can only do this if the indexes are physically different; for example, when one index is created as a B-tree index, and the second index as a bitmap index. Additionally, there can be only one visible index for the same combination of columns on a table.

Indexing Guidelines

Oracle indexes provide efficient access to large data sets. Deciding on using an index involves determining whether the improvement in performance SELECT statements is worth the cost of space consumed, and overhead when the table is updated. Table 1-2 summarizes the guidelines for efficiently using indexes.

Table 1-2. *Guidelines for Creating Indexes*

Guideline	Reasoning
Create as many indexes as you need, but try to keep the number to a minimum. Add indexes judiciously. Test first to determine quantifiable performance gains.	Indexes increase performance, but also consume disk space and processing resources. Don't add indexes unnecessarily.
The required performance of queries you execute against a table should form the basis of your indexing strategy.	Indexing columns used in SQL queries helps performance the most.
Consider using the SQL Tuning Advisor for indexing recommendations.	These tools provide recommendations and a second set of eyes on your indexing decisions.
Create primary key constraints for all tables.	This automatically creates a B-tree index (if the columns in the primary key aren't already indexed).
Create unique key constraints where appropriate.	This automatically creates a B-tree index (if the columns in the unique key aren't already indexed).
Create indexes on foreign key columns.	Foreign key columns are usually included in the WHERE clause when joining tables, and thus improve performance of SQL SELECT statements. Creating a B-tree index on foreign key columns also reduces locking issues when updating/deleting from parent tables.
Carefully select and test indexes on small tables (small being less than a few thousand rows).	Even on small tables, indexes can sometimes perform better than full table scans.
Use the correct type of index.	Correct index usage maximizes performance.
Use the basic B-tree index type if you don't have a verifiable performance gain from using a different index type.	B-tree indexes are suitable for most applications where you have high-cardinality column values.

(continued)

Table 1-2. (continued)

Guideline	Reasoning
Consider using bitmap indexes in data warehouse environments.	These indexes are ideal for low-cardinality columns where the values aren't updated often. Bitmap indexes work well on foreign key columns on star schema fact tables where you often run queries that use AND and OR join conditions.
Consider using a separate tablespace for indexes (separate from tables).	Table and index data may have different storage and/ or backup and recovery requirements. Using separate tablespaces lets you manage indexes separately from tables. If you don't have these types of requirements, it's fine to place tables and indexes in the same tablespace.
Let the index inherit its storage properties from the tablespace.	This makes it easier to manage and maintain index storage.
Use consistent naming standards.	This makes maintenance and troubleshooting easier.
Don't rebuild indexes unless you have a solid reason to do so.	Rebuilding indexes is generally unnecessary unless an index is corrupt or you want to move an index to different tablespace.
Monitor your indexes. Drop indexes that aren't used.	Doing this frees up physical space and improves the performance of data manipulation language (DML) statements.
Before dropping an index, consider marking it as unusable or invisible.	This allows you to better determine if there are any performance issues before you drop the index. These options let you rebuild or re-enable the index without requiring the data definition language (DDL) creation statement.

Refer to these guidelines as you create and manage indexes in your databases. These recommendations are intended to help you correctly use index technology.

Summary

Indexes exist primarily to increase query performance, so it's critical that you think carefully about how to implement indexes. A well-planned indexing strategy results in a well-performing database application. Conversely, a careless plan results in poor performance.

Indexes consume disk space and are stored separately from tables. However, indexes are defined on a table and one or more columns; in this sense, an index can't exist without the table.

Oracle provides a wide number of indexing types and features. In most situations, the default B-tree index is appropriate. Before using other index types, make sure that you understand the performance benefits. You should be aware of the indexing features that Oracle provides and under what circumstances you should employ specialized index types.

We recommend that you place indexes on primary key, unique key, and foreign key columns. This is a good starting point. Furthermore, analyze slowly performing SQL statements to see which columns are used. This will provide you additional candidate columns for indexing. These indexing recommendations lay the foundation for maximizing SQL query performance.

CHAPTER 2

■ ■ ■

B-tree Indexes

The B-tree index is the default index type in Oracle. This index type is known as *B-tree* because the table row identifier (ROWID) and associated column values are stored within index blocks in a *balanced* tree-like structure. Oracle B-tree indexes are used for the following reasons:

- Improving SQL statement performance

- Enforcing uniqueness of primary key and unique key constraints

- Reducing potential locking issues with parent and child table tables associated via primary and foreign key constraints

If a table column value (or combination of columns) is fairly unique within all rows in a table, then creating a B-tree index usually results in faster query performance. Additional performance improvements are realized when the index structure itself contains the required table column values to satisfy the result of the query. In this situation, the table data blocks need not be accessed. Understanding these concepts help you determine which columns to index and whether a concatenated index might be more efficient for certain queries but less optimal for others.

Also keep in mind that there is some overhead associated with indexes. When an index exists on a table, any subsequent update, insert, or delete requires that associated indexes also be modified. This consumes I/O, CPU, and memory. Too many indexes on a table can significantly slow down the performance of INSERT, UPDATE, and DELETE statements. Therefore, you should carefully consider the indexes that you choose to create on a table.

B-tree indexes also play a pivotal role in application design because these indexes are closely associated with certain types of constraints. Namely, Oracle uses B-tree indexes to enforce primary key and unique key constraints. In most scenarios, B-tree indexes are automatically created for you when implementing primary key and unique key constraints.

Indexes are often manually created to match foreign key constraint columns to improve the performance of queries that join tables on primary key and foreign key columns. Also, in certain circumstances, the lack of a B-tree index on a foreign key column(s) can cause locking problems.

This chapter begins with describing how Oracle uses B-tree indexes. It then covers typical strategies for implementing and managing B-tree indexes. Next, the role B-tree indexes have in relation to primary, unique, and foreign key constraints are explained. The last portion of the chapter covers a few indexing features available since Oracle Database 12*c*.

© Darl Kuhn, Sam R. Alapati and Bill Padfield 2016
D. Kuhn et al., *Expert Oracle Indexing and Access Paths*, DOI 10.1007/978-1-4842-1984-3_2

Understanding How Oracle Uses B-tree Indexes

This section helps you understand how Oracle uses B-tree indexes. The goal is to help you fully comprehend B-tree index internals to enable intelligent indexing decisions when building database applications. An example with a good diagram helps illustrate the mechanics of a B-tree index. Even if you've been working with B-tree indexes for quite a while, this example may illuminate the technical aspects of using an index. To get started, suppose you have a table created as follows:

```
create table cust(
 cust_id number
,last_name varchar2(30)
,first_name varchar2(30));
```

You also anticipate that queries will frequently execute against the table using the LAST_NAME column. Therefore, you create a B-tree index as follows:

```
create index cust_idx1
on cust(last_name);
```

Next, some seed data is inserted into the table:

```
insert into cust (cust_id, last_name, first_name) values(1,  'STARK','JIM');
insert into cust (cust_id, last_name, first_name) values(2,  'GREY','BOB');
insert into cust (cust_id, last_name, first_name) values(3,  'KHAN','BRAD');
insert into cust (cust_id, last_name, first_name) values(4,  'ACER','SCOTT');
insert into cust (cust_id, last_name, first_name) values(5,  'DOSS','JOE');
insert into cust (cust_id, last_name, first_name) values(6,  'WYNN','SUE');
insert into cust (cust_id, last_name, first_name) values(7,  'FIX', 'MAY');
insert into cust (cust_id, last_name, first_name) values(8,  'MOSS','BETH');
-- Insert some random data here
insert into cust
select level + 16
  ,dbms_random.string('U',dbms_random.value(3,15)) rand_last_name
  ,dbms_random.string('U',dbms_random.value(3,15)) rand_first_name
from dual
connect by level <= 100000;
--
insert into cust (cust_id, last_name, first_name) values(9,  'QUIN','JAY');
insert into cust (cust_id, last_name, first_name) values(10, 'POPE','TODD');
insert into cust (cust_id, last_name, first_name) values(11, 'XUI', 'ANN');
insert into cust (cust_id, last_name, first_name) values(12, 'ACER','SID');
insert into cust (cust_id, last_name, first_name) values(13, 'TAFT','HAL');
insert into cust (cust_id, last_name, first_name) values(14, 'ZIMM','KATE');
insert into cust (cust_id, last_name, first_name) values(15, 'LEE', 'KIM');
insert into cust (cust_id, last_name, first_name) values(16, 'OLDS','JEFF');
```

As rows are inserted into the table, Oracle allocates extents that consist of physical database blocks. Oracle also allocates blocks for the index. For each record inserted into the table, Oracle creates an entry in the index that consists of the ROWID and column value (the value in LAST_NAME in this example). The ROWID for each index entry points to the data file and block in which the table column value is stored.

Recall that the Oracle query optimizer relies on good statistics to generate efficient execution plans. Therefore, before proceeding with this example, let's first ensure that there are good statistics available for the optimizer:

```
exec dbms_stats.gather_table_stats( user, 'CUST' );
```

Recall that the ROWID contains the physical location of the row on disk. The ROWID identifies the data file, block, and row number of the row. You can view the ROWID information via the following query:

```
select
  cust_id, last_name, first_name,
  dbms_rowid.rowid_to_absolute_fno(rowid, user, 'CUST') absolute_fno,
  dbms_rowid.rowid_block_number(rowid) blocknumber,
  dbms_rowid.rowid_row_number(rowid) rownumber
from cust
where cust_id <= 16
order by cust_id;
```

Here is some sample output for this example:

CUST_ID	LAST_NAME	FIRST_NAME	ABSOLUTE_FNO	BLOCKNUMBER	ROWNUMBER
1	STARK	JIM	9	1421	0
2	GREY	BOB	9	1421	1
3	KHAN	BRAD	9	1421	2
4	ACER	SCOTT	9	1421	3
5	DOSS	JOE	9	1421	4
6	WYNN	SUE	9	1421	5
7	FIX	MAY	9	1421	6
8	MOSS	BETH	9	1421	7
9	QUIN	JAY	9	2117	255
10	POPE	TODD	9	2117	256
11	XUI	ANN	9	2117	257
12	ACER	SID	9	2117	258
13	TAFT	HAL	9	2117	259
14	ZIMM	KATE	9	2117	260
15	LEE	KIM	9	2117	261
16	OLDS	JEFF	9	2117	262

Figure 2-1 is a graphical representation of how data is stored in the table and the corresponding B-tree index.

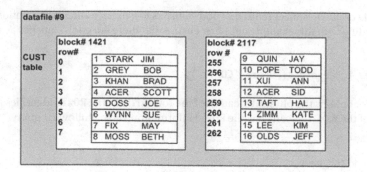

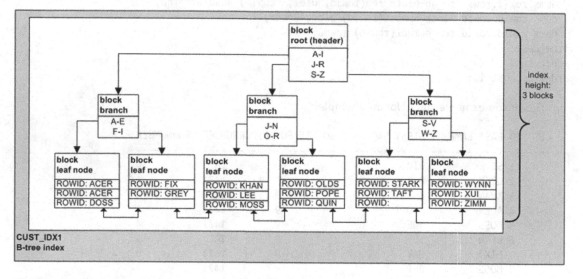

Figure 2-1. *Physical layout of a table and B-tree index*

The lowest blocks in Figure 2-1 are called *leaf nodes* (or *leaf blocks*). These blocks contain the ROWID and column values. The middle level blocks in Figure 2-1 are known as *branch blocks*. The branch blocks are used for navigation within the index structure. For example, if you wanted to find the value of ACER, you would start at the top root node, then navigate to the branch block that contains a pointer to leaf node blocks with values A-I, and then navigate to the leaf block containing the ROWIDs and values.

Notice that the leaf nodes in the B-tree index structure are implemented internally as a doubly linked list (indicated with double-headed arrows at the bottom of the diagram). The linked list allows indexes to efficiently provide the results of queries that have ranges in the WHERE clause, such as:

```
where last name < 'F'
```

This makes it possible for range scanning through the leaf nodes without having to traverse up and down through branch blocks (known as an *index range scan*).

One aspect of the B-tree structure is that the leaf nodes should all appear at the same *height*. The height of an index is defined as the number of blocks it takes to travel from the root to a leaf node. Typically, B-tree indexes have a height of two or three, even for indexes on tables with millions of rows. This means that it only takes two or three I/O operations to find a key value.

You can display the height of a B-tree index in two different ways. One way is to analyze an index and then query the INDEX_STATS view, as follows:

```
analyze index cust_idx1 validate structure;
```

Now you can select from INDEX_STATS to view the height of the index:

```
select name, height from index_stats;

NAME                 HEIGHT
-------------        ----------
CUST_IDX1                 3
```

The other way to determine the height of an index is to examine the BLEVEL column of USER_INDEXES. The branch level doesn't include the root node, so the height of the index is BLEVEL plus one, for example:

```
select blevel from user_indexes where index_name='CUST_IDX1';

    BLEVEL
----------
         2
```

Now with this understanding of a B-tree index structure, consider the following query:

```
select cust_id, last_name, first_name from cust where last_name='ACER';


  CUST_ID LAST_NAME    FIRST_NAME
---------- ------------ ------------
        4 ACER         SCOTT
       12 ACER         SID
```

Figure 2-2 depicts how Oracle first retrieves the ROWID from the index and then accesses the table by ROWID. Here's roughly what happens:

1. The index root node is accessed and points to a branch node.

2. The index branch node is accessed and points to leaf nodes.

3. The ROWID is read from the index leaf node.

4. The table is accessed by ROWID.

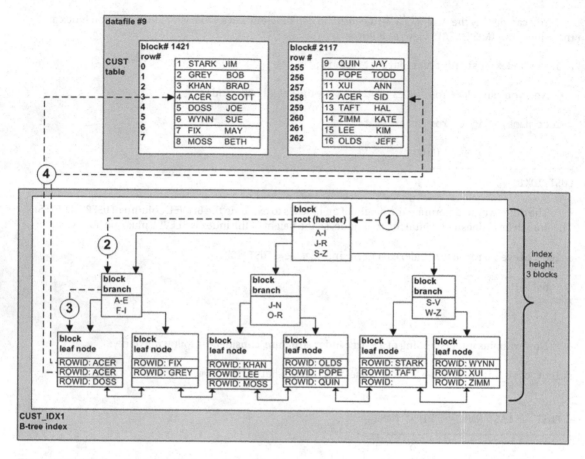

Figure 2-2. *Oracle using an index to retrieve table data*

You can also visualize the use of an index this by enabling tracing and rerunning the query:

```
set autotrace on;
select cust_id, last_name, first_name from cust where last_name='ACER';
set autotrace off;
```

Here is a partial snippet of the output:

```
---------------------------------------------------------------------------------
| Id  | Operation                            | Name      | Rows  | Bytes | Cost (%CPU)| Time     |
|
---------------------------------------------------------------------------------
|   0 | SELECT STATEMENT                     |           |     1 |    18 |3    (0)| 00:00:01 |
|   1 |   TABLE ACCESS BY INDEX ROWID BATCHED| CUST      |     1 |    18 |3    (0)| 00:00:01 |
|*  2 |    INDEX RANGE SCAN                  | CUST_IDX1 |     1 |       |1    (0)| 00:00:01 |
---------------------------------------------------------------------------------
```

```
...

Statistics
----------------------------------------------------------------
          0  recursive calls
          0  db block gets
          5  consistent gets
          0  physical reads
          0  redo size
        766  bytes sent via SQL*Net to client
        551  bytes received via SQL*Net from client
          2  SQL*Net roundtrips to/from client
          0  sorts (memory)
          0  sorts (disk)
          2  rows processed
```

The consistent gets value indicates there were five read operations from memory (db block gets plus consistent gets equals the total read operations from memory). That's about the number of reads you would expect because there are three index blocks that are read and two table blocks that are also accessed to retrieve the data.

Keep in mind that the consistent gets output in Autotrace isn't always a 100% accurate; rather, it's a close estimate. The main point here is that through using an index, a very small number of read operations are required to retrieve the data (even in this example, where the table has more than 100,000 records).

Prepping for B-tree Indexes

Before creating a B-tree index, it's prudent to make a few architectural decisions that will impact maintainability and availability. The following are manageability features that you should consider before building indexes:

- Estimate the size of the index before creating it.

- Consider designating a tablespace just for indexes (separate from tables). This allows you to more easily manage indexes separately from tables for tasks such as backup and recovery.

- Allow objects to inherit storage parameters from their tablespace.

- Define naming standards to be used when creating indexes.

- For partitioned tables, determine local and global indexing strategies.

These decision points are detailed in the following subsections.

Estimating the Size of an Index Before Creation

Before creating an index on a large table, you may want to estimate the space that it will consume (and the time that it takes). The best way to predict the size of an index is to create it in a test environment that has a representative set of production data. If you can't build a complete replica of production data, a subset of data can often be used to extrapolate the size required in production. If you don't have the luxury of using a copy of production data, you can also estimate the size of an index by using the DBMS_SPACE.CREATE_INDEX_COST procedure. For example, this code estimates the size of creating an index on the FIRST_NAME column of the CUST table:

```
set serverout on
exec dbms_stats.gather_table_stats(user,'CUST');
variable used_bytes number
variable alloc_bytes number
exec dbms_space.create_index_cost( 'create index cust_idx2 on cust(first_name)', -
                :used_bytes, :alloc_bytes );
print :used_bytes
print :alloc_bytes
```

Here is some sample output for this example:

```
USED_BYTES
----------
   1000160

ALLOC_BYTES
-----------
   3284992
```

The used_bytes variable gives you an estimate of how much room is required for the index data. The alloc_bytes variable provides an estimate of how much space is allocated within the tablespace.

Next, go ahead and create the index.

```
create index cust_idx2 on cust(first_name);
```

The actual amount of space consumed is shown by this query:

```
select bytes from user_segments where segment_name='CUST_IDX2';
```

The output indicates that the estimated amount of allocated bytes is in the ballpark of the amount of space actually consumed.

```
     BYTES
----------
   3538944
```

Your results may vary depending on the number of records, the number of columns, the datatypes, and the accuracy of statistics.

In addition to the initial sizing, keep in mind that the index will grow as records are inserted into the table. You'll have to monitor the space consumed by the index and ensure that there's enough disk space to accommodate future growth requirements.

Creating Separate Tablespaces for Indexes

For critical applications, you must give some thought to how much space tables and indexes consume and how fast they grow. Space consumption and object growth has a direct impact on database availability. If you run out of space, your database will become unavailable. The best way to manage this is by creating tablespaces tailored to space requirements and by explicitly creating objects naming the tablespaces. With that in mind, consider creating separate tablespaces for tables and indexes for the following reasons:

- It allows differing backup and recovery requirements. You may want the flexibility of backing up the indexes at a different frequency than the tables. Or you may choose not to back up indexes because you know that you can re-create them.

- If you let the table or index inherit its storage characteristics from the tablespace, when using separate tablespaces, you can tailor storage attributes for objects created within the tablespace. Tables and indexes may have different storage requirements (such as extent size, logging, and so on).

- When running maintenance reports, it's sometimes easier to manage tables and indexes when the reports have sections separated by tablespace.

If these reasons are valid for your environment, it's probably worth the extra effort to employ different tablespaces for tables and indexes. If you don't have any of the prior needs, then it's fine to put tables and indexes together in the same tablespace.

We should point out that DBAs sometimes consider placing indexes in a separate tablespace for performance reasons. If you have the luxury of setting up a storage system from scratch and can set up mount points that have their own sets of disks and controllers, you may see some I/O benefits by separating tables and indexes into different tablespaces. Nowadays, storage administrators often give you a large slice of storage in a SAN, and there's no way to guarantee that data and indexes will be stored physically on separate disks (and controllers). Thus you typically don't gain any performance benefits by separating tables and indexes into different tablespaces. In other words, the benefit isn't caused by having separate tablespaces but by achieving evenly distributed I/O across all available devices.

■ **Note** Oracle's Automatic Storage Management (ASM) solution provides striping across disks and rebalancing to remove I/O hotspots.

The following code shows an example of building separate tablespaces for tables and indexes:

```
create tablespace reporting_data
  datafile '/u01/dbfile/O1212/reporting_data01.dbf' size 1G;
--
create tablespace reporting_index
  datafile '/u01/dbfile/O1212/reporting_index01.dbf' size 1G;
```

After the tablespaces are created, you can then specify the appropriate tablespace; for instance:

```
create table cust(
 cust_id number
,last_name varchar2(30)
,first_name varchar2(30))
tablespace reporting_data;

create index cust_idx1
on cust(last_name)
tablespace reporting_index;
```

Inheriting Storage Parameters from the Tablespace

When creating a table or an index, there are a few tablespace-related technical details to be aware of. For example, if you don't specify storage parameters when creating tables and indexes, then the table and index inherit storage parameters from the tablespace. This is the desired behavior in most circumstances. This saves you from having to manually specify these parameters. If you need to create an object with different storage parameters from its tablespace, then you can do so within the CREATE TABLE/INDEX statement.

Also, keep in mind that if you don't explicitly specify a tablespace, by default, tables and indexes are created in the default tablespace for the user. This is acceptable for development and test environments. For production environments, you should consider explicitly naming tablespaces in the CREATE TABLE/INDEX statements.

Naming Standards

When you're creating and managing indexes, it's highly desirable to develop some standards regarding naming. Consider the following motives:

- Diagnosing issues is simplified when error messages contain information that indicates the table, index type, and so on.

- Reports that display index information are more easily grouped and more readable, and it's easier to spot patterns and issues.

Given these needs, here are some sample index-naming guidelines:

- Primary key index names should contain the table name and a suffix, such as _PK.

- Unique key index names should contain the table name and a suffix, such as _UKN, where N is a number.

- Indexes on foreign key columns should contain the foreign key table and a suffix, such as _FKN, where N is a number.

- For indexes that aren't used for constraints, use the table name and a suffix, such as _IDXN, where N is a number.

- Function-based index names should contain the table name and a suffix, such as _FCN, where N is a number.

Some shops use prefixes when naming indexes. For example, a primary key index would be named PK_CUST (instead of CUST_PK).

■ **Tip** Our personal preference is to use a suffix for index naming standards. The advantage of using a suffix is that when querying the data dictionary, you can quickly view all indexes for each table, instead of grouping by a prefix such as PK. Having said that, all of these various naming standards are valid. It usually doesn't matter what the standard is, just as long as everybody follows the same standard.

Implementing B-tree Indexes

This section describes the typical tasks that you encounter when working with B-tree indexes, including the following:

- Creating indexes

- Reporting on indexes

- Displaying code required to re-create an index

- Dropping indexes

These tasks are detailed in the following subsections.

Creating a B-tree Index

Listed next is a sample script that creates a table and its associated indexes in separate tablespaces. The tables and indexes inherit their storage attributes from the tablespace; this is because no storage parameters are specified in either the CREATE TABLE or CREATE INDEX statements.

```
CREATE TABLE cust(
 cust_id    NUMBER
,last_name  VARCHAR2(30)
,first_name VARCHAR2(30))
TABLESPACE reporting_data;
--
ALTER TABLE cust ADD CONSTRAINT cust_pk PRIMARY KEY (cust_id)
USING INDEX TABLESPACE reporting_index;
--
ALTER TABLE cust ADD CONSTRAINT cust_uk1 UNIQUE (last_name, first_name)  ·
USING INDEX TABLESPACE reporting_index;
--
CREATE TABLE address(
 address_id NUMBER
,cust_id    NUMBER
,street     VARCHAR2(30)
,city       VARCHAR2(30)
,state      VARCHAR2(30))
TABLESPACE reporting_data;
--
ALTER TABLE address ADD CONSTRAINT addr_fk1
FOREIGN KEY (cust_id) REFERENCES cust(cust_id);
--
CREATE INDEX addr_fk1 ON address(cust_id)
TABLESPACE reporting_index;
```

33

In this script, two tables are created. The parent table is CUST and its primary key is CUST_ID. The child table is ADDRESS and its primary key is ADDRESS_ID. The CUST_ID column exists in ADDRESS as a foreign key mapping back to the CUST_ID column in the CUST table.

Three B-tree indexes are also created; one is automatically created when the primary key constraint is created. A second index is automatically created when the unique constraint is created. A third index is explicitly created in the ADDRESS table on the CUST_ID foreign key column. All three indexes are created in the REPORTING_INDEX tablespace, whereas the tables are created in the REPORTING_DATA tablespace.

Reporting on Indexes

The index creation details for the example in the prior section can be verified by querying the data dictionary.

```
select index_name, index_type, table_name, tablespace_name, status
from user_indexes
where table_name in ('CUST','ADDRESS');
```

Here is some sample output:

INDEX_NAME	INDEX_TYPE	TABLE_NAME	TABLESPACE_NAME	STATUS
CUST_PK	NORMAL	CUST	REPORTING_INDEX	VALID
CUST_UK1	NORMAL	CUST	REPORTING_INDEX	VALID
ADDR_FK1	NORMAL	ADDRESS	REPORTING_INDEX	VALID

Run the following query to verify the columns on which the indexes are created:

```
select index_name, column_name, column_position
from user_ind_columns
where table_name in ('CUST','ADDRESS')
order by index_name, column_position;
```

Here is some sample output:

INDEX_NAME	COLUMN_NAME	COLUMN_POSITION
ADDR_FK1	CUST_ID	1
CUST_PK	CUST_ID	1
CUST_UK1	LAST_NAME	1
CUST_UK1	FIRST_NAME	2

To display the number of extents and space used, run the following query:

```
select a.segment_name, a.segment_type, a.extents, a.bytes
from user_segments a, user_indexes  b
where a.segment_name = b.index_name
and   b.table_name in ('CUST','ADDRESS');
```

Depending on the version of Oracle that you're using, the prior query may return no rows:

```
no rows selected
```

For example, starting with Oracle Database 11g Release 2, when you create a table, the creation of the associated segment (and extents) is deferred until the first row is inserted into the table. This means that any associated indexes also don't have segments created until rows are inserted into the related tables. To illustrate this, let's insert one row into the CUST table and one in the ADDRESS table, like so:

```
insert into cust values(1,'STARK','JIM');
insert into address values(100,1,'Vacuum Ave','Portland','OR');
```

Rerunning this query (that reports on segment usage) yields the following output:

```
SEGMENT_NAME      SEGMENT_TYPE          EXTENTS     BYTES
---------------   -------------------   ---------   ---------
CUST_UK1          INDEX                         1   65536
CUST_PK           INDEX                         1   65536
ADDR_FK1          INDEX                         1   65536
```

Displaying Index Code

From time to time, you'll need to drop an index. This could be because of an obsolete application or you've established that an index is no longer used. Prior to dropping an index, we recommend that you generate the data definition language (DDL) that would be required to re-create the index. This allows you to re-create the index (as it was before it was dropped) in the event that dropping the index has a detrimental impact on performance and needs to be re-created.

Use the DBMS_METADATA.GET_DDL function to display an object's DDL. Make sure that you set the LONG variable to an appropriate value so that the returned CLOB value is displayed in its entirety. Here's an example:

```
set long 1000000
select dbms_metadata.get_ddl('INDEX','ADDR_FK1') from dual;
```

Here is the output:

```
DBMS_METADATA.GET_DDL('INDEX','ADDR_FK1')
--------------------------------------------------------------------------------

  CREATE INDEX "MV_MAINT"."ADDR_FK1" ON "MV_MAINT"."ADDRESS" ("CUST_ID")
  PCTFREE 10 INITRANS 2 MAXTRANS 255 COMPUTE STATISTICS
  STORAGE(INITIAL 65536 NEXT 1048576 MINEXTENTS 1 MAXEXTENTS 2147483645
  PCTINCREASE 0 FREELISTS 1 FREELIST GROUPS 1
  BUFFER_POOL DEFAULT FLASH_CACHE DEFAULT CELL_FLASH_CACHE DEFAULT)
  TABLESPACE "REPORTING_INDEX"
```

This code shows all the aspects of the index that are required to re-create it. Many of these values reflect default settings or storage parameters that were inherited from the index tablespace.

If you want to display all index metadata for the currently connected user, run the following code:

```
select dbms_metadata.get_ddl('INDEX', index_name) from user_indexes;
```

If the currently connected user has many indexes, this query will produce a great deal of output.

Dropping a B-tree Index

If you determine that you aren't using an index anymore, then it should be dropped. Before you drop an index, take the necessary precautions to ensure that there won't be an adverse impact on performance. Also, large indexes require a great deal of system resources and time to rebuild. Therefore, you should ensure that the index isn't used before dropping. If possible, the best way to determine adverse performance implications is by dropping an index in a test environment that reflects the production environment (in terms of hardware, data, load, and so on). If it's not possible to thoroughly test, then consider doing one of the following before dropping:

- Enable monitoring for the index.

- Make the index invisible.

- Make the index unusable.

The idea is to try to determine that the index is not used for any purpose before actually dropping it (see Chapter 7 for details on monitoring an index). Monitoring an index gives you an idea if the application is using it for SELECT statements. Index monitoring does not tell you if the index is used for other internal purposes, like enforcing a constraint or preventing locking issues.

An invisible index is an index that exists but is not visible to the query optimizer. Keep in mind that an invisible index is still maintained by Oracle as a DML on the table occurs and it may still be used internally by Oracle to prevent locking issues or to enforce constraints. Therefore, making an index invisible isn't a completely reliable way to determine if it's used. Here's an example of making an index invisible:

```
alter index addr_fk1 invisible;
```

This code makes the index invisible to the query optimizer so that it can't be used to retrieve rows for a query. However, the index structure is still maintained by Oracle as records are modified in the table. If you determine that the index was critical for performance, you can easily make it visible to the optimizer again, like this:

```
alter index addr_fk1 visible;
```

Your other option before dropping an index is to make it unusable, as follows:

```
alter index addr_fk1 unusable;
```

This code renders the index unusable, but doesn't drop it. Unusable means that the optimizer won't use the index and Oracle won't maintain the index as DML statements operate on its table. Furthermore, an unusable index can't be used internally to enforce constraints or to prevent locking issues.

If you need to re-enable an unusable index, then you'll have to rebuild it. Be aware that rebuilding a large index can take a considerable amount of time and resources.

```
alter index addr_fk1 rebuild;
```

After you're sure that an index isn't required, use the DROP INDEX statement to remove it. This permanently drops the index. The only way to get the index back is to re-create it.

```
drop index addr_fk1;
```

Managing B-tree Indexes with Constraints

B-tree indexes and primary key and unique key constraints are inseparable. This is because Oracle uses these indexes to enforce primary key and unique key constraints. You can't have an enabled primary key or unique key constraint without an associated B-tree index.

When you create a primary key or unique key constraint, you have the option of having Oracle automatically create the corresponding index. In this scenario, if you drop or disable the constraint, Oracle also automatically drops the corresponding index.

You can also create the index separately from the constraint. When you create the index and constraint separately, this allows you to drop or disable the constraint without automatically dropping the corresponding index. If you work with large tables/indexes, you may want the flexibility of disabling a constraint without dropping the corresponding index.

Oracle doesn't automatically create an index when a foreign key constraint is defined, so you must manually create an index on columns associated with a foreign key constraint. In most scenarios, it's beneficial to create a B-tree index on foreign key columns because it helps prevent locking issues and assists with the performance of queries that join parent/child tables via the primary key and foreign key columns.

■ **Note**   Sometimes people confuse the terms *indexes* and *keys*. An *index* is the underlying physical object created in the database. Oracle uses indexes to enforce primary key and unique key constraints. The *key* (constraint) is the business rule being enforced.

Creating B-tree Index on Primary Key Columns

A *primary key constraint* guarantees that values in a column (or combination of columns) can be used to always uniquely identify a record within a table. There can be only one primary key constraint per table. A primary key constraint can't contain null values. You can think of a primary key constraint as a combination of unique and not null constraints. There are several good reasons to create a primary key index for each table.

- It enforces the business requirement that the primary key columns must be unique within a table. Yes, in some cases you may have a table (like a logging table) where you don't need a primary key, but for most situations, a primary key is required for each table.

- Many of the columns in the primary key are frequently used within the WHERE clause of queries accessing the application. An index on these columns improves the query performance.

- Oracle won't allow you to create foreign key constraints on a child table unless a primary key or unique key constraint has been defined for the parent table. Therefore, if you require foreign key constraints, you must use primary key or unique key constraints.

Oracle requires a corresponding index for any enabled primary key. There are several techniques for creating a primary key constraint and its corresponding index.

- First, create the table. Then, in a separate ALTER TABLE statement, add the primary key constraint. The ALTER TABLE statement creates both the primary key constraint and an index.

- Specify the primary key constraint inline (with the column) or out-of-line in a CREATE TABLE statement.

37

- Create the table, use a `CREATE INDEX` statement to create an index that contains the primary key columns, and then use `ALTER TABLE...ADD CONSTRAINT` to add the primary key constraint.

Examples of each of these techniques are shown in the following subsections.

Use ALTER TABLE to Create a Primary Key Constraint and Index

In our opinion, the technique shown next is the most preferable method for creating a primary key constraint and the associated index. This approach allows you to manage the table creation separate from the constraint and index definition. When you work with applications that contain thousands of tables, constraints, and indexes, it's often easier to manage and diagnose installation issues when you separate the creation of tables from corresponding constraints and indexes. This isn't a written-in-stone guideline; rather, it's a preference that has evolved from troubleshooting problems.

In this example, the primary key constraint is created separately from the table creation. First, the table is created without any constraint definitions.

```
create table cust(
 cust_id      number
,first_name  varchar2(200)
,last_name   varchar2(200));
```

Now a primary key constraint is added.

```
ALTER TABLE cust ADD CONSTRAINT cust_pk PRIMARY KEY (cust_id);
```

If you want to specify which tablespace the index is placed in, then you can do so as follows:

```
ALTER TABLE cust ADD CONSTRAINT cust_pk PRIMARY KEY (cust_id)
USING INDEX TABLESPACE reporting_index;
```

In this code example, the `ALTER TABLE...ADD CONSTRAINT` statement creates both a primary key constraint and a unique index. Both the constraint and index are named `CUST_PK`.

Use CREATE TABLE to Create a Primary Key Constraint and Index

Another common way to create a primary key constraint and index is with the `CREATE TABLE` statement. You can directly specify a constraint inline (with the column). The advantage of this approach is that it's very simple. If you're experimenting in a development or test environment, this approach is quick and effective. One downside to this approach is that it doesn't allow for a primary key to be defined on multiple columns. Here's an example:

```
create table cust(
 cust_id      number          primary key
,first_name  varchar2(30)
,last_name   varchar2(30));
```

In this code, Oracle creates both a primary key constraint and a corresponding unique index. Oracle automatically generates a random name like `SYS_C123456` (both the constraint and index are given the same name).

If you want to explicitly provide a name (for the constraint and index), you can do so as follows:

```
create table cust(
 cust_id       number           constraint cust_pk primary key
,first_name  varchar2(30)
,last_name   varchar2(30));
```

You can also specify the placement of the tablespace for the index, as shown:

```
create table cust(
 cust_id       number constraint cust_pk primary key
                    using index tablespace reporting_index
,first_name  varchar2(30)
,last_name   varchar2(30));
```

You can define the primary key constraint out-of-line (from the column) within the CREATE TABLE statement. Here's an example of defining a primary key constraint out-of-line:

```
create table cust(
 cust_id number
,first_name  varchar2(30)
,last_name   varchar2(30)
,constraint cust_pk primary key (cust_id)
using index tablespace reporting_index);
```

This technique is called *out-of-line* because the constraint declaration is separated (by a comma) from the column definition. The out-of-line approach has one advantage over the inline approach in that you can specify multiple columns for the primary key.

Create a B-tree Index and Primary Key Constraint Separately

You have the option of first creating an index and then altering the table to apply the primary key constraint. For completeness of this example, the CREATE TABLE statement is shown.

```
create table cust(
 cust_id number
,first_name  varchar2(30)
,last_name   varchar2(30));
```

```
create unique index cust_pk
on cust(cust_id);
```

```
alter table cust
add constraint cust_pk
primary key (cust_id);
```

The advantage to this approach is that you can drop or disable the primary key constraint independently of the index. Sometimes in large database environments, you may want to drop or disable constraints while loading data for performance reasons. You may need the flexibility of being able to drop the constraint but not the index. In large database environments, re-creating an index can take a long time and consume considerable system resources.

Another slight twist to this scenario is that it is possible to create an index with columns defined differently than the primary key constraint. Here is an example:

```
create index cust_pk
on cust(cust_id, first_name, last_name);

alter table cust
add constraint cust_pk
primary key (cust_id);
```

We're not recommending that you create primary key indexes with different columns than the constraint; rather we're pointing out that it's possible. In the prior code, only the CUST_ID column is unique, whereas the other columns are non-unique. The application using this table may assume that all columns are unique because they are present in the index. This will most likely cause confusion.

Viewing Primary Key Constraint and Index Details

You can confirm the details of the index as follows:

```
select index_name, index_type, uniqueness
from user_indexes
where table_name = 'CUST';
```

Here is the output for this example:

```
INDEX_NAME           INDEX_TYPE       UNIQUENES
-------------------- ---------------- ---------
CUST_PK              NORMAL           UNIQUE
```

Here is a query to verify the constraint information:

```
select constraint_name, constraint_type
from user_constraints
where table_name = 'CUST';
```

Here is the corresponding output:

```
CONSTRAINT_NAME      CONSTRAINT_TYPE
-------------------- ---------------
CUST_PK              P
```

Dropping the Primary Key Constraint and Index

An index that was automatically created (when the primary key constraint was created) can't be directly dropped. In this scenario, if you attempt to drop the following index:

```
drop index cust_pk;
```

You'll receive this error:

```
ORA-02429: cannot drop index used for enforcement of unique/primary key
```

To remove the index, you must do so by dropping or disabling the primary key constraint. For example, any of the following statements would drop an index that was automatically created when the constraint was created:

```
alter table cust disable constraint cust_pk;
alter table cust drop constraint cust_pk;
alter table cust drop primary key;
```

When you drop or disable a primary key constraint, you have the option of not dropping the associated index. Use the KEEP INDEX clause of the DROP/DISABLE CONSTRAINT clause to retain the index, as shown in this example:

```
alter table cust drop constraint cust_pk keep index;
```

This code instructs Oracle to drop the constraint but keep the index. If you're working with large tables, you may want to disable or drop the constraint for performance reasons while loading or manipulating the data. Dropping the index associated with a large table may take considerable time and resources to recreate.

One other aspect to be aware of is that if a primary key or unique key is referenced by an enabled foreign key, and you attempt to drop the constraint on the parent table, as follows:

```
alter table cust drop primary key;
```

You'll receive this error:

```
ORA-02273: this unique/primary key is referenced by some foreign keys
```

In this situation, you need to first drop or disable the referenced foreign key or use the CASCADE clause to automatically drop the foreign key constraint when the primary key constraint is dropped or disabled. For example, any of the following removes the constraint:

```
alter table cust drop constraint cust_pk cascade;
alter table cust disable constraint cust_pk cascade;
alter table cust drop primary key cascade;
```

■ **Note** Cascading the dropping of constraints only drops any dependent foreign key constraints. It doesn't delete any data from children tables.

Creating a B-tree Index on Unique Key Columns

The main purpose of a unique key constraint is to enforce uniqueness on columns that aren't part of the primary key. If there is a business requirement that non-primary key columns be unique within a table, then a unique key constraint should be used. For example, you may have a primary key defined on CUST_ID in the customer table, but may also require a unique key constraint on a combination of the LAST_NAME and FIRST_NAME columns.

■ **Note** Unique keys differ from primary keys in two ways. First, a unique key can contain NULL values. Second, there can be more than one unique key defined per table (whereas there can only be one primary key defined per table).

If you have a requirement for a unique constraint on a column, you can implement this requirement in several different ways.

- Use the ALTER TABLE statement to create a unique constraint. This automatically creates a unique B-tree index.

- Use the CREATE TABLE statement to create a unique constraint. This automatically creates a unique B-tree index.

- Create a B-tree index and constraint separately. Use this approach if you want to manage the index and constraint separately when disabling or dropping the constraint.

- Create a unique B-tree index only. Don't bother with a unique key constraint. Use this approach if the columns within the index won't ever be referenced by a child table foreign key.

These topics are discussed in detail in the following subsections.

Use the ALTER TABLE to Create a Unique Constraint and Index

This approach is our preferred method for enabling unique key constraints and creating the corresponding index. As mentioned with primary key constraints and indexes, it's often easier to troubleshoot installation issues when the table creation statement is separated from the constraint and index creation.

The following example demonstrates how to create a table and then add a unique key constraint on non-primary key columns. For example, suppose you have a CUST table created, as follows:

```
create table cust(
 cust_id     number
,first_name  varchar2(30)
,last_name   varchar2(30));
```

Next, use the ALTER TABLE statement to create a unique constraint named CUST_UX1 on the combination of the LAST_NAME and FIRST_NAME columns of the CUST table.

```
alter table cust add constraint cust_uk1 unique (last_name, first_name);
```

The prior statement creates the unique constraint. Additionally, Oracle automatically creates an associated index with the same name.

If you want to include the tablespace as part of the command, do so as follows:

```
alter table cust add constraint cust_uk1 unique (last_name, first_name)
using index tablespace reporting_index;
```

Use CREATE TABLE to Create a Unique Constraint and Index

The advantage of using the CREATE TABLE approach is that it's simple and encapsulates the constraint and index creation within one statement. When you define a unique constraint within the CREATE TABLE statement, it can be either inline or out-of-line.

This first example shows how to create a unique key constraint and index on a column inline. Since an inline unique key constraint can be defined on only one column, we've added an SSN column that has a unique key constraint defined on it inline.

```
create table cust(
 cust_id      number constraint cust_pk primary key
,first_name   varchar2(30)
,last_name    varchar2(30)
,ssn          varchar2(15) constraint cust_uk1 unique);
```

Here's the same code as the prior script, except this adds the code to separate the index and tablespaces into different tablespaces:

```
create table cust(
 cust_id      number constraint cust_pk primary key
              using index tablespace reporting_index
,first_name   varchar2(30)
,last_name    varchar2(30)
,ssn          varchar2(15) constraint cust_uk1 unique
              using index tablespace reporting_index
)
tablespace reporting_data;
```

This next example creates a unique constraint using the out-of-line technique on the combination of the FIRST_NAME and LAST_NAME columns:

```
create table cust(
 cust_id      number constraint cust_pk primary key
,first_name   varchar2(30)
,last_name    varchar2(30)
,ssn          varchar2(15)
,constraint cust_uk1 unique (first_name, last_name));
```

Here's the same code as the prior script, except this includes the lines to separate the index and tablespaces into different tablespaces:

```
create table cust(
 cust_id       number constraint cust_pk primary key
               using index tablespace reporting_index
,first_name   varchar2(30)
,last_name    varchar2(30)
,ssn          varchar2(15)
,constraint cust_uk1 unique (first_name, last_name)
               using index tablespace reporting_index)
tablespace reporting_data;
```

The out-of-line definition has the advantage of allowing you to create a unique key constraint on multiple columns.

Create a B-tree Index and Unique Key Constraint Separately

If you need to manage the index and constraint separately, then first create the index and then the constraint, as shown in this example:

```
create unique index cust_uk1 on cust(first_name, last_name) tablespace reporting_index;
alter table cust add constraint cust_uk1 unique(first_name, last_name);
```

The advantage of creating the index separate from the constraint is that you can drop or disable the constraint without dropping the underlying index. When working with big data, you may want to consider this approach. If you need to disable the constraint for any reason and then re-enable it later, you can do so without dropping the index (which may take a long time for large indexes).

Creating Only a Unique Index

You can create a unique index without adding the unique constraint. If you never plan on referencing a unique key from a foreign key, then it's okay to only create a unique index without defining the unique constraint. Here's an example of creating a unique index without an associated constraint:

```
create unique index cust_uk1 on cust(first_name, last_name);
```

When you explicitly create only a unique index (as in the prior statement), Oracle creates a unique index but doesn't add an entry for a constraint in DBA/ALL/USER_CONSTRAINTS. Why does this matter? Consider this scenario:

```
insert into cust values (1, 'JAMES', 'STARK');
insert into cust values (2, 'JAMES', 'STARK');
```

Here's the corresponding error message that is thrown:

```
ORA-00001: unique constraint (MV_MAINT.CUST_UK1) violated
```

If you're asked to troubleshoot this issue, the first place to look is in USER_CONSTRAINTS for a constraint named in the error message. However, there is no information.

```
select
  constraint_name
from user_constraints
where constraint_name='CUST_UK1';
```

```
no rows selected
```

The "no rows selected" message can be confusing: the error message thrown when you insert into the table indicates that a unique constraint has been violated, yet there is no information in the constraint-related data dictionary views. In this situation, you have to look at DBA_INDEXES to view the details of the unique index that has been created. Here's an example:

```
select index_name, uniqueness
from user_indexes where index_name='CUST_UK1';
```

Here's some sample output:

```
INDEX_NAME            UNIQUENES
-------------------- ----------
CUST_UK1              UNIQUE
```

If you want to be able to use the constraint related data dictionary views to report on unique key constraints, you should also define a constraint.

When creating a unique index, if the table contains duplicate values on the unique columns, then you'll receive the following error:

```
ORA-01452: cannot CREATE UNIQUE INDEX; duplicate keys found
```

In this situation, you need to remove the duplicate values before creating the unique index. Here's a simple script to identify duplicate records (based on the FIRST_NAME and LAST_NAME columns):

```
select first_name, last_name
from cust
group by first_name, last_name
having count(*) > 1;
```

To remove the duplicate records, you can use a script such as the following:

```
delete from cust a
where a.rowid <
(select max(b.rowid)
 from cust b
 where a.first_name = b.first_name
 and   a.last_name  = b.last_name);
```

The prior script leaves one record in the table for any records that contain duplicates of the FIRST_NAME and LAST_NAME columns.

Dropping a Unique Key Constraint and Index

If an index was automatically created when the unique key constraint was created, then you can't directly drop the index. In this scenario, you must drop or disable the unique key constraint and the associated index is automatically dropped, as follows:

```
alter table cust drop constraint cust_uk1;
```

This line drops both constraint and the index. If you want to keep the index, then specify the KEEP INDEX clause, like so:

```
alter table cust drop constraint cust_uk1 keep index;
```

If you created the index and unique key constraint separately, or if there is no unique key constraint associated with a unique index, then you can directly drop the index.

Indexing Foreign Key Columns

Foreign key constraints ensure that when inserting into a child table, a corresponding parent table record exists. This is the mechanism to guarantee that data conforms to parent/child business relationship rules. Foreign keys are also referred to as *referential integrity constraints*.

Unlike primary key and unique key constraints, Oracle doesn't automatically create indexes on foreign key columns. Therefore, you must manually create a foreign key index based on the columns defined as the foreign key constraint. In most scenarios, you should create indexes on columns associated with a foreign key. Here are two good reasons:

- Oracle can often make use of an index on foreign key columns to improve the performance of queries that join a parent table and a child table (using the foreign key columns).

- If no B-tree index exists on the foreign key columns, deleting from the child table, the parent table will be locked. Without an index on the foreign key column(s), Oracle places a lock on the parent table. This means that no modifications are allowed on the parent table until the transaction commits.

Let's first discuss an example that demonstrates the unnecessary locking. Next, let's go over creating a B-tree index on a foreign key column. Then, let's look at some techniques for detecting unindexed foreign key columns.

Unnecessary Locking

This section provides a simple example that demonstrates the locking issue when foreign key columns are not indexed. First, create two tables, associate them with a foreign key constraint, and insert some data:

```
create table parent (pid int primary key);
create table child (cid references parent);
--
insert into parent values (1);
insert into parent values (2);
insert into parent values (3);
--
insert into child values (2);
insert into child values (3);
commit;
```

Now open two terminal sessions. From one, delete a record from the child table (don't commit).

```
delete from child where cid = 2;
```

Now from a different terminal session, attempt to delete from the parent table some data not impacted by the child table delete.

```
delete from parent where pid = 1;
```

The delete from the parent table hangs until the child table transaction is committed. Without a regular B-tree index on the foreign key column in the child table, the parent table is locked and no deletes are allowed.

Now run the prior experiment; except this time, also create an index on the foreign key column of the child table.

```
create index child_fk on child(cid);
```

You should be able to independently run the prior two DELETE statements. When you have a B-tree index on the foreign key columns, Oracle will not excessively lock parent rows.

Implementing an Index on a Foreign Key Column

Let's say that you have a requirement that every record in the ADDRESS table be assigned a corresponding CUST_ID column that exists in the CUST table. To enforce this relationship, you create a foreign key constraint on the ADDRESS table, as follows:

```
alter table address add constraint addr_fk1
foreign key (cust_id) references cust(cust_id);
```

■ **Note**   A foreign key column must reference a column in the parent table that has a primary key or a unique key constraint defined on it; otherwise, you'll receive the ORA-02270: no matching unique or primary key for this column-list error.

You realize the foreign key column is used extensively when joining the CUST and ADDRESS tables and that an index on the foreign key column increases performance. You have to manually create an index in this situation. For example, a regular B-tree index is created on the foreign key column of CUST_ID in the ADDRESS table.

```
create index addr_fk1
on address(cust_id);
```

You don't have to name the index the same as the foreign key name (as you did in these lines of code). It's a personal preference as to whether you do that. We feel that it's easier to maintain environments when the constraint and corresponding index have the same name.

When creating an index, if you don't specify the tablespace name, Oracle places the index in the user's default tablespace. It's usually a good idea to explicitly specify which tablespace the index should be placed in; for instance:

```
create index addr_fk1
on address(cust_id)
tablespace reporting_index;
```

■ **Note**   An index on foreign key columns doesn't have to be of type B-tree. In data warehouse environments, it's common to use bitmap indexes on foreign key columns in star schema fact tables. Unlike B-tree indexes, bitmap indexes on foreign key columns don't resolve parent/child table-locking issues. Applications that use star schemas typically are not deleting or modifying the child record from fact tables; therefore, locking is less of an issue in data warehouse environments that use bitmap indexes on foreign key columns.

Determining if Foreign Key Columns Are Indexed

If you're creating an application from scratch, it's fairly easy to create the code and ensure that each foreign key constraint has a corresponding index. However, if you've inherited a database, it's prudent to check if the foreign key columns are indexed.

Let's query the data dictionary to determine if there are any foreign keys that don't have a corresponding index. The query will need to inspect for the case of multicolumn foreign keys. It doesn't matter if the constraint is defined in a different order from the index columns, as long as the indexed columns are in the leading edge of the index. In other words, if the constraint is defined to be COL1 and COL2, then it's okay to have a B-tree index defined on the leading edge of COL2 and then COL1.

Another issue is that a B-tree index protects you from locking issues, but a bitmap index does not. In this situation, the query should also check the index type.

Having said all of that, the following query uses the LISTAGG analytical function to compare columns (returned as a string in one row) in a foreign key constraint to corresponding indexed columns:

```
SELECT
 CASE WHEN ind.index_name IS NOT NULL THEN
   CASE WHEN ind.index_type IN ('BITMAP') THEN
     '** Bitmp idx **'
   ELSE
     'indexed'
   END
 ELSE
   '** Check idx **'
 END checker
,ind.index_type
,cons.owner, cons.table_name child_table, cons.cols, ind.index_name, cons.constraint_name
,(SELECT r.table_name
   FROM dba_constraints r
   WHERE cons.owner        = r.owner
   AND cons.r_constraint_name = r.constraint_name
   ) parent_table
```

```
FROM (SELECT
           c.owner, c.table_name, c.constraint_name, c.r_constraint_name
          ,LISTAGG(cc.column_name, ',' ) WITHIN GROUP (ORDER BY cc.column_name) cols
       FROM dba_constraints   c
           ,dba_cons_columns cc
       WHERE c.owner           = cc.owner
       AND   c.owner = UPPER('&&schema')
       AND   c.constraint_name = cc.constraint_name
       AND   c.constraint_type = 'R'
       GROUP BY c.owner, c.table_name, c.constraint_name, c.r_constraint_name) cons
LEFT OUTER JOIN
(SELECT
  table_owner, table_name, index_name, index_type, cbr
 ,LISTAGG(column_name, ',' ) WITHIN GROUP (ORDER BY column_name) cols
 FROM (SELECT
           ic.table_owner, ic.table_name, ic.index_name
          ,ic.column_name, ic.column_position, i.index_type
          ,CONNECT_BY_ROOT(ic.column_name) cbr
       FROM dba_ind_columns ic
           ,dba_indexes      i
       WHERE ic.table_owner = UPPER('&&schema')
       AND   ic.table_owner = i.table_owner
       AND   ic.table_name  = i.table_name
       AND   ic.index_name  = i.index_name
       CONNECT BY PRIOR ic.column_position-1 = ic.column_position
       AND PRIOR ic.index_name = ic.index_name)
  GROUP BY table_owner, table_name, index_name, index_type, cbr) ind
ON  cons.cols       = ind.cols
AND cons.table_name = ind.table_name
AND cons.owner      = ind.table_owner
ORDER BY checker, cons.owner, cons.table_name;
```

This query prompts you for a schema name and then displays foreign key constraints that don't have corresponding indexes. This query also checks for the index type. Bitmap indexes may exist on foreign key columns but don't prevent locking issues.

Multiple Indexes on the Same Column Combinations

Prior to Oracle Database 12c, you could not have multiple indexes defined on one table with the exact same combination of columns. For example, this would not work:

```
create table d(x int);
create index d_idx1 on d(x);
create bitmap index d_bidx1 on d(x) invisible;
```

Here is the error thrown in this situation:

```
ERROR at line 1:
ORA-01408: such column list already indexed
```

Starting with 12c, you can create multiple indexes on the same set of columns. However, you can only do this if the indexes are physically different; for example, when one index is created as a B-tree index and the second index is created as a bitmap index. Also, there can be only one visible index for the same combination of columns on a table. Therefore, running the prior CREATE INDEX statements works in an Oracle 12c database:

```
create table d(x int);
create index d_idx1 on d(x);
create bitmap index d_bidx1 on d(x) invisible;
```

Why would you want two indexes defined on the same set of columns? Perhaps you had originally built a data warehouse star schema with all B-tree indexes on the fact table foreign key columns, and later discover through testing that bitmap indexes perform better for the types of queries applied to the star schema. Therefore, you want to convert to bitmap indexes as seamlessly as possible. So you first build the bitmap indexes as invisible. Then when you're ready, you can drop the B-tree indexes and then alter the bitmap indexes to be visible.

Extended Data Types

Before discussing indexing extended columns, first some explanation is required regarding the nature of an extended data type. With the advent of 12c, the VARCHAR2, NVARCHAR2, and RAW data types can be configured to store up to 32,767 bytes of information (previously, the limit was 4,000 bytes for VARCHAR2 and NVARCHAR2, and 2000 bytes for RAW). Prior to Oracle 12c, the maximum length allowed for VARCHAR2 and NVARCHAR2 data types was 4,000 bytes, and 2,000 bytes for the RAW data type. Starting with Oracle 12c, these data types can be configured to store up to 32,767 bytes.

For reference, listed next are the steps for enabling extended data types for a non-container, single instance database. These steps must be performed as SYS:

```
shutdown immediate;
startup upgrade;
alter system set max_string_size=extended;
@?/rdbms/admin/utl32k.sql
shutdown immediate;
startup;
```

■ **Note**   Refer to the Oracle Database Reference for complete details on implementing extended data types for all types of databases (single instance, container, RAC, and Data Guard Logical Standby).

Be aware that once you've modified the MAX_STRING_SIZE to EXTENDED, you can't modify the value back to the default (of STANDARD). It's a one-way operation. When you try this, first ensure that this operation is performed on a test database before applying the change to a production database. If you need to switch back, you have to perform a recovery to a point in time before the change was made—meaning you'll need RMAN backups (taken prior to the change) or have the flashback database enabled. You can also take a Data Pump export from a database with extended data types enabled and import into a database without extended data types enabled, with the caveat that any tables with extended columns will fail on the import.

After enabling the extended data type, you can create a table with an extended column, as follows:

```
create table ext_demo(x varchar2(32727));
```

If you describe the table, it shows the large definition:

```
desc ext_demo
```

```
Name                            Null?    Type
----------------------------    -------- --------------------
X                                        VARCHAR2(32727)
```

You can manipulate the extended VARCHAR2 column via SQL just as you would a non-extended column. This is an example:

```
insert into ext_demo values(rpad('abc',10000,'abc'));
select substr(x,9500,10) from ext_demo where UPPER(x) like 'ABC%';
```

```
SUBSTR(X,9500,10)
----------------------------------------
bcabcabcab
```

The extended data type is internally implemented as a LOB. Assuming that the EXT_DEMO table is created in a schema not containing any other objects, you'll get the following when querying USER_OBJECTS:

```
select object_name, object_type from user_objects;
```

```
OBJECT_NAME              OBJECT_TYPE
------------------------ -----------------------
EXT_DEMO                 TABLE
SYS_IL0000041073C00001$$ INDEX
SYS_LOB0000041073C00001$$ LOB
```

You can further verify the LOB segment details by querying USER_LOBS:

```
select table_name, column_name, segment_name, tablespace_name, in_row
from user_lobs where table_name='EXT_DEMO';
```

```
TABLE_NAME   COLUMN_NAME  SEGMENT_NAME                TABLESPACE_NAME IN_
------------ ------------ --------------------------- --------------- ---
EXT_DEMO     X            SYS_LOB0000041073C00001$$   USERS           YES
```

You have no direct control over the LOB associated with the extended column. This means that you cannot manipulate the underlying LOB column with the DBMS_LOB package. Also, the internal LOB associated with the extended data type column is not visible to you via DBA_TAB_COLUMNS or COL$.

The LOB segment and associated LOB index are always stored in the tablespace of the table that the extended data type was created in. Following normal LOB storage rules, Oracle stores the first 4,000 bytes inline within the table. Anything greater than 4,000 bytes is stored in the LOB segment. If the tablespace that the LOB is created in is using Automatic Segment Space Management (ASSM), then the LOB is created as a SecureFiles LOB; otherwise, it is created as a BasicFiles LOB.

If you have an application that deals with character data greater than 4,000 bytes but less than or equal to 32,727 bytes, then you may want to consider using extended data types. Also, if you're migrating from a non-Oracle database (that supports large character columns) to an Oracle database, the extended data type feature will help make that migration easier, as you can now define large sizes for VARCHAR2, NVARCHAR2, and RAW columns natively in Oracle.

Indexing Extended Columns

Now that you understand extended data types, now we'll demonstrate how to index extended columns. Let's start by creating a table with an extended column and then try to create a regular B-tree index on that column:

```
create table ext_demo(x varchar2(32767));
```

■ **Note** If you attempt to create a table with a VARCHAR2 column greater than 4,000 bytes in a database that hasn't been configured for extended data types, Oracle will throw an ORA-00910: specified length too long for its datatype message.

Next, attempt to create an index on the extended column:

```
create index ext_demo_idx1 on ext_demo(x);

ERROR at line 1:
ORA-01450: maximum key length (6398) exceeded
```

An error is thrown because Oracle imposes a maximum length on the index key, which is about three-fourths of the block size (the block size for the database in this example is 8K). Even though there aren't any entries in this index yet, Oracle knows that it's possible that the index key could be larger than 6,398 bytes for a column that can contain up 32,767 bytes, and therefore it won't allow you to create an index in this scenario.

That doesn't mean you can't index extended columns; rather you have to use techniques that limit the length of the index key to less than 6,398 bytes. With that in mind, a few options become apparent:

- Create virtual column based on SUBSTR or STANDARD_HASH functions, and then create an index on the virtual column.

- Create a function-based index using SUBSTR or STANDARD_HASH functions.

- Create a tablespace based on a larger block size; for example, a 16K block size allows index keys the size of approximately 12,000 bytes. Having said that, if you need 12,000 bytes for an index key, then you're probably doing something wrong and you need to rethink what you're doing. This method is not explored in this book.

Let's start by looking at the virtual column solution.

Virtual Column Solution

The idea here is to first create a virtual column applying a SQL function on the extended column that returns a value less than 6,398 bytes. Then that virtual column can be indexed, which provides a mechanism for better performance when issuing queries against extended columns. An example will demonstrate this. First, create a table with an extended column:

```
create table ext_demo(x varchar2(32767));
```

Next, insert some test data into the table:

```
insert into ext_demo select to_char(level)|| rpad('abc',10000,'xyz')
   from dual connect by level < 1001
   union
   select to_char(level)
   from dual connect by level < 1001;
```

Suppose that you know that the first ten characters of the extended column are sufficiently selective enough to return small portions of the rows in the table. Therefore, you create a virtual column based on a substring of the extended column:

```
alter table ext_demo add (xv as (substr(x,1,10)));
```

Now create an index on the virtual column and gather statistics:

```
create index ext_demo_idx1 on ext_demo(xv);
exec dbms_stats.gather_table_stats(user,'EXT_DEMO');
```

When querying the virtual column, the optimizer can take advantage of the index in equality and range predicates in the WHERE clause, as shown in this example:

```
explain plan for select count(*) from ext_demo where x = '800';
select * from table(dbms_xplan.display(null,null,'BASIC +COST'));
```

```
---------------------------------------------------------------------
| Id | Operation                            | Name          | Cost (%CPU)|
---------------------------------------------------------------------
|  0 | SELECT STATEMENT                     |               |    2   (0)|
|  1 |  SORT AGGREGATE                      |               |           |
|  2 |   TABLE ACCESS BY INDEX ROWID BATCHED| EXT_DEMO      |    2   (0)|
|  3 |    INDEX RANGE SCAN                  | EXT_DEMO_IDX1 |    1   (0)|
---------------------------------------------------------------------
```

Notice that even though the index is on the virtual column, the optimizer can still use it when querying directly against the extended column X (and not the virtual column XV). The optimizer can also use this type of index in a range-type search:

```
explain plan for select count(*) from ext_demo where x >'800' and x<'900';
select * from table(dbms_xplan.display(null,null,'BASIC +COST'));
```

```
--------------------------------------------------------------------
| Id  | Operation                          | Name          | Cost (%CPU)|
--------------------------------------------------------------------
|   0 | SELECT STATEMENT                   |               |    4   (0)|
|   1 |  SORT AGGREGATE                    |               |           |
|   2 |   TABLE ACCESS BY INDEX ROWID BATCHED| EXT_DEMO     |    4   (0)|
|   3 |    INDEX RANGE SCAN                | EXT_DEMO_IDX1 |    2   (0)|
--------------------------------------------------------------------
```

Like the SUBSTR function, you can also base a virtual column on the STANDARD_HASH function. The STANDARD_HASH function can be applied to a long character string and return a fairly unique RAW value much less than 6,398 bytes. Let's look at a couple of examples using a virtual column based on STANDARD_HASH.

Assuming the same table and seed data as used with the prior SUBSTR examples, here you add a virtual column to the table using STANDARD_HASH, create an index, and generate statistics:

```
drop table ext_demo;
create table ext_demo(x varchar2(32727));
alter table ext_demo add (xv as (standard_hash(x)));
create index ext_demo_idx1 on ext_demo(xv);
exec dbms_stats.gather_table_stats(user,'EXT_DEMO');
```

The STANDARD_HASH works well when using equality predicates in the WHERE clause; for example:

```
explain plan for select count(*) from ext_demo where x='300';
select * from table(dbms_xplan.display(null,null,'BASIC +COST'));
```

```
--------------------------------------------------------------------
| Id  | Operation                          | Name          | Cost (%CPU)|
--------------------------------------------------------------------
|   0 | SELECT STATEMENT                   |               |    1   (0)|
|   1 |  SORT AGGREGATE                    |               |           |
|   2 |   TABLE ACCESS BY INDEX ROWID BATCHED| EXT_DEMO     |    1   (0)|
|   3 |    INDEX RANGE SCAN                | EXT_DEMO_IDX1 |    1   (0)|
--------------------------------------------------------------------
```

The index on a STANDARD_HASH–based virtual column allows efficient equality-based searches, but does not work for range-based searches, as the data is stored in an index based on the randomized hash value, as shown in this example:

```
explain plan for select count(*) from ext_demo where x >'800' and x<'900';
select * from table(dbms_xplan.display(null,null,'BASIC +COST'));
```

```
----------------------------------------------------
| Id  | Operation            | Name     | Cost (%CPU)|
----------------------------------------------------
|   0 | SELECT STATEMENT     |          |    2   (0)|
|   1 |  SORT AGGREGATE      |          |           |
|   2 |   TABLE ACCESS FULL  | EXT_DEMO |    2   (0)|
----------------------------------------------------
```

Function-Based Index Solution

The concept here is that you're building an index and applying a function to it in a way that limits the length of the index key and also results in a usable index. Here we use the same code (as in the prior section) to create a table with an extended column and then populate it with test data:

```
drop table ext_demo;
create table ext_demo(x varchar2(32767));

insert into ext_demo
  select to_char(level)|| rpad('abc',10000,'xyz')
  from dual connect by level < 1001
  union
  select to_char(level)
  from dual connect by level < 1001;
```

Now suppose you're familiar with the data and know that the first ten characters of the extended columns are usually sufficient for identifying a row; therefore, you create an index on the substring of the first ten characters and generate statistics for the table:

```
create index ext_demo_idx1 on ext_demo(substr(x,1,10));
exec dbms_stats.gather_table_stats(user,'EXT_DEMO');
```

The optimizer can use an index like this when there are equality and range predicates in the WHERE clause. Some examples will illustrate this:

```
explain plan for select count(*) from ext_demo where x = '800';
select * from table(dbms_xplan.display(null,null,'BASIC +COST'));
```

Id	Operation	Name	Cost (%CPU)
0	SELECT STATEMENT		2 (0)
1	SORT AGGREGATE		
2	TABLE ACCESS BY INDEX ROWID BATCHED	EXT_DEMO	2 (0)
3	INDEX RANGE SCAN	EXT_DEMO_IDX1	1 (0)

This example uses a range predicate:

```
explain plan for select count(*) from ext_demo where x>'200' and x<'400';
select * from table(dbms_xplan.display(null,null,'BASIC +COST'));
```

Id	Operation	Name	Cost (%CPU)
0	SELECT STATEMENT		6 (0)
1	SORT AGGREGATE		
2	TABLE ACCESS BY INDEX ROWID BATCHED	EXT_DEMO	6 (0)
3	INDEX RANGE SCAN	EXT_DEMO_IDX1	3 (0)

Assuming the same table and seed data as used with the prior SUBSTR examples, here you add a function-based index using STANDARD_HASH:

```
drop index ext_demo_idx1;
create index ext_demo_fnidx1 on ext_demo(standard_hash(x));
```

Now verify that an equality-based search uses the index:

```
explain plan for select count(*) from ext_demo where x = '800';
select * from table(dbms_xplan.display(null,null,'BASIC +COST'));
```

```
--------------------------------------------------------------------------------
| Id  | Operation                           | Name            | Cost (%CPU)|
--------------------------------------------------------------------------------
|   0 | SELECT STATEMENT                    |                 |     4   (0)|
|   1 |  SORT AGGREGATE                     |                 |            |
|   2 |   TABLE ACCESS BY INDEX ROWID BATCHED| EXT_DEMO       |     4   (0)|
|   3 |    INDEX RANGE SCAN                 | EXT_DEMO_FNIDX1 |     1   (0)|
--------------------------------------------------------------------------------
```

This allows efficient equality-based searches, but does not work for range-based searches, as the data is stored in an index based on the randomized hash value.

Summary

B-tree indexes are the default index type used in Oracle databases. For most applications, B-tree indexes are sufficient. With high-cardinality columns, a B-tree index usually provides considerable performance benefits.

When creating an index, we recommend that you place the index in a tablespace separate from its corresponding table. This allows you more options for storage management and backup and recovery. This isn't a hard-and-fast rule, but rather a guideline to help with maintenance and manageability.

B-tree indexes are closely associated with primary key and unique key constraints. Oracle automatically creates a B-tree index for you when the primary key or unique key constraint is created. When an index is automatically created with the constraint, the index is also automatically dropped when you drop or disable the constraint. You have the option of creating the index and constraint separately if you are required to manage these two objects separately.

Oracle doesn't automatically create an index for you when creating a foreign key constraint. Indexes on foreign key columns must be manually created. It's usually advisable to create an index on foreign key columns because this prevents locking issues and helps with the performance of queries that join parent/child tables on primary key and foreign key columns.

A couple of Oracle Database 12*c* topics were discussed toward the end of the chapter: multiple indexes on the same column combinations and indexing extended columns. When indexing the same column combinations, you must use different physical index types, and only one index can be designated as visible. With indexing extended columns, this requires either using a virtual column and an associated index or a function-based index. These features provide you with additional options that can be utilized to enhance performance in new and creative ways.

CHAPTER 3

■ ■ ■

Bitmap Indexes

Bitmap indexes are best suited for data warehouse or decision support systems (DSS). Common to the data warehouse is the star schema, in which a central fact table contains all the detailed information for a particular subject, such as customer revenue, and the number of related dimension tables containing associated reference type data on a particular dimension, such as time or geography. In a star schema, the dimension tables are the parent and the central fact table is the child table. Figure 3-1 shows a sample data model of a simple star schema.

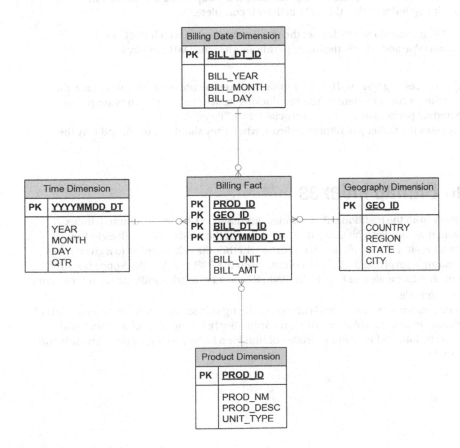

Figure 3-1. *Sample star schema*

© Darl Kuhn, Sam R. Alapati and Bill Padfield 2016

D. Kuhn et al., *Expert Oracle Indexing and Access Paths*, DOI 10.1007/978-1-4842-1984-3_3

With Oracle, the database configuration specific for the star schema is called *star transformation*. This configuration is specifically designed to help performance with querying against the star schema. With star transformation, there are some Oracle initialization parameters that need to be configured. In addition, to get the star transformation to occur, it is essential to place, at a minimum, bitmap indexes on the foreign keys in the fact table of the star schema.

As mentioned, star transformation is built to aid in the performance of queries against star schemas. Improving performance of such queries is one of the most common uses of bitmap indexes, although not the only manner in which they can or should be used. While there are distinct advantages to bitmap indexes, they have drawbacks and limitations in certain applications. Some of the guidelines for bitmap indexes are as follows:

- Should generally be used on low-cardinality columns.

- Best used in data warehouse or DSS systems.

- Best used on star schemas (common in the data warehouse environment).

- Efficient when there are many queries that join or filter on indexed columns.

- Data manipulation language (DML) activity on tables with bitmap indexes enabled should be minimized or avoided.

- To perform DML on tables, drop the bitmap indexes prior to updating the tables and re-create the bitmap indexes after the DML activity is complete.

- To perform DML on partitioned tables, set the given partitions on which DML is occurring to unusable and rebuild the index partitions after the DML activity is complete.

For online transaction processing systems (OLTP), bitmap indexes are not appropriate because there are many DML operations that occur consistently; also row-locking issues can occur with bitmap indexes. This can greatly impede update performance, which is crucial for OLTP systems.

The next section discusses the makeup of bitmap indexes, when they should be used, and why they are useful.

Understanding Bitmap Indexes

Bitmap indexes differ greatly from the traditional B-tree index discussed in Chapter 2. A bitmap index is composed of several strings of bits. Each bit string represents one of the valid distinct values in the underlying column. Each bit is either on or off, which indicates whether the value applies to a given row.

Table 3-1 shows an example involving the GENDER column from the EMPLOYEES table. Notice how the index has a bit string for each value: male and female. Individual bits in each string indicate whether a given row has the value of male or female.

Bitmap indexes can be created very quickly and can end up being very small in relation to a comparable B-tree index. Bitmap indexes are built for columns with low cardinality (a low number of distinct, valid values). The GENDER column in Table 3-1 is an appropriate column for a bitmap index, as there are only two valid values: male and female.

Table 3-1. Bitmap Index on the GENDER Column of the EMPLOYEES Table

			Bitmap Index on GENDER Column	
Row Number	Employee_ID	Employee Name	GENDER/Male Bitmap	GENDER/Female Bitmap
1	107	Lorentz,Diana	0	1
2	108	Greenberg,Nancy	0	1
3	109	Faviet,Daniel	1	0
4	110	Chen,John	1	0
5	111	Sciarra,Ismael	1	0

It is also possible to create a bitmap index on the combination of several columns from the underlying table. The rules still apply, as each column of a composite bitmap index should be a low-cardinality column. Table 3-2 shows a composite bitmap index on the GENDER column, which only has two valid values, and on the REGION column, which only has four valid values.

Table 3-2. Composite Bitmap Index on the GENDER and REGION Columns of the EMPLOYEES Table

			Composite Bitmap Index on Gender and Region Columns					
Row	Employee_ID	Employee Name	Gender Male	Gender Female	Region East	Region West	Region North	Region South
1	107	Lorentz,Diana	0	1	1	0	0	0
2	108	Greenberg,Nancy	0	1	0	1	0	0
3	109	Faviet,Daniel	1	0	1	0	0	0
4	110	Chen,John	1	0	0	0	1	0
5	111	Sciarra,Ismael	1	0	0	1	0	0

When choosing whether a column is appropriate for a bitmap index, the basic rule that it should be a low-cardinality column needs to be put into perspective. Based on your application, the makeup of your data, and the tables in your database, what is appropriate for a bitmap index may vary greatly. One basic rule of thumb that can be used is that if the valid values for a column make up less than 1% of the overall rows in the table, it is a feasible candidate for a bitmap index. It's better to use a percentage rather than strictly go off of the number of valid values for a given column. For example, let's say that your table contains 1,000 rows. If you use the 1% guideline, it means if a column's valid values number 10 or less, it would be a viable candidate as a column for a bitmap index. On a much grander scale, if you have a one-billion-row table, 1% of that is 10 million rows. While some may not believe that 10 million valid values for a column is a good candidate for a bitmap index, it actually may be a viable candidate. You need to look at that cardinality in relation to the data volume as a whole. One easy way to determine cardinality is by querying the DBA_TAB_COL_STATISTICS table to determine the number of distinct values for a column. Take a look at the following example:

```
select table_name, column_name, num_distinct from dba_tab_col_statistics
where table_name = 'EMPLOYEES'
order by num_distinct;
```

TABLE_NAME	COLUMN_NAME	NUM_DISTINCT
EMPLOYEES	GENDER	2
EMPLOYEES	COMMISSION_PCT	7
EMPLOYEES	DEPARTMENT_ID	11
EMPLOYEES	MANAGER_ID	18
EMPLOYEES	JOB_ID	19
EMPLOYEES	SALARY	57
EMPLOYEES	FIRST_NAME	91
EMPLOYEES	HIRE_DATE	98
EMPLOYEES	LAST_NAME	102
EMPLOYEES	EMPLOYEE_ID	107
EMPLOYEES	PHONE_NUMBER	107
EMPLOYEES	EMAIL	107

Based on this example, the GENDER and COMMISSION_PCT columns are examples of low-cardinality columns in our EMPLOYEES table.

With bitmap indexes, nulls are handled differently than with B-tree indexes. Unlike B-tree indexes, null values with an indexed column *are* stored within a bitmap index. In B-tree indexes, null values are not stored, at least within single-column indexes. To clarify, nulls can be stored in composite or multiple-column B-tree indexes as long as one of the columns contains a non-null value.

Because the bitmap index stores a value for each row in your table, it includes any null values that exist on the indexed column. This has performance implications when issuing queries on columns that have a bitmap index associated with that column. Since B-tree indexes may not store null values, if a query on a column with a single-column index that contains null values is issued, it needs to either perform a full table scan or use another existing index and then filter the null value after the row has been retrieved. This is not the case with bitmap indexes. The index can still be used in certain circumstances where functions such as COUNT are used.

See the following example of a query against the GENDER column of your EMPLOYEES table, which has been indexed using a bitmap index. You can see from this query that the GENDER column has not yet been populated for any of the rows, and thus is null.

```
SQL> select count(*), count(gender) from employees_nulltest;

  COUNT(*) COUNT(GENDER)
---------- -------------
  42074112             0
```

When you issue a query against the GENDER column, the explain plan shows that even with null values in the table, an index is used.

```
SELECT count(*) FROM employees_nulltest
WHERE gender = 'F';
```

Id	Operation	Name
0	SELECT STATEMENT	
1	SORT AGGREGATE	
2	BITMAP CONVERSION COUNT	
3	BITMAP INDEX SINGLE VALUE	EMPLOYEES_B9

If you index the same column on the same table with a B-tree index, the explain plan shows that the query will perform a full table scan.

```
-----------------------------------------------------
| Id  | Operation            | Name                 |
-----------------------------------------------------
|   0 | SELECT STATEMENT     |                      |
|   1 |   SORT AGGREGATE     |                      |
|   2 |    TABLE ACCESS FULL | EMPLOYEES_NULLTEST    |
-----------------------------------------------------
```

If you decide to implement bitmap indexes within your application, it's a good idea to occasionally check the makeup of the data within the columns that are bitmap indexed. This is especially important if you have bitmap index maintenance operations as part of your overall application. If you miscalculate the cardinality of any columns with bitmap indexes, it could cause negative ramifications for your application, such as the following:

- Storage for the bitmap indexes will increase.

- Query performance will degrade.

- Rebuild operation times will increase.

It is especially important to review the makeup of the data with new applications where the makeup of the data isn't known initially. Sometimes you have to make assumptions during application design, which you should reassess after you start seeing "real" data. After the initial implementation of your application, take time to reassess cardinality on columns at least once to validate any assumptions you relied upon for bitmap indexes. You can then take steps to modify your application appropriately, which may include converting some bitmap indexes to B-tree indexes, or vice versa. Modifications also may include the restructuring or the removal of index maintenance operations if you need to remove bitmap indexes, or the addition of some index maintenance operations if you need to add bitmap indexes.

Creating a Bitmap Index

Once you have determined that bitmap indexes are appropriate for your environment, it is fairly straightforward to create a bitmap index. The syntax is the same as it is for a B-tree index, except that you need to include the BITMAP keyword when creating the index; for example:

```
CREATE BITMAP INDEX EMPLOYEES_B1
ON EMPLOYEES (GENDER)
NOLOGGING;
```

Because the physical structure of a bitmap index is so simple, and therefore much smaller than a B-tree index, you can create them much faster than a B-tree index. Note that the NOLOGGING keyword is used in the previous example. We recommend you always create bitmap indexes with NOLOGGING because DML operations on bitmap indexes perform so poorly that it's a good idea to destroy and rebuild them rather than maintain them. Of course, as with any database objects with NOLOGGING specified, you need to rebuild any bitmap indexes if any database recovery is required. In the following example, you create an index on the GENDER column of the EMPLOYEES table. Note the time that it took to create the bitmap index.

```
SQL> CREATE BITMAP INDEX EMPLOYEES_B2
  2  ON EMPLOYEES (GENDER)
  3* NOLOGGING;

Index created.

Elapsed: 00:00:10.01
```

Creating the same index on the gender column using a B-tree index takes about 18 times longer, and this is with the NOLOGGING option, which is not recommended for B-tree indexes. Note the following example:

```
SQL> CREATE INDEX EMPLOYEES_I2
  2  ON EMPLOYEES (GENDER)
  3* NOLOGGING;

Index created.

Elapsed: 00:03:01.24
```

Not only do you save time in creating bitmap indexes, you save space over B-tree indexes as well, as long as your bitmap index column(s) are low cardinality. If bitmap indexes are created on columns with somewhat higher cardinality, the space used by the bitmap indexes will increase and the space savings over the equivalent B-tree indexes will be reduced.

Using the previous example of the indexes you created on the GENDER column, note the size difference between a B-tree and bitmap index using the following query from DBA_SEGMENTS. Noting the size in megabytes, the B-tree index takes up 37 times more space than the bitmap index.

```
SQL> SELECT sum(bytes)/1048576
  2  FROM dba_segments
  3* WHERE segment_name = 'EMPLOYEES_B2';

SUM(BYTES)/1048576
------------------
                16

SQL> SELECT sum(bytes)/1048576
  2  FROM dba_segments
  3* WHERE segment_name = 'EMPLOYEES_I2';

SUM(BYTES)/1048576
------------------
               600
```

Creating a Partitioned Bitmap Index

Bitmap indexes can be created on partitioned tables, but they must be created as local partitioned indexes. Here's an example:

```
CREATE BITMAP INDEX employees_part_1i
ON employees_part (department_id)
LOCAL;
```

Oracle will not allow you to create bitmap indexes on partitioned tables unless they are local partitioned indexes. If you attempt to create a non-partitioned bitmap index on a partitioned table, you will receive the following error:

```
SQL> CREATE BITMAP INDEX employees_part_1i
2 ON employees_part (department_id);

on employees_part (department_id)
    *
ERROR at line 2:
ORA-25122: Only LOCAL bitmap indexes are permitted on partitioned tables
```

In the same manner, globally partitioned bitmap indexes are also not allowed on partitioned tables.

```
SQL> CREATE BITMAP INDEX employees_part_1i
2  ON employees_part (department_id)
3  GLOBAL;

GLOBAL
*
ERROR at line 3:
ORA-25113: GLOBAL may not be used with a bitmap index
```

Creating a Bitmap Index on an Index-Organized Table

Bitmap indexes can be created on index-organized tables (IOT) as secondary indexes on the IOT, but they must be created with a mapping table. The following is an example of creating the IOT:

```
CREATE TABLE employees_part
(
 EMPLOYEE_ID          NUMBER(6)         NOT NULL
 ,FIRST_NAME          VARCHAR2(20)
 ,LAST_NAME           VARCHAR2(25)      NOT NULL
 ,EMAIL               VARCHAR2(25)      NOT NULL
 ,PHONE_NUMBER        VARCHAR2(20)
 ,HIRE_DATE           DATE              NOT NULL
 ,JOB_ID              VARCHAR2(10)      NOT NULL
 ,SALARY              NUMBER(8,2)
 ,COMMISSION_PCT      NUMBER(2,2)
 ,MANAGER_ID          NUMBER(6)
 ,DEPARTMENT_ID       NUMBER(4)
 ,CONSTRAINT employees_part_pk PRIMARY KEY (employee_id, hire_date)
)
ORGANIZATION INDEX
MAPPING TABLE;
```

Since the mapping table has been specified on the IOT, bitmap indexes can be created on the IOT.

```
SQL> CREATE BITMAP INDEX employees_part_1i
2  ON employees_part (department_id)
3  NOLOGGING
3  LOCAL;
```

```
Index created.
```

If no mapping table is specified on the IOT, you will receive the following error when attempting to create the bitmap index:

```
ON employees_part (department_id)
   *
ERROR at line 2:
ORA-28669: bitmap index can not be created on an IOT with no mapping table
```

If you are trying to create a bitmap index on an existing IOT with no mapping, simply alter the table, as seen in this example:

```
SQL> alter table employees_part move mapping table;

Table altered.
```

■ **Note**   You can't use bitmap indexes in conjunction with reverse key indexes.

Performance Implications of Querying with Bitmap Indexes

Bitmap indexes are primarily built to aid in performance, especially in the data warehouse environment. The key performance benefits of using bitmap indexes include the following:

- Query speed improves with the use of a bitmap index over the traditional B-tree index.

- Creation speed of a bitmap index is far faster than that of a comparable B-tree index.

- Maintenance operations such as rebuilding indexes are much faster with a bitmap index.

One of the key reasons for some of these benefits is simply because the bitmap index is so much *smaller* than its B-tree equivalent. Of course, this assumes that you have created the bitmap index on lower cardinality columns. All of these benefits said, the primary reason to build a bitmap index is to get superior query performance. Take a look at the following example of a query against your table using two scenarios; the first is a query against a B-tree indexed column and the second is a query against the same column indexed with a bitmap index.

In the following example, you are querying against the EMPLOYEES_BIG_BTREE table with a B-tree index on the GENDER column. Note that there is a filter on the indexed GENDER column. The optimizer does use the B-tree index and runs in 5.1 seconds. In the statistics for the query, the database performed 124,685 physical reads.

```
SQL> SELECT count(*) FROM employees_big_btree
  2* WHERE gender = 'F';

  COUNT(*)
----------
  21233664
```

Elapsed: 00:00:05.10

```
-----------------------------------------------------------------------
| Id | Operation            | Name         | Rows | Bytes | Cost (%CPU)| Time     |
-----------------------------------------------------------------------
|  0 | SELECT STATEMENT     |              |    1 |     2 | 20366  (3)| 00:04:05 |
|  1 |  SORT AGGREGATE      |              |    1 |     2 |           |          |
|* 2 |   INDEX FAST FULL SCAN| EMPLOYEES_I2 |  21M |   40M | 20366  (3)| 00:04:05 |
-----------------------------------------------------------------------
```

Predicate Information (identified by operation id):
----

   2 - filter("GENDER"='F')

Statistics
----
         0 recursive calls
         0 db block gets
    124904 consistent gets
    124865 physical reads
         0 redo size
       529 bytes sent via SQL*Net to client
       523 bytes received via SQL*Net from client
         2 SQL*Net roundtrips to/from client
         0 sorts (memory)
         0 sorts (disk)
         1 rows processed

Now perform the exact same query on a table with the exact same number of rows, except the table has a bitmap index on the GENDER column rather than a B-tree index. As you can see, the query uses an index, runs in less than 1 second, and performs only 996 physical reads, rather than the 124,685 physical reads performed against a similar table with a B-tree index on the GENDER column.

```
SQL> SELECT count(*) FROM employees_big_bitmap
  2* WHERE gender = 'F';

  COUNT(*)
----------
  21233664
```

Elapsed: 00:00:00.02

```
------------------------------------------------------------------------------
| Id | Operation                  | Name         | Rows | Bytes | Cost (%CPU)| Time     |
------------------------------------------------------------------------------
|  0 | SELECT STATEMENT           |              |    1 |     2 |  975   (0)| 00:00:12 |
|  1 |  SORT AGGREGATE            |              |    1 |     2 |           |          |
|  2 |   BITMAP CONVERSION COUNT  |              |  21M |   40M |  975   (0)| 00:00:12 |
|* 3 |    BITMAP INDEX SINGLE VALUE| EMPLOYEES_B2 |      |       |           |          |
------------------------------------------------------------------------------
```

```
Predicate Information (identified by operation id):
-----------------------------------------------------

   3 - access("GENDER"='F')

Statistics
------------------------------------------------------------
          0  recursive calls
          0  db block gets
        996  consistent gets
        996  physical reads
          0  redo size
        529  bytes sent via SQL*Net to client
        523  bytes received via SQL*Net from client
          2  SQL*Net roundtrips to/from client
          0  sorts (memory)
          0  sorts (disk)
          1  rows processed
```

With the star schema, bitmap indexes are essential to obtain successful query performance, and bitmap indexes are, at a minimum, needed on all foreign key columns in the fact table. In addition, you should have your database configured for star transformation. Table 3-3 presents the Oracle initialization parameters that should be configured or analyzed for the proper value.

Table 3-3. Initialization Parameters for Star Transformation

Parameter Name	Value
star_transformation	TRUE (FALSE is the default).
memory_target	Variable. This parameter is used to configure both System Global Area (SGA) and Program Global Area (PGA). Star transformation needs PGA memory configured.
pga_aggregate_target	Configure this parameter if operating in versions 9*i* or 10*g* of the Oracle Database.

The following "star query" notes a query against a star schema that uses star transformation. This can be verified by running an explain plan on your query.

```
SQL> show parameter star_transformation

NAME                                  TYPE         VALUE
------------------------------------- -----------  -------------------------------
star_transformation_enabled           string       TRUE

SELECT pr.prod_category, c.country_id,
t.calendar_year, sum(s.quantity_sold), SUM(s.amount_sold)
FROM sales s, times t, customers c, products pr
WHERE s.time_id = t.time_id
AND    s.cust_id = c.cust_id
AND    pr.prod_id = s.prod_id
AND    t.calendar_year = '2016'
```

```
GROUP BY pr.prod_category, c.country_id, t.calendar_year;
```

```
---------------------------------------------------------------------
| Id | Operation                          | Name                     |
---------------------------------------------------------------------
|  0 | SELECT STATEMENT                   |                          |
|  1 |  HASH GROUP BY                     |                          |
|  2 |   HASH JOIN                        |                          |
|  3 |    HASH JOIN                       |                          |
|  4 |     HASH JOIN                      |                          |
|  5 |      PARTITION RANGE ALL           |                          |
|  6 |       TABLE ACCESS BY LOCAL INDEX ROWID| SALES                |
|  7 |        BITMAP CONVERSION TO ROWIDS |                          |
|  8 |         BITMAP AND                 |                          |
|  9 |          BITMAP MERGE              |                          |
| 10 |           BITMAP KEY ITERATION     |                          |
| 11 |            BUFFER SORT             |                          |
| 12 |             TABLE ACCESS FULL      | CUSTOMERS                |
| 13 |             BITMAP INDEX RANGE SCAN | SALES_CUST_BIX          |
| 14 |          BITMAP MERGE              |                          |
| 15 |           BITMAP KEY ITERATION     |                          |
| 16 |            BUFFER SORT             |                          |
| 17 |             VIEW                   | index$_join$_016         |
| 18 |              HASH JOIN             |                          |
| 19 |               INDEX FAST FULL SCAN | PRODUCTS_PK              |
| 20 |               INDEX FAST FULL SCAN | PRODUCTS_PROD_CAT_IX     |
| 21 |             BITMAP INDEX RANGE SCAN | SALES_PROD_BIX          |
| 22 |      TABLE ACCESS FULL             | TIMES                    |
| 23 |     TABLE ACCESS FULL              | CUSTOMERS                |
| 24 |    VIEW                            | index$_join$_004         |
| 25 |     HASH JOIN                      |                          |
| 26 |      INDEX FAST FULL SCAN          | PRODUCTS_PK              |
| 27 |      INDEX FAST FULL SCAN          | PRODUCTS_PROD_CAT_IX     |
---------------------------------------------------------------------
```

Note

    - star transformation used for this statement

Keep in mind that the optimizer may choose to ignore star transformation if it determines a cheaper cost alternative to execute your query. If you think that you should be achieving star transformation and you're not, try adding a STAR_TRANSFORMATION hint, and if needed, also a FACT hint, and see if the query then uses star transformation. Sometimes both hints are needed for the query to achieve star transformation. Then you can compare the performance between the results using star transformation to the one that is not to see which of the two is the better performing query. The following examples show how to use the hints related to star transformation:

```
SELECT /*+ star_transformation */ pr.prod_category, c.country_id, ...

SELECT /*+ fact(s) */ pr.prod_category, c.country_id, ...

SELECT /*+ star_transformation fact(s) */ pr.prod_category, c.country_id, ...
```

If you executed this query without star transformation enabled, then you can see from the following explain plan output that the optimizer bypassed the use of star transformation in the execution plan and the bitmap indexes were not utilized:

```
---------------------------------------------------------------
| Id | Operation                      | Name         |
---------------------------------------------------------------
|  0 | SELECT STATEMENT               |              |
|  1 |  HASH GROUP BY                 |              |
|  2 |   NESTED LOOPS                 |              |
|  3 |    NESTED LOOPS                |              |
|  4 |     NESTED LOOPS               |              |
|  5 |      NESTED LOOPS              |              |
|  6 |       PARTITION RANGE ALL      |              |
|  7 |        TABLE ACCESS FULL       | SALES        |
|  8 |        TABLE ACCESS BY INDEX ROWID| PRODUCTS  |
|  9 |         INDEX UNIQUE SCAN      | PRODUCTS_PK  |
| 10 |       TABLE ACCESS BY INDEX ROWID | CUSTOMERS |
| 11 |        INDEX UNIQUE SCAN       | CUSTOMERS_PK |
| 12 |      INDEX UNIQUE SCAN         | TIMES_PK     |
| 13 |     TABLE ACCESS BY INDEX ROWID | TIMES       |
---------------------------------------------------------------
```

Performance Implications of Loading Data with Bitmap Indexes

The biggest payoff for using bitmap indexes is that they help the speed of queries. Bitmap indexes can be created very quickly in comparison to B-tree indexes, and they consume much less space than B-tree indexes. The trade-off for gains with these distinct advantages is the impact that bitmap indexes have on DML operations on tables containing bitmap indexes. Bitmap indexes can be created quickly and can be scanned quickly to help query performance, but they are not designed to support DML operations very well.

What the following example demonstrates is that it is actually much faster to simply drop and re-create bitmap indexes before and after a load operation. In the following example, you have a star schema with a central fact table, with dimension tables surrounding the fact table. In order to achieve star transformation, at minimum you need foreign keys on the fact tables pointing back to the parent dimension primary keys. In this example, you have a total of 11 bitmap indexes on the fact table that are created on the foreign key columns from the dimension tables. There is also a primary key index and two B-tree indexes. Columns with date-based data types are not good candidates for bitmap indexes because of their cardinality, so for date-based columns, a normal B-tree index is recommended.

The following query shows your indexes:

```
SQL> select index_name, index_type, partitioned
  2  from user_indexes
  3* where table_name = 'BILLING_FACT';
```

```
INDEX_NAME                      INDEX_TYPE                  PAR
------------------------------  --------------------------  ---
BILLING_FACT_BNAPNXX            NORMAL                      YES
BILLING_FACT_BIXFK103           BITMAP                      YES
BILLING_FACT_BIXFK104           BITMAP                      YES
BILLING_FACT_BIXFK109           BITMAP                      YES
BILLING_FACT_BIXFK111           BITMAP                      YES
BILLING_FACT_BIXFK113           BITMAP                      YES
BILLING_FACT_BIXFK114           BITMAP                      YES
BILLING_FACT_BIXFK115           BITMAP                      YES
BILLING_FACT_BIXFK117           BITMAP                      YES
BILLING_FACT_BIXFK118           BITMAP                      YES
BILLING_FACT_BIXFK120           BITMAP                      YES
BILLING_FACT_IXFK01             NORMAL                      YES
BILLING_FACT_BBNPANXX           BITMAP                      YES

13 rows selected.
```

It is very common to have many bitmap indexes on a fact table, and the number increases as the number of dimension tables increases in a star schema. It is cases like this where performance suffers with DML operations on tables with a large number of bitmap indexes. This degradation occurs, of course, in a typical star schema configured for star transformation.

For demonstration purposes, insert one million rows into the fact table. See the following DML operation and note the time that it takes to complete the operation:

```
insert into billing_fact
select * from billing_fact_temp;

1000000 rows created.

Elapsed: 00:01:46.68
```

You can see that it took 1 minute and 47 seconds to insert the rows into your fact table. At a glance, the time taken appears reasonable. Keep in mind that in the data warehouse environment, it is common to process hundreds of millions of rows a day. If you extrapolated this number to 100 million rows, it could take over 2 hours to load 100 million rows.

In contrast, the preferred mechanism for DML when operating with bitmap indexes is simply to drop the bitmap indexes prior to a DML operation, or, if you have large, partitioned tables in the data warehouse environment, mark the indexes for the given partitions(s) that are being loaded unusable prior to the load.

The steps required to perform bitmap index maintenance in this regard are as follows:

1. Drop all bitmap indexes. Or, for a partitioned table, mark the bitmap indexes for the targeted partitions for DML operations as unusable.

2. Perform the DML load operation.

3. Rebuild all bitmap indexes. Or, for a partitioned table, rebuild the bitmap indexes for the affected partitions.

In the following example, follow these steps using the BILLING_FACT table and the same data as used in the prior test. Use the 1 minute and 47 seconds as a benchmark for comparison. The BILLING_FACT table is a partitioned table, and you are loading March 2016 data. You will therefore mark all bitmap indexes as unusable for the March partitions.

```
Starting marking index subpartitions unusable at 20160402.1449.49

alter index BILLING_FACT_BBNPANXX modify subpartition BFACT1603PREC unusable;
alter index BILLING_FACT_BIXFK103 modify subpartition BFACT1603PREC unusable;
alter index BILLING_FACT_BIXFK104 modify subpartition BFACT1603PREC unusable;
alter index BILLING_FACT_BIXFK109 modify subpartition BFACT1603PREC unusable;
alter index BILLING_FACT_BIXFK111 modify subpartition BFACT1603PREC unusable;
alter index BILLING_FACT_BIXFK113 modify subpartition BFACT1603PREC unusable;
alter index BILLING_FACT_BIXFK114 modify subpartition BFACT1603PREC unusable;
alter index BILLING_FACT_BIXFK115 modify subpartition BFACT1603PREC unusable;
alter index BILLING_FACT_BIXFK117 modify subpartition BFACT1603PREC unusable;
alter index BILLING_FACT_BIXFK118 modify subpartition BFACT1603PREC unusable;
alter index BILLING_FACT_BIXFK120 modify subpartition BFACT1603PREC unusable;
alter index BILLING_FACT_BNAPNXX modify subpartition BFACT1603PREC unusable;
alter index BILLING_FACT_IXFK01 modify subpartition BFACT1603PREC unusable;

Completed marking index subpartitions unusable at 20160402.1450.03
```

The operation to mark the indexes as unusable took less than one second. Next, perform the identical DML operation that took the 1 minute and 47 seconds—only this time, all affected partitions for the bitmap indexes have been marked unusable, and therefore the load operation doesn't build the index entries for the new rows inserted.

```
insert into billing_fact
select * from billing_fact_temp;

1000000 rows created.

Elapsed: 00:00:41.17
```

The load operation is obviously significantly faster without the bitmap indexes, taking 41 seconds. Lastly, you need to rebuild the index partitions for the bitmap indexes that you marked unusable in the first step.

Take a look at the rebuild syntax that follows and the associated time that it took to rebuild the affected March 2016 partition for the 11 bitmap indexes:

```
Starting index rebuilds at 20160402.1454.29

alter index BILLING_FACT_BIXFK103 rebuild subpartition BFACT1603PREC;
alter index BILLING_FACT_BIXFK104 rebuild subpartition BFACT1603PREC;
alter index BILLING_FACT_BIXFK113 rebuild subpartition BFACT1603PREC;
alter index BILLING_FACT_BBNPANXX rebuild subpartition BFACT1603PREC;
alter index BILLING_FACT_IXFK01 rebuild subpartition BFACT1603PREC;
alter index BILLING_FACT_BIXFK117 rebuild subpartition BFACT1603PREC;
alter index BILLING_FACT_BIXFK115 rebuild subpartition BFACT1603PREC;
alter index BILLING_FACT_BIXFK109 rebuild subpartition BFACT1603PREC;
alter index BILLING_FACT_BIXFK111 rebuild subpartition BFACT1603PREC;
alter index BILLING_FACT_BIXFK120 rebuild subpartition BFACT1603PREC;
alter index BILLING_FACT_BIXFK114 rebuild subpartition BFACT1603PREC;
alter index BILLING_FACT_BNAPNXX rebuild subpartition BFACT1603PREC;
alter index BILLING_FACT_BIXFK118 rebuild subpartition BFACT1603PREC;

Completed index rebuilds at 20160402.1454.44
```

It took 15 seconds to rebuild all the March partitions for your bitmap indexes. For partitioned tables, you have the added flexibility of running many rebuilds at one time, which can also speed the overall rebuild time. So, although it's more complex than performing a single DML insert operation on your fact table, by splitting up the work into three pieces, the total time to insert one million rows took about half the time as the straight INSERT statement. As stated, if you have bitmap indexes on large partitioned tables, it is recommended to perform partition-level operations on the indexes rather than completely drop the bitmap indexes. Even though bitmap indexes create very quickly, if you have millions to billions of rows in a table, it can still take time. Furthermore, if you can isolate DML operations to a given partition or set of partitions, you can simply mark the indexes as unusable before the DML operation begins and then rebuild only those partitions after the DML operation is completed.

Alternatively, you can also issue the following command, which can save you from having to issue a statement for each index:

```
alter table billing_fact modify subpartition BFACT1603PREC rebuild unusable local indexes;
```

The trade-off of the simplicity of this command is that the indexes for a given partition are built serially. If you issue a command to rebuild a partition for each given index, you have the option to issue multiple statements at once, which can speed index creation time because you are then essentially rebuilding the indexes in parallel.

Understanding Bitmap Join Indexes

Bitmap join indexes, like normal bitmap indexes, are useful in data warehouse applications, specifically with the star schema. One of the key benefits of a bitmap join index is implied in the name of the index: the *join*. The basic premise of a bitmap join index is as follows: when creating a bitmap join index, which is a join of indexed values between two tables, the join results are stored within the index itself. Doing the join upfront and storing the results saves you from having to scan the indexes to get join values between the two tables.

Within a star schema, the base elements for the bitmap join index are the large fact table and the dimension table. In a normal star schema, there are foreign keys on the child fact table back to the parent dimension table. The join piece of the bitmap join index is an equi-inner join on these foreign key columns between the fact and dimension tables.

To illustrate the situation further, materialized views are also popular in the realm of the data warehouse. They are typically created to store the results of a join or aggregation for easy and quick repeated access by the user. Bitmap join indexes are, in essence, a materialized join of indexed columns between two tables, processed and stored once. They can be accessed over and over by the user without having to reprocess a given join condition.

Let's say that you create an index on your sample billing fact table and the geography dimension. The join column between these two tables would be the primary key for the geography dimension (GEO_ID) and the associated foreign key column on the billing fact table (also called GEO_ID).

To illustrate an example of a bitmap join index, refer to Tables 3-4 and 3-5. In Table 3-4, a sample of rows and values is shown for both the BILLING_FACT and the GEOGRAPHY_DIMENSION tables. In Table 3-5, it shows the actual makeup of a bitmap join index based on the relationship with the GEO_ID column. Table 3-5 shows an example of how the actual bitmap join index would be stored in the database. There are four unique ROWID values shown for the BILLING_FACT table and two associated ROWID values for the matching row on the GEOGRAPHY_DIMENSION table. If your query joins the BILLING_FACT and GEOGRAPHY_DIMENSION tables and is searching for the GEO_ID of 24010 by scanning the bitmap index, the ROWID values for each table are stored together and the data can quickly be retrieved from the two tables.

Table 3-4. *Foreign Key Relationship Between Fact and Dimension Table*

Billing Fact

Row	Prod_ID	Geo_ID	Bill_date_id	YYMMDD_DDDATE	Bill_Unit	Bill_Amt
1	107	10	11011	2011-06-28	US	124.47
2	108	14	10037	2011-06-24	US	252.14
3	109	14	12001	02011-07-01	US	83.16
4	110	12	11021	2011-06-28	US	99.45
5	111	11	10147	2011-06-26	US	157.15

Geography Dimension

Row	Geo_ID	Country	Region	State	City
1	10	USA	East	Maine	Portland
2	11	USA	East	Maryland	Baltimore
3	12	USA	North	North Dakota	Fargo
4	13	USA	South	Texas	Houston
5	14	USA	West	Oregon	Portland

Table 3-5. *Bitmap Join Index Values Between Star Schema Fact Table and Joined Dimension Table*

BILLING FACT ROWID	GEOGRAHY DIMENSION ROWID	Matching GEO_ID
AAARm6ABDAAAMz1ABB	AAAUWMABiAAAS9KAAr	23099
AAARm6ABCAAAUiHAA6	AAAUWMABiAAAS9KAAr	23099
AAARm9AAAABAUjBAA9	AAAUWMABiAAAS9CBAm	24010
AAARm9AAAABCUhBACC	AAAUWMABiAAAS9CBAm	24010
AAAHm6ACBAABCUbBBB	AAAUWMABiAAAS9CBAm	24010

If you employ the star schema within your environment, bitmap join indexes should seriously be considered. They offer distinct performance benefits in data warehouse environments employing the star schema. Join operations take time, and when you have a central fact table and many dimensions on which to join, the time to perform join operations can significantly increase as tables are added to a join condition. Because the bitmap join index is essentially a materialized join between join columns on the fact and dimension tables, join operations at execution time are already complete because the join operation was done and stored in the bitmap join index when it was created. Bitmap join indexes are tailor-made for star schemas and should be considered to help the query efficiency when accessing tables within the star schema.

Creating a Bitmap Join Index

Creating a bitmap join index is similar to creating a normal bitmap index in that you need the BITMAP keyword, but different in that you also need the FROM and WHERE clauses. Here's an example:

```
CREATE BITMAP INDEX BILLING_FACT_BJIX01
ON BILLING_FACT (GEO.GEO_ID)
```

```
FROM BILLING_FACT BF, GEOGRAPHY_DIMENSION GEO
WHERE BF.GEO_ID = GEO.GEO_ID
tablespace BILLING_FACT_S
PCTFREE 5
PARALLEL 4
LOCAL
NOLOGGING;
```

You can create locally partitioned indexes on bitmap join indexes, as noted in the previous example with the LOCAL keyword. You can also create bitmap join indexes between the fact table and multiple dimension tables; for example:

```
CREATE BITMAP INDEX BILLING_FACT_BJIX02
ON BILLING_FACT (GEO.GEO_ID, TM.YYYYMMDD_DT)
FROM BILLING_FACT BF, GEOGRAPHY_DIMENSION GEO, TIME_DIMENSION TM
WHERE BF.GEO_ID = GEO.GEO_ID
AND BF.YYYYMMDD_DT = TM.YYYYMMMDD_DT
tablespace BILLING_FACT_S
PCTFREE 5
PARALLEL 4
LOCAL
NOLOGGING;
```

If you have a snowflake schema, which is an extension of a star schema with child entities off of the dimension tables, you can also create a bitmap join index off of the dimension tables in a snowflake schema. In essence, the syntax is identical.

Duplicating Indexes for Performance

With Oracle 12c, you can create multiple indexes on the same set of columns, provided that the characteristics of the indexes are different. For instance, you can create a B-tree index and a bitmap index on the same set of columns. Let's say that you have a database used more as an OLTP database during the day, and the same database is used for reporting and querying during the evening. You can utilize a B-tree index during the day for OLTP purposes, and utilize a bitmap index on the same set of columns, which can be used for reporting in the evening. The caveat in using this feature is that you cannot have both indexes visible at the same time.

If you attempt to create two visible indexes, you will encounter an error when creating the second index, as shown in the following example:

```
SQL> CREATE BITMAP INDEX "BILLING_FACT_BBNPANXX"
  2  ON "BILLING_FACT" ("BTN_NPA_NXX")
  3  NOLOGGING
  4  TABLESPACE "USERS" LOCAL;

Index created.

SQL> CREATE INDEX "BILLING_FACT_BNAPNXX"
  2  ON "BILLING_FACT" ("BTN_NPA_NXX")
  3  NOLOGGING
  4  TABLESPACE "USERS" LOCAL;
          *
```

```
ERROR at line 2:
ORA-01408: such column list already indexed
```

In order to accomplish this, the first index needs to be invisible, and then you can create the second index:

```
  1* alter index BILLING_FACT_BBNPANXX invisible
SQL> /
```

Index altered.

```
  1  CREATE INDEX "BILLING_FACT_BNAPNXX"
  2  ON "BILLING_FACT" ("BTN_NPA_NXX")
  3  NOLOGGING
  4* TABLESPACE "USERS" LOCAL;
```

Index created.

If you then try to flip the second index you created to visible, you will get the following error message:

```
alter index BILLING_FACT_BBNPANXX visible
*
ERROR at line 1:
ORA-14147: There is an existing VISIBLE index defined on the same set of
columns.
```

Using this functionality with Oracle 12c should be done based on specific requirements within your application such that there is a benefit in doing so. The aforementioned example of creating a B-tree index and a bitmap index using the same column list is one example of where a performance benefit may be obtained by creating both indexes. You would need to examine your specific database environment and circumstances to see if this functionality is beneficial to your specific application.

Reporting on Bitmap Indexes

It is fairly simple to get information on bitmap indexes from the data dictionary. Take a look at the following query from the USER_INDEXES view to get information on both bitmap and bitmap join indexes:

```
SELECT index_name, index_type, join_index FROM dba_indexes
WHERE index_type = 'BITMAP';
```

```
INDEX_NAME                     INDEX_TYPE                   JOI
------------------------------ ---------------------------- ---
BILLING_FACT_BIXFK102          BITMAP                       NO
BR_FACT_BJIX002                BITMAP                       YES
```

If you want to get the specific join information on any bitmap join indexes that you have in your database, you can get it from the USER_JOIN_IND_COLUMNS data dictionary view. This view shows the tables used in the join condition for bitmap join indexes, as well as the columns joined, as shown in the following example:

```
SQL> SELECT index_name, inner_table_name inner_table, inner_table_column inner_column,
  2          outer_table_name outer_table, outer_table_column outer_column
  3  FROM user_join_ind_columns
  4* WHERE index_name = 'BR_FACT_BJIX002';
```

INDEX_NAME	INNER_TABLE	INNER_COLUMN	OUTER_TABLE	OUTER_COLUMN
BL_FACT_BJIX002	BILLING_FACT	GEO_ID	GEOGRAPHY_DIM	GEO_ID

Summary

The bitmap and bitmap join indexes are most commonly used in the data warehouse environment. The simple bitmap index can also be used outside of the data warehouse, but the bitmap join index is specifically designed to be used within the star schema, which is a data model built for the data warehouse environment.

They key advantages with bitmap indexes are that they can be created very quickly and generally take up much less space than a B-tree counterpart index. This fact makes rebuild operations much more attractive, as they can be rebuilt very quickly. Query performance is aided by bitmap indexes, as they can be scanned quickly because they are smaller.

The biggest drawback of bitmap indexes is that DML operations can be much slower. If you use bitmap indexes, the DML performance problems can be avoided simply by disabling or dropping the indexes prior to the DML operation(s), and then enabling or rebuilding them after the DML operation is complete.

The existence of bitmap join indexes within your star schema can aid query performance because joined columns between the fact and dimension tables were stored at index creation time, which helps query performance at execution time.

■ ■ ■

## CHAPTER 4

Index-Organized Tables

The simplest explanation of an index-organized table is that it is accessed like any other Oracle table (typically a heap-organized table) but is physically stored like an Oracle B-tree index. Index-organized tables are typically created on "thin" tables (tables without too many columns). Typically, multiple columns of the table make up the primary key of the index-organized table. The non-key columns can also be stored as part of the B-tree index. The proper configuration and use of index-organized tables is fairly specific and does not meet all application needs.

Understanding the Structure

From a user or developer perspective, an index-organized table (IOT) appears like a normal table. IOTs are stored in a B-tree structure. There must be a primary key on an index-organized table, as the data is stored in primary key order. Since there is no data segment, there are no physical ROWID values for index-organized tables. Figure 4-1 presents an example of an IOT.

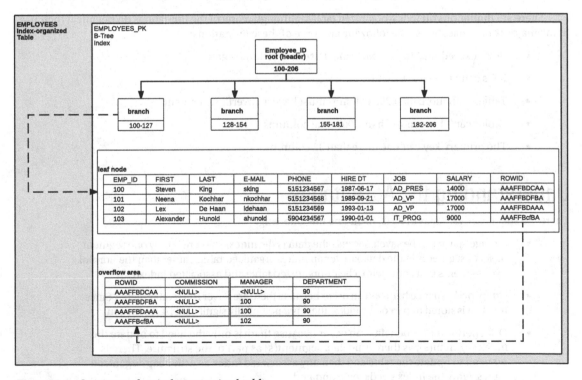

Figure 4-1. *Structure of an index-organized table*

© Darl Kuhn, Sam R. Alapati and Bill Padfield 2016
D. Kuhn et al., *Expert Oracle Indexing and Access Paths*, DOI 10.1007/978-1-4842-1984-3_4

IOTs support many of the same features found in heap-organized tables, such as

- Constraints

- Partitioning

- Triggers

- LOB columns

- Parallelism

- Indexes (e.g., secondary indexes on IOTs)

- Global hash-partitioned indexes

- Online reorganization

Because all of the data within an index-organized table is stored within the index itself, there are physical differences in the way an index-organized table is stored, as compared to a normal B-tree index that supports a normal heap-organized table. Some of the unique aspects of IOTs are as follows:

- Secondary indexes use logical ROWIDs rather than physical ROWIDs.

- They *require* a primary key.

- Primary key compression can be used to save storage and reduce the size of an IOT.

- An overflow segment can be used for non-key column data.

- Secondary bitmap indexes require a defined mapping table.

- Non-key column data is stored in the leaf blocks of an IOT.

There are limitations on index-organized tables, although many of the limitations do not affect their use in the majority of applications. The following are some of these limitations:

- Rows exceeding 50% of a block must use an overflow segment.

- IOTs can't use virtual columns.

- Tables with more than 255 columns must have an overflow segment.

- Tables can't have more than 1,000 total columns.

- The primary key can't be more than 32 columns.

Understanding the Advantages

There are specific advantages of IOTs, including the following:

- Storage space can be saved because the data is the index, so there is only one segment or set of segments in the database for an index-organized table, rather than the normal two segments that come with a heap-organized table and associated index(es).

- Query performance benefits can occur because there are fewer I/O requirements. Since the data is stored as part of the index, there is a potentially significant I/O reduction.

- DML performance benefits can occur because there is only the need to update the index segment(s), as there is no data segment(s) as part of the structure. There is no need to update the table and then any associated index as with heap-organized tables. Only the index needs to be updated.

Index-organized tables are most beneficial in OLTP environments for the following reasons:

- IOTs allow fast primary key access.

- IOTs allow online reorganization, which is essential in an OLTP environment.

- IOTs allow fast data retrieval in applications like Internet search engines.

The biggest challenge with index-organized tables is deciding when to use them. If you have tables that have several columns that make up the primary key, and the table itself is not dense as far as the number of columns, it *may* be a candidate as an IOT. However, this by itself is not reason enough to make a table into an index-organized table. There should be a tangible benefit gained from having a table structure be index-organized, and this may require some testing of your application. Generally, index-organized tables provide fast lookup of the primary key. They can be slower for inserts. Likewise, secondary index access isn't as fast as a normal B-tree index because index-organized table rows don't have the physical ROWID that would be found in a heap-organized table. Instead, IOTs use a logical ROWID, which isn't as exact as a physical ROWID and can become outdated over time. Because of this, index-organized tables may have to be rebuilt periodically for performance reasons. All in all, the use of index-organized tables should be limited and specific to a particular need. They are best used when fast primary key access is required. As mentioned, performing DML on index-organized tables is slower and over time can cause a degradation of query performance. Therefore, IOTs are best suited for data that is fairly static, with minimal DML activity.

Creating an Index-Organized Table

The data definition language (DDL) for an index-organized table is very similar to the DDL for a heap-organized table. The key difference is the use of the ORGANIZATION INDEX clause, which tells Oracle that you are creating an index-organized table; for example:

```
SQL> CREATE TABLE locations_iot
  2  (LOCATION_ID          NUMBER(4)          NOT NULL
  3  ,STREET_ADDRESS       VARCHAR2(40)
  4  ,POSTAL_CODE          VARCHAR2(12)
  5  ,CITY                 VARCHAR2(30)       NOT NULL
  6  ,STATE_PROVINCE       VARCHAR2(25)
  7  ,COUNTRY_ID           CHAR(2)
  8  ,CONSTRAINT locations_iot_pk PRIMARY KEY (location_id)
  9  )
 10  ORGANIZATION INDEX;

Table created.
```

As previously stated, you must have a primary key defined on an IOT. Since the IOT is stored in a B-tree index structure, there is no physical ROWID stored with each row. That's why you must have a primary key on an IOT—so that each row can be uniquely identified.

The B-tree structure of an index-organized table is based on the primary key values. If you don't specify a primary key, you will get the following error:

```
SQL> CREATE TABLE locations_iot
  2  (LOCATION_ID          NUMBER(4)          NOT NULL
  3  ,STREET_ADDRESS       VARCHAR2(40)
  4  ,POSTAL_CODE          VARCHAR2(12)
  5  ,CITY                 VARCHAR2(30)       NOT NULL
```

```
  6   ,STATE_PROVINCE        VARCHAR2(25)
  7   ,COUNTRY_ID            CHAR(2)
  8   )
  9   ORGANIZATION INDEX;

organization index
              *
ERROR at line 10:
ORA-25175: no PRIMARY KEY constraint found
```

For the most part, index-organized tables can be partitioned just like a heap-organized table. You can partition index-organized tables using the following partitioning methods: range, list, or hash partitioning. Using the LOCATIONS_IOT from the previous example, you can list partition the table by STATE_PROVINCE based on whether it is a domestic or an international state province, as shown in the following DDL:

```
SQL> CREATE TABLE locations_iot
  2   (LOCATION_ID           NUMBER(4)              NOT NULL
  3   ,STREET_ADDRESS        VARCHAR2(40)
  4   ,POSTAL_CODE           VARCHAR2(12)
  5   ,CITY                  VARCHAR2(30)           NOT NULL
  6   ,STATE_PROVINCE        VARCHAR2(25)           NOT NULL
  7   ,COUNTRY_ID            CHAR(2)
  8   ,constraint locations_iot_pk primary key (location_id, state_province)
  9   )
 10   ORGANIZATION INDEX
 11   partition by list(STATE_PROVINCE)
 12   (partition p_intl values
 13   ('Maharashtra','Bavaria','New South Wales', 'BE','Geneve',
 14    'Tokyo Prefecture', 'Sao Paulo','Manchester','Utrecht',
 15    'Ontario','Yukon','Oxford'),
 16   partition p_domestic values ('Texas','New Jersey','Washington','California'));

Table created.
```

You can't use composite partitioning in relation to index-organized tables. The following DDL snippet is attempting to create a composite range-list partitioned table:

```
SQL> CREATE TABLE locations_iot
  2   ...
 17   organization index
 18   partition by range(hire_date)
 19   subpartition by list( DEPARTMENT_ID)
 20   subpartition template
 21   (SUBPARTITION JOB10 VALUES ('10')
 22   ,SUBPARTITION JOB20 VALUES ('20')
 23   ,SUBPARTITION JOB30 VALUES ('30')
 24   ,SUBPARTITION JOB40 VALUES ('40')
 25   ,SUBPARTITION JOB50 VALUES ('50')
 26   ,SUBPARTITION JOB60 VALUES ('60')
 27   ,SUBPARTITION JOB70 VALUES ('70')
 28   ,SUBPARTITION JOB80 VALUES ('80')
```

```
29  ,SUBPARTITION JOB90 VALUES ('90')
30  ,SUBPARTITION JOB100 VALUES ('100')
31  ,SUBPARTITION JOB110 VALUES ('110')
32  (
33  partition p1990 values less than ('1991-01-01'),
...
45  );

subpartition template
*
ERROR at line 20:
ORA-25198: only range, list, and hash partitioning are supported for
index-organized table
```

This error clearly indicates that composite partitioning is not supported. For more information on the features of IOTs and their limitations, see the *Oracle Database Administrator's Guide* for your release of the database.

Adding an Overflow Segment

For index-organized tables, it is common, and even recommended, to create an overflow area for row data as part of the overall index-organized table structure. The typical index-organized table that includes an overflow area is structured as follows:

- B-tree index entry, which includes the following:

    - Primary key columns

    - Some non-key columns, depending on PCTTHRESHOLD and INCLUDING clause values specified

    - A physical ROWID pointer to the overflow segment

- Overflow segment, which contains the remaining non-key column values

In a normal B-tree index, the leaf node contains the index column key value, and then the ROWID for the row in the data segment. With index-organized tables, all the non-key column values are stored within the leaf blocks of the index by default. If the row data becomes very wide, the B-tree entries can become very large. This can slow data retrieval simply because the index must traverse more index blocks.

The overflow segment can aid in the efficiency of the overall B-tree index of an index-organized table by storing some of the non-key column values in an overflow data segment of the IOT, which is used solely to store these non-key column values. Associated with the overflow area is the PCTTHRESHOLD parameter, which specifies how column data goes to the overflow segment. If the length of a row is greater than the percentage of the index block specified by the PCTTHRESHOLD parameter (the default is 50), every column that exceeds the threshold will be stored in the overflow area. Also, you can specify the overflow segment to a specific tablespace, if desired.

■ **Tip** Use the ANALYZE TABLE...LIST CHAINED ROWS command to determine if you have set PCTTHRESHOLD appropriately.

In contrast to the PCTTHRESHOLD parameter, there is the INCLUDING clause, which specifies the last table column for the row data that will be stored in the B-tree index segment. All columns *after* the column specified by the INCLUDING clause will be stored in the overflow area. It is possible to specify both the PCTTHRESHOLD and INCLUDING clauses, as shown in the following example:

```
SQL> CREATE TABLE employees
  2  (
  3    EMPLOYEE_ID          NUMBER(6)          NOT NULL
  4    ,FIRST_NAME          VARCHAR2(20)
  5    ,LAST_NAME           VARCHAR2(25)       NOT NULL
  6    ,EMAIL               VARCHAR2(25)       NOT NULL
  7    ,PHONE_NUMBER        VARCHAR2(20)
  8    ,HIRE_DATE           DATE               NOT NULL
  9    ,JOB_ID              VARCHAR2(10)       NOT NULL
 10    ,SALARY              NUMBER(8,2)
 11    ,COMMISSION_PCT      NUMBER(2,2)
 12    ,MANAGER_ID          NUMBER(6)
 13    ,DEPARTMENT_ID       NUMBER(4)
 14    ,CONSTRAINT employees_pk PRIMARY KEY (employee_id)
 15  )
 16  ORGANIZATION INDEX
 17  TABLESPACE empindex_s
 18  PCTTHRESHOLD 40
 19  INCLUDING salary
 20  OVERFLOW TABLESPACE overflow_s

Table created.
```

Figure 4-1 shows an illustration of an index-organized EMPLOYEES table row as stored in the table, as well as the overflow segment. In the example, you can see that the primary key in the EMPLOYEES table is the EMPLOYEE_ID, and the root block, branch blocks, and leaf blocks are structured based on the primary key. Within the leaf blocks themselves is the primary key, as well as all of the non-key columns up through the SALARY column, which corresponds to the INCLUDING clause in the CREATE TABLE DDL statement. All column data after the SALARY column is therefore stored in the overflow segment.

For performance reasons, the order of columns within an index-organized table is important, unlike normal heap-organized tables. This is simply because of the overflow segment. The most queried columns should *not* be placed in the overflow segment, simply because it is an extra I/O operation to retrieve the remaining column data for a given row. For this reason, the least queried columns should be placed on the trailing end of the table DDL, especially those after the column specified in the INCLUDING clause. In the table example, let's say that you determine through user interviews that the most queried columns on your EMPLOYEES table will be the JOB_ID, DEPARTMENT_ID, and MANAGER_ID columns. The initial DDL placed the DEPARTMENT_ID and MANAGER_ID columns in the overflow segment.

Based on the user interviews, it may be beneficial to move these two columns *above* the INCLUDING clause and possibly shift some other columns below the INCLUDING clause. The following example shows a modified DDL that rearranges the column order such that the DEPARTMENT_ID and MANAGER_ID are moved above the INCLUDING clause, and thus out of the overflow segment:

```
CREATE TABLE employees
(
 EMPLOYEE_ID            NUMBER(6)           NOT NULL
 ,FIRST_NAME            VARCHAR2(20)
 ,LAST_NAME             VARCHAR2(25)        NOT NULL
 ,EMAIL                 VARCHAR2(25)        NOT NULL
 ,PHONE_NUMBER          VARCHAR2(20)
 ,HIRE_DATE             DATE                NOT NULL
 ,JOB_ID                VARCHAR2(10)        NOT NULL
 ,SALARY                NUMBER(8,2)
 ,MANAGER_ID            NUMBER(6)
 ,DEPARTMENT_ID         NUMBER(4)
 ,COMMISSION_PCT        NUMBER(2,2)
 ,MANAGER_ID            NUMBER(6)
 ,DEPARTMENT_ID         NUMBER(4)
 ,CONSTRAINT employees_pk PRIMARY KEY (employee_id)
)
ORGANIZATION INDEX
TABLESPACE empindex_s
PCTTHRESHOLD 40
INCLUDING DEPARTMENT_ID
OVERFLOW TABLESPACE overflow_s;
```

Based on your user interviews, it may also mean (based on the necessary queries against the EMPLOYEES table) that you decide not to create an overflow segment for the EMPLOYEES table. Creation of the overflow segment, and which columns to place there, should be done after careful analysis based on the proposed usage of the table columns.

If you choose to specify an INCLUDING clause within the DDL for an IOT, you must specify an OVERFLOW area, else you will receive the following error:

```
create table employees_iot
*
ERROR at line 1:
ORA-25186: INCLUDING clause specified for index-organized table without
OVERFLOW
```

Also, the Oracle data dictionary can become cluttered with entries for the overflow areas that have been dropped from an index-organized table. Recyclebin objects are normally seen in the DBA_SEGMENTS view, but for IOT overflow segments, you can see them in the USER_TABLES view (or appropriate ALL or DBA views), including those that have been dropped. The following query and results provide an example:

```
SQL> select table_name, iot_type from user_tables
  2  where iot_type like '%IOT%';

TABLE_NAME                       IOT_TYPE
-------------------------------- ------------
SYS_IOT_OVER_77689               IOT_OVERFLOW
SYS_IOT_OVER_77692               IOT_OVERFLOW
SYS_IOT_OVER_77697               IOT_OVERFLOW
EMPLOYEES_IOT                    IOT
```

Therefore, purge the recyclebin to get rid of superfluous overflow entries.

```
SQL> purge recyclebin;
```

Recyclebin purged.

After you purge the recyclebin, the dropped overflow objects no longer show in the data dictionary.

```
SQL> select table_name, iot_type from user_tables
  2  where iot_type like '%IOT%''

TABLE_NAME                           IOT_TYPE
------------------------------       ------------
SYS_IOT_OVER_77697                   IOT_OVERFLOW
EMPLOYEES_IOT                        IOT
```

■ **Tip**   Always attempt to keep the most frequently accessed columns within the table itself—and outside of the overflow segment—for better access performance.

Compressing an Index-Organized Table

You can use a concept called *key compression* on index-organized tables to save storage space and compress data. It's called "key compression" because it can eliminate repeated values of the key columns. You can use key compression with either a CREATE TABLE statement or an ALTER TABLE statement. The following is a sample DDL of a CREATE TABLE statement with key compression enabled:

```
SQL> CREATE TABLE employees_iot
  2  (
  3    EMPLOYEE_ID         NUMBER(7)        NOT NULL
  4    ,FIRST_NAME         VARCHAR2(20)
  5    ,LAST_NAME          VARCHAR2(25)     NOT NULL
  6    ,EMAIL              VARCHAR2(25)     NOT NULL
  7    ,PHONE_NUMBER       VARCHAR2(20)
  8    ,HIRE_DATE          DATE             NOT NULL
  9    ,JOB_ID             VARCHAR2(10)     NOT NULL
 10    ,SALARY             NUMBER(8,2)
 11    ,COMMISSION_PCT     NUMBER(2,2)
 12    ,MANAGER_ID         NUMBER(6)
 13    ,DEPARTMENT_ID      NUMBER(4)
 15    ,CONSTRAINT employees_iot_pk PRIMARY KEY (employee_id, job_id)
 17  )
 18  ORGANIZATION INDEX COMPRESS 1
 19  TABLESPACE empindex_s
 20  PCTTHRESHOLD 40
 21  INCLUDING salary
 22  OVERFLOW TABLESPACE overflow_s;

Table created.
```

If you have a pre-existing table on which you want to enable key compression, you can simply use the `ALTER TABLE...MOVE` statement to enable the compression.

```
SQL> ALTER TABLE employees_iot MOVE TABLESPACE empindex_s COMPRESS 1;

Table altered.
```

You can only use key compression when there are multiple columns as part of the primary key; otherwise, you receive the following message when creating the table:

```
CREATE TABLE employees_iot
*
ERROR at line 1:
ORA-25193: cannot use COMPRESS option for a single column key
```

For obvious reasons, you can't use the same number of key columns as is within the primary key for the key compression factor specified in the `COMPRESS` clause because that represents a unique value, and therefore no key compression is possible. You receive the following error if you attempt to create the table with the same compression factor as the number of primary key columns:

```
CREATE TABLE employees_iot
*
ERROR at line 1:
ORA-25194: invalid COMPRESS prefix length value
```

The compression occurs when there are duplicates within the columns of the primary key. For instance, if the employee with `EMPLOYEE_ID` 100 worked several jobs over the years, they would have several entries for the `EMPLOYEE_ID/JOB_ID` combination. For rows with duplicates of the `EMPLOYEE_ID` itself, all repeated values would be compressed. Table 4-1 provides a brief example of the results from key compression.

Table 4-1. Example of Key Compression for Employee_ID 100

Employee_ID	Job_ID	Employee_ID Value Compressed?
100	AD_ASST	NO (first entry)
100	IT_PROG	YES
100	AD_VP	YES
100	...	YES for all subsequent entries

Building Secondary Indexes

The index-organized table can be viewed the same as a heap-organized table in that if other indexes are needed to speed query performance, secondary indexes can be added to index-organized tables because they can be added on heap-organized tables. The following example shows how to create a secondary index on `DEPARTMENT_ID` in the `EMPLOYEES_IOT` table:

```
SQL> CREATE INDEX employees_iot_1i
  2  ON employees_iot (department_id);
```

You can also create secondary indexes on partitioned IOTs.

```
SQL> CREATE INDEX employees_iot_1i
  2  on employees_iot (department_id)
  3  LOCAL;
```

The key difference between secondary indexes on heap-organized tables and secondary indexes on index-organized tables is that there is no physical ROWID for each row in an index-organized table because the table data is stored as part of the B-tree index. Therefore, all access to data within an index-organized table is based on the primary key.

Instead of the normal physical ROWIDs to locate table rows, index-organized tables use a logical ROWID, which is used by any secondary indexes on the IOT in order to retrieve data. The logical ROWID is the equivalent to a physical guess of the row location based on the ROWID when the index entry was first created. Based on the physical guess, Oracle scans through leaf blocks searching for a match. The physical guess doesn't change over time, even if a row's physical location changes. For instance, leaf block splits can occur over time, which can fragment the index and change a row's physical location. Because the physical guess is not updated even if a row location changes, the physical guesses can become outdated or stale over time.

You can get information from the data dictionary to determine if the physical guesses for an IOT are stale by querying the PCT_DIRECT_ACCESS column of USER_INDEXES, as follows:

```
SQL> select index_name, index_type, pct_direct_access
  2  from user_indexes;
```

INDEX_NAME	INDEX_TYPE	PCT_DIRECT_ACCESS
EMPLOYEES_IOT_PK	IOT - TOP	0
EMPLOYEES_PART_1I	NORMAL	100

If the PCT_DIRECT_ACCESS value falls below 100, it means that the secondary index entries are becoming migrated, and the physical guess can start to be inaccurate enough that extra I/O operations start occurring and performance starts to degrade. Once the PCT_DIRECT_ACCESS falls below 80, performance degradation starts becoming more noticeable, and the index may be a good candidate for a rebuild operation.

In order to refresh the logical ROWIDs over time, there are two primary ways to address the issue:

- Rebuild the secondary index.
- Update the block references for the index.

The first way to refresh the logical ROWIDs within secondary indexes is simply by rebuilding the index(es). Rebuilding secondary indexes built on index-organized tables is no different from rebuilding indexes on heap-organized tables.

```
SQL> ALTER INDEX employees_1i REBUILD;
```

Of course, depending on the size of the table, rebuilding one or more secondary indexes can take time, and with shrinking maintenance windows and ever-increasing availability windows on databases, it can be problematic to rebuild indexes on large tables on a regular basis.

An alternative to rebuilding your secondary indexes and a quick way to fix stale physical guesses within your secondary indexes is to use the ALTER INDEX...UPDATE BLOCK REFERENCES command, which quickly realigns stale physical guesses without having to rebuild an entire index.

```
SQL> ALTER INDEX employees_part_1i UPDATE BLOCK REFERENCES;
```

You can also place bitmap indexes on IOTs as secondary indexes. Refer to Chapter 3 for examples of creating bitmap indexes on an IOT. Within the bitmap index, since there is an entry for each row in a given table, there is normally a ROWID, along with the bitmap and data value corresponding to the indexed column. Since there are no physical ROWID values with an index-organized table, a bitmap index that is built on an index-organized table must be managed differently. When creating the bitmap index on the IOT, you must include a mapping table within the bitmap index. Again, see Chapter 3 for an example of how to build a bitmap index on an index-organized table.

A mapping table is simply a heap-organized table that is used to store the logical ROWID values. The mapping table is essentially an object that replaces the physical ROWID representation with a logical ROWID representation for the rows in the table. So, within the bitmap index itself, the physical ROWID is from the mapping table, rather than from the base table. Then the mapping table is accessed to retrieve the logical ROWID in order to access the data from the index-organized table. Figure 4-2 shows an example of a bitmap index with a mapping table.

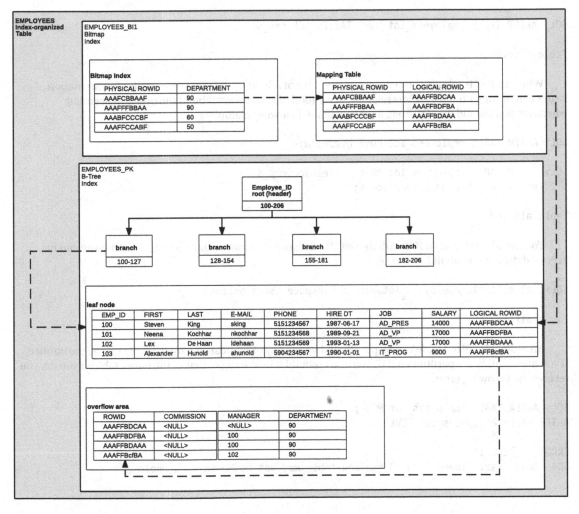

Figure 4-2. *A bitmap index within an index-organized table*

Rebuilding an Index-Organized Table

An index-organized table is a B-tree index. It can become fragmented over time and can incur the same issues as a normal B-tree index: an expanded index depth over time, an unbalanced tree, and sparse blocks, to name a few. Therefore, you can rebuild an index-organized table as you would a normal B-tree index. The obvious difference is that because it is regarded as a table, you rebuild an IOT with the ALTER TABLE command, as shown in the following example:

```
SQL> ALTER TABLE employees_iot MOVE;

Table altered.
```

If you want to move the IOT to a different tablespace, simply specify the tablespace within the ALTER TABLE clause, as shown in the following example:

```
SQL> ALTER TABLE employees_iot MOVE TABLESPACE emp_s;

Table altered.
```

When an IOT is rebuilt, the overflow segment is not rebuilt by default. Since similar fragmentation issues can occur with the overflow segment, it's a good idea to always rebuild the overflow segment whenever you rebuild the IOT itself, as shown in the following examples:

```
SQL> ALTER TABLE employees_iot MOVE overflow;

SQL> ALTER TABLE employees_iot MOVE tablespace emp_s
  2  overflow tablespace overflow_s;

Table altered.
```

You can also rebuild an IOT with the ONLINE clause, which means that the existing structure can be accessed during the rebuild operation.

```
SQL>  alter table employees_iot move tablespace users online;

Table altered.
```

An index-organized table can be partitioned just as any other heap-organized table can be partitioned. If you are rebuilding a partitioned IOT, you can't rebuild it in one step—that is, the entire table; if you do, you receive the following error:

```
SQL> ALTER TABLE employees_iot MOVE;
ALTER TABLE employees_iot MOVE
            *
ERROR at line 1:
ORA-28660: Partitioned Index-Organized table may not be MOVEd as a whole
```

If you wish to rebuild an entire partitioned IOT, you must do it one partition at a time. You need to get the partition names from the index itself using the USER_IND_PARTITIONS view (or, of course, optionally the equivalent ALL or DBA views), and then issue the ALTER TABLE…MOVE PARTITION command in order to move each partition of an IOT, as shown in the following example:

```
SQL> select partition_name
  2  from user_ind_partitions
  3* where index_name = 'EMPLOYEES_IOT_PK';

PARTITION_NAME
------------------------------
P1990
...
P1999
P2000
PMAX

SQL> ALTER TABLE employees_iot MOVE PARTITION p1990;

Table altered.
```

You must rebuild the IOT with an ALTER TABLE command. If you attempt to rebuild an IOT via the primary key index, you receive the following error:

```
SQL> alter index employees_iot_pk rebuild;
alter index employees_iot_pk rebuild
*
ERROR at line 1:
ORA-28650: Primary index on an IOT cannot be rebuilt
```

Converting to or from an Index-Organized Table

You may have an existing table that you want to convert either to an index-organized table or from an index-organized table due to application needs. In either case, the conversion process is straightforward. The simplest method is to use the "create table as select" syntax. The following examples show how to perform these conversions using this method.

First, let's say you have a heap-organized table that meets the fundamental requirements of an index-organized table, and you wish to convert that table to an IOT, as follows:

```
CREATE TABLE locations_iot
 (LOCATION_ID
 ,STREET_ADDRESS
 ,POSTAL_CODE
 ,CITY
 ,STATE_PROVINCE
 ,COUNTRY_ID
 ,CONSTRAINT locations_iot_pk PRIMARY KEY (location_id)
 )
 ORGANIZATION INDEX
 as select * from locations;

Table created.
```

Conversely, if you have an index-organized table that is causing performance problems, and you want to convert to a heap-organized table, you could do as shown in the following example:

```
CREATE TABLE locations
 (LOCATION_ID
 ,STREET_ADDRESS
 ,POSTAL_CODE
 ,CITY
 ,STATE_PROVINCE
 ,COUNTRY_ID
 ,CONSTRAINT locations_pk PRIMARY KEY (location_id)
 )
 as select * from locations_iot;

Table created.
```

After you have completed the operation, you'd then have to drop the original table, of course, and if necessary, rename the newly created table to the desired name.

Based on how an application and its data can change over time, you may need to convert a table from a heap-organized table to an IOT or from an IOT to a heap-organized table. The aforementioned examples are one simple way to do this.

Reporting on Index-Organized Tables

Getting information from the Oracle data dictionary on index-organized tables is straightforward. Look at the following query, which gives the fundamental information regarding the IOTs within your database:

```
SQL> select i.table_name, i.index_name, i.index_type, i.pct_threshold,
  2         nvl(column_name,'NONE') include_column
  3  from user_indexes i left join user_tab_columns c
  4  on (i.table_name = c.table_name)
  5  and (i.include_column = c.column_id)
  6  where index_type = 'IOT - TOP';
```

TABLE_NAME	INDEX_NAME	INDEX_TYPE	PCT_THRESHOLD	INCLUDE_COLUMN
LOCATIONS_IOT	LOCATIONS_IOT_PK	IOT - TOP	50	NONE
EMPLOYEES_PART	EMPLOYEES_PART_PK	IOT - TOP	50	NONE
COUNTRIES	COUNTRY_C_ID_PK	IOT - TOP	50	NONE
EMPLOYEES_IOT	EMPLOYEES_IOT_PK	IOT - TOP	40	SALARY

From this query, you get the following information:

- The table name

- The index name(s), which includes the primary key and any secondary indexes on the table

- The index type, which will be designated as 'IOT - TOP' for index-organized tables

- The PCTTHRESHOLD for the table

- The INCLUDING column, if specified

You need to do an outer join to the USER_TAB_COLUMNS view to get the column name for the column specified by the INCLUDING clause, which is optional when creating an index-organized table. The COLUMN_ID column on the USER_INDEXES view specifies the column number of the column for the INCLUDING clause. If there is no INCLUDING clause specified on the index-organized table, the COLUMN_ID column will be populated with a default value of '0' or with the value from the USER_TAB_COLUMNS COLUMN_ID column.

If you look at the USER_TABLES view, both the IOT itself and the overflow segment are shown.

```
SQL> select table_name, iot_type, segment_created from user_tables;

TABLE_NAME                       IOT_TYPE      SEG
-----------------------------    ------------  ---
SYS_IOT_OVER_77704               IOT_OVERFLOW  YES
EMPLOYEES_IOT                    IOT           YES
```

If querying DBA_SEGMENTS to get the actual physical characteristics of the IOT itself, as well as the overflow segment, remember to use the primary key segment_name; the table name itself will not be specified within the DBA_SEGMENTS view, since the IOT is essentially an index segment.

```
  1  select segment_name, segment_type
  2  from dba_segments
  3* where segment_name like '%IOT%'
SQL> /

SEGMENT_NAME                     SEGMENT_TYPE
-----------------------------    ------------------
SYS_IOT_OVER_77704               TABLE
EMPLOYEES_IOT_PK                 INDEX
```

Summary

Index-organized tables have a specific niche in applications and are not really suitable for extensive use. The following are some guidelines to determine if a table is a good candidate for an IOT:

- Is it a table with a small number of columns?

- Is it a table made up of a composite primary key (several columns of the table)?

- Does the table require fast primary key access?

- Is the data in the table fairly static—with little DML activity?

IOTs are generally better suited for OLTP applications than data warehouse applications, simply because OLTP applications often have a requirement for very fast lookup of primary key data. IOTs are generally avoided in the data warehouse simply because a data warehouse typically does bulk loading of data, and the performance of inserts on IOTs is slower. This is especially noticeable with a large volume of data. Also, if there are access requirements to place many secondary indexes on the IOT, it can generally be slower just because no physical ROWID exists within an IOT. This can slow the access of data, especially over time, as physical guesses become stale. Of course, these are guidelines. Deciding whether to use IOTs within your application depends on your specific data loading and data retrieval requirements. You should also consider your available maintenance windows, which can be used in part to rebuild IOTs when they become fragmented.

All this said, the index-organized table is a valuable tool. Knowing the features, advantages, and disadvantages can help you decide where and when to properly implement an index-organized table within your application.

■ ■ ■

## CHAPTER 5

Specialized Indexes

Thus far, you've learned how to create normal Oracle indexes, which include both B-tree indexes as well as bitmap indexes. You also learned how to create and manage index organized tables. This chapter explains several specialized indexes that you can create for serving various needs. Most of these specialized indexes are actually B-tree indexes, so it's not the organization of the index that makes them special. For example, an invisible index is an index that's not automatically available to the cost-based optimizer, unless you make it available by setting a specific initialization parameter. You use invisible indexes mainly for testing the use of an index and to make sure that an index is redundant before you drop it.

The chapter explains how to use function-based indexes when your application applies functions to a column value. Besides using Oracle-provided functions, you can create custom functions and create indexes based on those functions. Function-based indexes let you create indexes based on arithmetical expressions. You will also learn how to use the CASE construct to generate indexes based only on some rows in a table. This chapter explains the rationale behind the use of reverse key indexes and discusses alternatives to these indexes when dealing with index contention in an Oracle RAC environment. The chapter also introduces application domain indexes, which help you create your own index structures to implement index types that Oracle doesn't currently provide.

Invisible Indexes

When you create any index, by default, the optimizer is aware of the index and it starts taking account of the index in all its cost estimations. However, there are occasions when you may want to create an index but control when the optimizer can use the index. For example, you may decide to create an invisible index when you build a new index, validate an index, or test the impact of a new index. You can hide an index from the optimizer by creating an index as an "invisible" index. You can also alter the status of an existing index by making it invisible. You can toggle the status of the index between visible and invisible as you please.

■ **Note** Since the database must continue to maintain a visible index when inserts, deletes, and updates occur, it is important that you're fully aware of any invisible indexes.

When to Create an Invisible Index

In Chapter 7, you'll learn how to monitor the usage of an index by using the monitoring clause in an alter index (or create index) statement. If your analysis reveals that a certain index isn't being used by any queries, you may want to get rid of that index. You can use invisible indexes in any situation where you're considering either dropping an index or making it unusable. Both of these actions are very expensive if you

© Darl Kuhn, Sam R. Alapati and Bill Padfield 2016
D. Kuhn et al., *Expert Oracle Indexing and Access Paths*, DOI 10.1007/978-1-4842-1984-3_5

need to use the index later on. If you drop the index, you have to re-create it; if you made an index unusable, you have to rebuild it. Invisible indexes are very helpful when you have a situation where specific modules of an application benefit from an index but the index adversely affects other parts of the application. In this case, you can make the index visible only to those modules of the application where the index is beneficial.

The biggest use of an invisible index is when you want to test if you should drop an index. There are times when an index helps just one or two queries perform better but degrades the performance of a bunch of other queries. In cases like this, you're faced with the dilemma as to whether to retain the index or to get rid of it. Well, invisible indexes let you have the cake and eat it, too. You can specify the use of the index only when you want to and let the index remain invisible the rest of the time! Before Oracle introduced invisible indexes, you had to make an index unusable first and then test the performance of your queries. If you decided that performance was better without the index, you could then drop the index. If you decided to keep the index, you had to rebuild the unusable index to make it usable again. All this takes time and effort. Of course, invisible indexes make all this work unnecessary. You simply alter the status of a normal index to that of an invisible index and test.

A good time to use an invisible index is when one or two ad hoc queries require an index. You can make the index visible only to these queries and change its status to an invisible index for all other queries.

Often you find that an application is running slow because of a large full table scan. You figure out that you can avoid the full table scan by creating an index. However, this is not a simple decision in most cases because that index, while it helps avoid the full table scan for the specific query you are troubleshooting, may adversely affect other queries. Invisible indexes are perfect for cases such as this where you want to selectively expose an index to the optimizer.

Creating an Invisible Index

You can create an invisible index by including the INVISIBLE clause in an index creation statement, like so:

```
SQL>  create index test_idx1 on products(prod_id) invisible tablespace products_tbsp;

     Index created.

SQL>
```

You can make an existing index invisible by using the following alter index statement:

```
SQL> alter index test_idx1 invisible;

Index altered.

SQL>
```

And you can toggle the status of the index back to visible by doing this:

```
SQL> alter index test_idx1 visible;
Index altered.
SQL>
```

Finding Invisible Indexes in Your Database

You can check the visibility status of an index by executing the following query:

```
SQL> select index_name, visibility from dba_indexes
 2* where visibility='INVISIBLE';

INDEX_NAME                     VISIBILITY
-----------                    --------------
TEST_IDX1                      INVISIBLE

SQL>
```

This query helps you easily keep track of all invisible indexes in your database. You should know about them because the database engine does need to maintain them. They are invisible, not free of cost.

Making an Invisible Index Available to the Optimizer

Once you make an index invisible, the optimizer doesn't use that index. Even specifying the INDEX hint won't make the optimizer see an invisible index. However, you can make an invisible index available to the optimizer at the session level or the system level by setting the optimizer_use_invisible_indexes parameter to true. The optimizer_use_invisible_indexes parameter controls the use of an invisible index. When you set this parameter to true, an invisible index is considered the same as a normal, visible index. If you set this parameter to false (the default value), the optimizer ignores the invisible index. By default, the optimizer_use_invisible_indexes initialization parameter is set to false, as shown here:

```
SQL> show parameter invisible

NAME                                 TYPE          VALUE
-----------------------------------  -----------   ----------
    optimizer_use_invisible_indexes  boolean       FALSE
SQL>
```

If you have an invisible index on a column, by default, the optimizer won't use that index. You can confirm this by running an explain plan for a SQL statement that involves the index. You'll notice that the database does a full table scan instead of using the invisible index.

You can make an invisible index available to the optimizer by using an index hint in a query. But first, you must set the optimizer_use_invisible_indexes parameter to true at the session or system level before you can specify the INDEX hint.

You can make all invisible indexes available to the optimizer by issuing the following alter session command:

```
SQL> alter session set optimizer_use_invisible_indexes=true;
Session altered.
SQL>
```

This statement makes all invisible statements available to all the users in the database.

Once you set the optimizer_use_invisible_indexes parameter to true, you're ready to specify the INDEX hint in a query to let the optimizer make use of the invisible index; for example:

```
SQL> select /*+ index(test_idx1) */ * from products where prod_id=9999;
```

If you've created a new index that you want to introduce into production, but you aren't quite sure how it's going to affect the queries that use the index, you can first test the efficacy of the index by making it visible to the optimizer through the alter session set optimizer_use_invisible_indexes=true statement, as explained earlier. Once you're satisfied with your testing, you can make the index visible to the optimizer in all sessions by issuing the alter index ...visible statement.

Maintaining an Invisible Index

The database maintains an invisible index the same way it does a normal visible index. You can also collect optimizer statistics on an invisible index, as shown here:

```
SQL> exec dbms_stats.gather_index_stats(user,'TEST_IDX1');
PL/SQL procedure successfully completed.
SQL>
```

Note that it's immaterial whether an index has the visible or invisible status when you collect statistics for that index. You can also rebuild an invisible index just as you would a regular index, as shown here:

```
SQL> alter index test_idx1 rebuild;
```

As you can see from these examples, there's absolutely no difference between visible and invisible indexes in regards to their maintenance.

Descending Indexes

Descending indexes are different from regular indexes in the sense that the data is ordered in descending order (by default, an Oracle database uses an ascending order of each column to create an index). Oracle treats a descending index as if it were a function-based index. Descending indexes are useful in cases where you order data in descending order, or when you search for the minimum or maximum value of a column that's indexed.

To create a descending index on a column, all you need to do is to add the DESC keyword at the end of the index creation statement, as shown here:

```
create index arrival_time_desc on flights (dest_airport, arrive_time desc);
Note: Reverse or bitmap indexes can't specify the DESC keyword
```

Descending indexes are ideal in situations where you need to specify a mixed sort of columns in a query. Let's use a simple example to understand how a descending index can help you.

1. First, create a test table.

```
SQL> create table object_test as
2    select object_name, object_id, created, owner
3    from dba_dobjects;
```

```
Table created.
SQL>
```

2. Create a regular index (not a descending index) on the OBJECT_NAME and OWNER columns.

```
SQL> create index test_idx11 on object_test (object_name, owner);

Index created.
SQL>
```

3. Gather statistics on the new index and then run the following query.

```
SQL> set autotrace traceonly explain;
SQL> select * from object_test
  2  where object_name between 'Y' and 'Z'
  3  order by object_name asc, owner desc;

Execution Plan
----------------------------------------------------------
Plan hash value: 293023843
--------------------
| Id  | Operation                             | Name        | Rows | Bytes | Cos
t (%CPU)| Time       |
-------------------------------------------------------------------
|   0 | SELECT STATEMENT                      |             |   64 |  2560 |
57   (2)| 00:00:01 |
|   1 |  SORT ORDER BY                        |             |   64 |  2560
57   (2)| 00:00:01 |
|   2 |   TABLE ACCESS BY INDEX ROWID BATCHED| OBJECT_TEST |   64 |  2560
56   (0)| 00:00:01 |
|*  3 |    INDEX RANGE SCAN                   | TEST_IDX11  |   64 |       |
3   (0)| 00:00:01 |
Predicate Information (identified by operation id):
---------------------------------------------------
   3 - access("OBJECT_NAME">='Y' AND "OBJECT_NAME"<='Z')
Note
   - dynamic statistics used: dynamic sampling (level=2)
SQL>
```

As the explain plan output reveals, Oracle sorts the values in the OWNER column in descending order, just as you requested. You can avoid this sort by creating an index that already has the OWNER column values in it, in descending order. Here's how you do it.

1. Create a new index. Specify that the owner column be indexed in descending order by adding the DESC clause.

```
SQL> create index test_idx22 on object_test (object_name, owner desc);
Index created.
SQL>
```

2. Run the following query to check its explain plan.

```
SQL> select * from object_test
  2       where object_name between 'Y' and 'Z'
  3* order by object_name asc, owner desc;
Execution Plan
----------------------------------------------------------
Plan hash value: 756387914

---------------------------------------------------------------------------
| Id  | Operation                   | Name        | Rows  | Bytes | Cost (%CPU)|
  Time       |
-----------
|   0 | SELECT STATEMENT            |             |    64 |  2560 |    56    (0)|
  00:00:01 |
|   1 |   TABLE ACCESS BY INDEX ROWID| OBJECT_TEST |    64 |  2560 |    56    (0)|
  00:00:01 |
|*  2 |    INDEX RANGE SCAN         | TEST_IDX22  |    64 |       |     3    (0)|
  00:00:01 |
-----------

Predicate Information (identified by operation id):
---------------------------------------------------
   2 - access("OBJECT_NAME">='Y' AND "OBJECT_NAME"<='Z')
Note
-----
   - dynamic statistics used: dynamic sampling (level=2)
SQL>
```

Note how the SORT operation (SORT ORDER BY) has disappeared. In this case, there is a descending index on the OWNER column, and hence the optimizer knows that it need not sort the rows in that column—the descending index contains the sorted values. To determine if a descending index is helpful, you need to evaluate the distribution of data in a column and the nature of your queries.

Function-Based Indexes

An Oracle database lets you create function-based indexes to facilitate queries that use values returned by a function. You can actually use a function or an expression to create a function-based index.

The advantage to using a function-based index is that the database computes the value of the function (or expression) that involves one or more columns ahead of time and stores it in the index that you create on the function. Since queries can use the precomputed values of expressions by looking up the index rather than having to compute the values at runtime, performance improves when using these indexes. Function-based indexes increase the probability of the database using the more efficient index range scan rather than an expensive full table scan. Note that while we classify a function-based index as a "specialized" index, it is still a regular B-tree index that is created based on a function (or expression) rather than a column.

Let's say that you've the following SQL statement with the WHERE clause specifying UPPER(LAST_NAME):

```
SQL>select first_name,last_name,phone_number
    from employees
    where UPPER(last_name) = UPPER('alapati');
```

As the query's explain plan output shows, the optimizer ignores the index on the LAST_NAME column and performs a full table scan.

```
Execution Plan
------------------------------------------------------------
Plan hash value: 1445457117
--------------------------------------------------------------------
| Id | Operation          | Name      | Rows | Bytes | Cost (%CPU)| Time     |
--------------------------------------------------------------------
|  0 | SELECT STATEMENT   |           |   1  |   30  |   3   (0)| 00:00:01 |
|* 1 | TABLE ACCESS FULL| EMPLOYEES |   1  |   30  |   3   (0)| 00:00:01 |
--------------------------------------------------------------------

Predicate Information (identified by operation id):
---------------------------------------------------
   1 - filter(UPPER("LAST_NAME")='ALAPATI')
```

The LAST_NAME column is indexed, but the optimizer skips the index and instead performs a full table scan. The reason for this is that the search is really not on the LAST_NAME; it's on UPPER(last_name). The database treats this as a different search and since there's no index on the UPPER function, it goes for a full table scan. In order for this query to use an index, you must create an index on the actual search expression, a function-based index. You can create the following function to make the database use an index on the LAST_NAME column:

```
SQL> create index emp_up_name
    on employees (upper(last_name));
```

If you issue the previous query now, the database uses your function-based index to retrieve the values of the LAST_NAME column. The following explain plan output shows that the query this time uses the function-based index:

```
Execution Plan
------------------------------------------------------------
Plan hash value: 3983250699
---------------------------------------------------------------------------
| Id | Operation                   | Name         | Rows | Bytes | Cost (%CPU) | Time     |
---------------------------------------------------------------------------
|  0 | SELECT STATEMENT            |              |   1  |   42  |   2   (0)  |00:00:01 |
|  1 | TABLE ACCESS BY INDEX ROWID | EMPLOYEES    |   1  |   42  |   2   (0)  |00:00:01 |
|* 2 | INDEX RANGE SCAN            | EMP_UPP_NAME |   1  |       |   1   (0)  |00:00:01 |
---------------------------------------------------------------------------

Predicate Information (identified by operation id):
---------------------------------------------------
   2 - access(UPPER("FIRST_NAME")='ALAPATI')
```

Creating a Function-Based Index

Function-based indexes are ideal for making queries run faster without changing the application logic and code. Function-based indexes are highly useful in case-sensitive searches and sorts and in searches on columns that have computations performed on them. The following are some examples that illustrate how to create a function-based index. Not only can you use Oracle-provided functions in a function-based index, but you can use any type of function you create as well. Case-insensitive searches are probably one of the most common reasons for creating a function-based index. The following example shows how to speed up case-insensitive searches by creating a function on the LAST_NAME column:

```
SQL> create index emp_lstname on employees (UPPER(LAST_NAME));
```

Index created.

SQL>

Once you create the function-based index as shown here, you can use the index expression in a query such as the following:

```
SQL> select *
  2  from employees
  3* where UPPER(LAST_NAME) LIKE 'S%_A'
```

The execution plan for this query shows that the optimizer is using the function-based index you created.

```
Execution Plan
----------------------------------------------------------
Plan hash value: 1134195146

--------------------------------------------------------------------------------
| Id  | Operation                   | Name        | Rows  | Bytes | Cost (%CPU)| Time     |
--------------------------------------------------------------------------------
|   0 | SELECT STATEMENT            |             |     5 |   425 |     2   (0)| 00:00:01 |
|   1 |  TABLE ACCESS BY INDEX ROWID| EMPLOYEES   |     5 |   425 |     2   (0)| 00:00:01 |
|*  2 |   INDEX RANGE SCAN          | EMP_LSTNAME |     1 |       |     1   (0)| 00:00:01 |
--------------------------------------------------------------------------------

Predicate Information (identified by operation id):
---------------------------------------------------
   2 - access(UPPER("LAST_NAME") LIKE 'S%_A')
       filter(UPPER("LAST_NAME") LIKE 'S%_A')
SQL>
```

This example showed how to create a function-based index using the Oracle function UPPER. You can create a function-based index based on expressions without ever using any function, as shown in the following example:

```
SQL> create index test_idx
          on weather ((maxtemp-mintemp) desc, maxtemp);
```

The index test_idx materializes the values of the expressions and stores the differences between maxtemp and mintemp. If you want to find all the rows where the difference in temperatures is less than 25 and the maximum temperature is greater than 80, you can do so by issuing the following statement:

```
SQL> select * from weather
       where ((maxtemp-mintemp) < '25' and maxtemp > '80');
```

You can also create an index on a CASE statement (or function) by using the following syntax:

```
SQL> create index case_tab_idx1 on case_tab (case source_tran when 'PO'
       then po_id when 'VOUCHER' then voucher_id else journal_id end);
Index created.
SQL>
```

This example shows how to use a function-based index for indexing only specific rows in a table. You can issue a query such as the following to query the case_tab table:

```
select source_tran, case when source_tran like 'GL%' then journal_id
when source_tran like 'PO%' then po_id
when source_tran like 'VO%' then voucher_id
...
```

The function for the index on case_tab returns a NULL for some rows, which aren't indexed. It also returns a non-null value for other rows that you want to index. In this case, you're interested only in the 'PO' and 'VOUCHER' values, and it's only these two values that are stored in the index case_tab_idx1. You usually do this when you're dealing with large tables. In this example, the table contains millions of records, but only a few of them have the value of 'PO' or 'VOUCHER' for the SOURCE_TRAN column. In essence, you are shrinking a potentially very large index into a much smaller, more manageable index that takes very little space compared the index on all the values for the column. More importantly, there is significant improvement in performance, because the index that you create will have a smaller height in terms of the number of index branches (BLEVEL).

The CASE construct can also be used to great benefit when you want to enforce a constraint such as preventing certain columns from having the same values. Let's say that you have a situation where you want all currently published books to have a distinct name, but you don't care what the book names in the publisher's backlist (list of previously published but currently selling books) are. You can then create the following function-based index:

```
SQL> create unique index current_books on case_tab
         (case when publish_date ='CURRENT' then list_name end);
```

As another example of a function-based index, consider the case where you create an index for precomputing arithmetic expressions. The following shows a test table and an index that is created on an arithmetic expression:

```
SQL> create table tt(
2   a integer,
3   b integer,
4   c integer);
Table created.

SQL> create index tt_idx1 on tt(a+b*(c-1),a,b);

Index created.

SQL>
```

If you issue a SQL statement such as the following, the query will use an index range scan instead of a full table scan because it uses the precomputed expression values created and stored in the index you've created on the arithmetic expression:

```
SQL> select a from tt where a+b*(c-1) <200;

no rows selected

SQL>
```

The following is an explain plan for a simple query that utilizes the index that was created based on the arithmetic expression.

```
SQL> set autotrace on explain
SQL> select a from tt where
  2  a + b * (c -1) < 100;

no rows selected

Execution Plan
----------------------------------------------------------
Plan hash value: 1814671983

------------------------------------------------------------------------------
| Id  | Operation          | Name    | Rows  | Bytes | Cost (%CPU)| Time     |
------------------------------------------------------------------------------
|   0 | SELECT STATEMENT   |         |     1 |    26 |     0   (0)| 00:00:01 |
|*  1 |   INDEX RANGE SCAN | TT_IDX1 |     1 |    26 |     0   (0)| 00:00:01 |
------------------------------------------------------------------------------

Predicate Information (identified by operation id):
---------------------------------------------------

   1 - access("A"+"B"*("C"-1)<100)

Note
-----
   - dynamic statistics used: dynamic sampling (level=2)

SQL>
```

Note that when you create a user-defined function, the function must be *deterministic,* which means that it should return the same value always for the same input. In the case of a user-defined function, you must ensure that you use the SUBSTR operator to limit the values returned by a function that returns VARCHAR2 or RAW types. The length of the value that a function returns is limited by the maximum length of the data type returned. If a function returns a VARCHAR2 value, Oracle truncates the value and returns the result without any error message if the length of the return value is over the maximum length. Note that you can create a function-based index on an object column or REF column.

Limitations of Function-Based Indexes

Function-based indexes come with a few limitations or restrictions.

- The data type of the index expression can't be VARCHAR2, RAW, LONGRAW, or a PL/SQL data type of indeterminate length.

- The database ignores function-based indexes while doing an OR expansion.

- The index expression must not invoke an aggregate function such as SUM.

Probably the biggest restriction or condition on the usage of a function-based index when you're creating the function yourself is that the function should be deterministic. That is, the function must return the same result always for the same parameters, In other words, the result of the function shouldn't be determined by the parameters. You must explicitly declare the function as deterministic in order for you to be able to use that function as the basis of a function-based index. By including the DETERMINISTIC keyword in your function definition, Oracle assumes that you've done your due diligence to make sure that your function is actually deterministic. Oracle won't verify that the code really is deterministic. Therefore, you could actually include the DETERMINISTIC keyword in a function that returned non-deterministic results. In other words, Oracle won't catch your mistake.

Note also that when using a complex user-defined function-based index, inserts (and updates) definitely run slower, but the big payoff is that the queries run much faster. The increase in response time to complete the DML is proportionate to how long it takes the function to execute and store the answer in the index. Plus, the more rows that are affected by the statement, the more likely the time difference will be noticed. On single row DML statements, the "slowness" may not even be noticeable. But on large inserts/updates, the slowness may rear its head in a more noticeable way.

■ **Tip**   Behind the scenes, the Oracle database represents expressions of function-based indexes as virtual columns. This enables you to gather statistics on these indexes. The database can also build histograms on such virtual columns.

Collecting Statistics for Function-Based Indexes

Oracle automatically collects statistics for an index upon its creation and thus you don't have to explicitly collect fresh statistics after creating an index. However, in the case of a function-based index, things work a bit differently. The database creates a hidden virtual column on the parent table when it creates a function-based index. The database creates this virtual column on the table to help the optimizer more accurately determine the function's selectivity and cardinality, thus helping it compute a more accurate cost of using the function-based index you've created.

When you create a function-based index, Oracle automatically computes index statistics such as the number of leaf blocks, BLEVEL, and clustering factor, but it won't compute other more critical statistics such as the number of distinct values (NDV) associated with the virtual column. The following example illustrates this fact:

```
SQL> create index emp_total_sal_idx
     on employees (12 * salary * commission_pct, salary, commission_pct);

Index created.
SQL>
```

Once you create the function-based index as shown here, check the statistics on the new hidden virtual column created by the database.

```
SQL> select column_name,num_distinct, hidden_column,virtual_column
     from dba_tab_ cols where table_name='EMPLOYEES';

COLUMN_NAME              NUM_DISTINCT      HID      VIR
-------------           ------------      ---      ----
SYS_NC00012$                              YES      YES
DEPARTMENT_ID                     11      NO       NO
MANAGER_ID                        18      NO       NO
...
13 rows selected.

SQL>
```

As the query's output shows, a new virtual column (SYS_NC00012$) was created following the creation of the function-based index. This column is both virtual and hidden. The NUM_DISTINCT column is empty, meaning that the database has no idea of the selectivity associated with this function-based index. The cost-based optimizer may thus end up with wrong execution plans, even though it uses your new function-based index. To avoid this problem, you must always collect statistics on the hidden virtual column after creating a function-based index.

```
You can collect statistics for this hidden virtual column by using the following syntax:
SQL> exec dbms_stats.gather_table_stats(ownname=>null,tabname=>'EMPLOYEES',-
> estimate_percent=>null,cascade=>true,method_opt=>-
> 'FOR ALL HIDDEN COLUMNS SIZE 1');

PL/SQL procedure successfully completed.

SQL>
```

You can check once again to confirm that the database has collected statistics for the hidden virtual column.

```
SQL> select column_name,num_distinct, hidden_column,virtual_column
  2*     from dba_tab_cols where table_name='EMPLOYEES'
SQL> /
COLUMN_NAME          NUM_DISTINCT    HID    VIR
---------------      ------------    ---    ---
SYS_NC00013$                   31    YES    YES
EMPLOYEE_ID                   107    NO     NO
FIRST_NAME                     91    NO     NO
...
13 rows selected.
SQL>
```

Alternately, you can directly collect statistics on the function expression, as shown in the following example:

```
SQL> execute dbms_stats.gather_table_stats (ownname=> USER,
> tabname=>'EMPLOYEES',
> method_opt=>'FOR ALL COLUMNS FOR COLUMNS (12 * salary * commission_pct)');

PL/SQL procedure successfully completed.

SQL>
```

Indexes on Virtual Columns

Before we discuss creating an index on a virtual column, it's a good idea to clarify exactly what a virtual column is. A virtual column represents data in a table just as a normal table, but it's not stored on disk (or elsewhere!). Instead, the database computes the values for the virtual column on the fly by computing a set of expressions or functions. It is important to understand that the value of a virtual column is computed only when that value is queried. That is, virtual columns are evaluated when a WHERE clause refers to the column in a SELECT statement.

The following is a simple example that shows how to create a virtual column named TOTAL_AMOUNT, which is calculated as the total value of a sale by taking the product of the AMOUNT_SOLD and QUANTITY_SOLD columns:

```
SQL>   create table sales_new
  2    (prod_id     number(6) not null,
  3     cust_id   number not null,
  4     time_id date not null,
  5     channel_id char(1) not null,
  6     quantity_sold number(3) not null,
  7     amount_sold number(10,2) not null,
  8*    total_amount AS (quantity_sold * amount_sold))
SQL> /
Table created.
SQL>
```

This example used the shorter syntax for defining a virtual column. The full syntax for creating a virtual column is as follows:

```
column_name  [datatype]  [GENERATED ALWAYS]  AS (expression)  [VIRTUAL]
```

So, for example, you can use both the following types of syntax to generate a virtual column:

```
salary as (ROUND(salary*(1+commission/100),2))
salary  NUMBER GENERATED ALWAYS AS (ROUND(salary*(1+commission)/100),2))
```

The GENERATED ALWAYS clause means that the column value is generated at runtime based on the values of the columns it is based on. A virtual column can also be derived from a constant instead of table's columns. The column can include SQL or user-defined PL/SQL functions.

Once you create a virtual column, you can use it as any regular column. Virtual columns reduce the need for using triggers. You can create an index on a virtual column just as you'd for a regular column.

You can also create constraints on a virtual column, as shown here:

```
SQL> create unique index test_pk on sales(total_amount);
Index created.
SQL>
SQL> alter table sales add
  2    constraint test_pk
  3    primary key(total_amount)
  4    using index;

Table altered.
SQL>
```

You can also reference the virtual column from a foreign key constraint. Simply create a foreign key on the child table that references the virtual column AMOUNT_SOLD in the SALES table. Any function you use in an expression must be deterministic, but you can recompile the function after the creation of the index to make it non-deterministic without making the virtual column invalid. You may want to do this when using a virtual column as a partitioning key because you normally can't use a deterministic function as a virtual column expression in this case. Once you recompile the function, you must rebuild the index on the virtual column. In addition, if you've any constraints on the virtual column, you must re-enable them after first disabling them. Finally, you must regather the table statistics.

Key Compressed Indexes

Often, an index includes multiple occurrences of key column prefix values. The Oracle database's key compression feature lets you separate an index key into two entries: a prefix and a suffix. Key compression lets the suffix entries in an index block share the prefix entries, thus letting you store more keys per index block. Of course, you save on storage and you improve performance as a result. Performance may be improved since there are fewer leaf blocks that may need to be accessed due to the compression. While it's obvious that compression saves storage space, it's natural to wonder if the overhead of compression is going to negate the benefits of compressing data. The online transaction processing (OLTP) table compression feature enables the compression of data during all DML operations and minimizes overhead during write operations, thus making it usable in online environments. Oracle doesn't have to uncompress the compressed data before reading it and the data stays in a compressed form in the cache, thus taking up a smaller amount of cache space.

You can use key compression to compress parts of primary key column in either a regular B-tree index or an index-organized table. Each index key has two components: a grouping piece and a unique piece. When you compress index keys, the database breaks the index key into a prefix entry (grouping piece) and a suffix entry (unique piece). The number of key columns determines the maximum prefix length in a non-unique index. In a unique index, it is the number of key columns minus one.

When Key Compression is Useful

Key compression is useful in any situation where the database needs to deal with duplicate values in the index keys. For example, if you have a unique index on two columns such as STOCK_TICKER and TRANSACTION_TIME, you can envisage numerous rows with the same stock ticker, such as NYT, but with different TRANSACTION_TIME values. When you compress this index, the database stores the value of the STOCK_TICKER column only once in each index block, as a prefix entry. It stores the TRANSACTION_TIME column values as suffix entries that reference the same STOCK_TICKER prefix entry.

In the case of a non-unique index, the database appends a ROWID to duplicate keys to distinguish between the rows. When you compress such an index, the database stores the duplicate key as a prefix entry in the index block. All the duplicate entries are stored as suffix entries, which consist only of a ROWID.

You can use key compression when dealing with indexing a VARRAY or a NESTED TABLE data type because the database repeats the same object ID for each of a collection data type's elements. In this case, you can employ key compression to reduce storage for the repeating object ID values.

■ **Note** An Oracle database compresses only leading columns in an index. In the case of a non-unique index, this can be all columns in an index. In the case of a unique index, it can be all but the last column.

There are cases when key compression actually has a negative impact on index storage. Note that the prefix table stores the unique compressed column values in an index leaf block. If your index's leading column or the compressed columns are extremely selective, the prefix table will have many distinct values. The database is forced to create a large prefix table to store the individual column values. The prefix entries aren't shared by many index row entries. Compressing such an index is actually counterproductive because the compression factor and thus the storage savings are very low. The database also has to deal with the additional burden of maintaining the large prefix table. You can potentially end up in a situation where the compressed index is larger than the uncompressed index!

An extreme example of a very selective index is a single column unique index, where by definition, there can't be duplicate column values. Each index row entry has a separate prefix index entry, and thus the compressed index is larger than the uncompressed version. Actually, Oracle doesn't even allow you to do this, because it issues an error if you try to use the COMPRESS option for a single column unique index, as the following two examples demonstrate. In the first example, you can compress a unique index on two columns (name,id) without a problem, but the database won't allow you to compress a single column (column name in this example) unique index.

```
SQL> create unique index tt2_idx1 on tt2(name,id) compress
SQL> /

Index created.

SQL> create unique index tt2_idx3 on tt2(name) compress;
create unique index tt2_idx3 on tt2(name) compress
                                               *
ERROR at line 1:
ORA-25193: cannot use COMPRESS option for a single column key

SQL>
```

In general, remember that the more heavily repeated a column value, the higher the storage savings when you compress the index. In a composite index, ensure that the low-cardinality columns are the leading columns for compression to show good results.

Creating a Compressed Index

Let's make use of the following example to understand how key compression helps reduce storage in an index. Let's create a composite index on the ORDERS table (OE schema) on the columns ORDER_MODE and ORDER_STATUS.

```
SQL> create index orders_mod_stat_idx on orders(order_mode,order_status);
Index created.
SQL>
```

Once you create this composite index, an index block will have the following entries:

```
Online,0,AAAPvCAAFAAAAFaAAa
Online,0,AAAPvCAAFAAAAFaAAg
Online,0,AAAPvCAAFAAAAFaAAl
Online,2,AAAPvCAAFAAAAFaAAm
Online,3,AAAPvCAAFAAAAFaAAq
Online,3,AAAPvCAAFAAAAFaAAt
```

The index block shows that the key prefix is a concatenation of the ORDER_MODE and ORDER_STATUS values. Now, compress the ORDERS_MOD_STAT_IDX index using default key compression, as shown here:

```
SQL> create index orders_mod_stat_idx on orders(order_mode,order_status)
  2  compress;

Index created.
```

SQL>

As a result of the compression, the key prefix, consisting of the concatenation of the ORDER_MODE and ORDER_STATUS column values, is compressed. All duplicate key prefixes, such as online, 0 and online, 2, are represented by a single, non-repeating value as a result of compression, as shown here:

```
Online,0
AAAPvCAAFAAAAFaAAa
AAAPvCAAFAAAAFaAAg
AAAPvCAAFAAAAFaAAl
Online,2
AAAPvCAAFAAAAFaAAm
Online,3
AAAPvCAAFAAAAFaAAq
AAAPvCAAFAAAAFaAAt
```

Compression of the index results in multiple suffix values referencing a single prefix entry. Note that both the prefix and suffix values are stored in the same index block. This example used default key compression, which compresses all the columns in the prefix.

Instead, you can specify a prefix length of 1, in which case the prefix would be just the value of the ORDER_MODE column. The suffix entry includes both the values of the ORDER_STATUS column and the ROWID. Here is how to specify a prefix length of 1 when compressing the index key:

```
SQL> create index orders_mod_stat_idx on orders(order_mode,order_status)
  2  compress 1;

Index created.

SQL>
```

The number after the COMPRESS command (1 in this case) tells the database the number of columns that it should compress. In the case of a non-unique index, the default is all columns. In the case of a unique index, it is all columns minus one.

The index block now compresses all repeated occurrences of the ORDER_MODE column, as shown here:

```
0,AAAPvCAAFAAAAFaAAa
0,AAAPvCAAFAAAAFaAAg
0,AAAPvCAAFAAAAFaAAl
2,AAAPvCAAFAAAAFaAAm
3,AAAPvCAAFAAAAFaAAq
3,AAAPvCAAFAAAAFaAAt
```

In this case, at most, the index will store a prefix once per leaf block.

You can disable key compression at any time by rebuilding the index with the nocompress clause, as shown here:

```
SQL> alter index orders_mod_stat_idx rebuild nocompress;

Index altered.

SQL>
```

You can use key compression to compress one or more partitions of an index, so long as it's a B-tree index. Here is an example:

```
SQL> create indexi_cost1 on costs_demop (prod_id) compress local
     (partition costsold,partition costs_q1_2015,
     partition costs_q2_2015, partition costs_recednt nocompress);
```

You can specify a number after the COMPRESS keyword to tell Oracle how many columns to compress, as in the following example:

```
SQL> create index tt2_idx1 on tt2(name,id) compress 2;

Index created.

SQL>
```

If you don't specify a number after the COMPRESS keyword, by default, an Oracle database compresses all columns in a non-unique index. In a unique index, it compresses all columns except the last column.

Key Compression and Storage

Key compression can reduce the number of leaf blocks in an index, as shown in the following example. First, let's create a regular uncompressed index on two columns in the table objects.

```
SQL> create index normal_idx on objects(owner,object_name);

Index created.

SQL>
```

Check the number of leaf blocks in the index with the following command:

```
SQL> select num_rows,blevel,leaf_blocks from user_indexes
  2* where index_name='NORMAL_IDX';
NUM_ROWS      BLEVEL        LEAF_BLOCKS
--------      ------        -----------
 2925312         2             16954
SQL>
```

Now, drop the uncompressed index and create a new compressed index on the same columns.

```
SQL> create index compress_idx on objects(owner,object_name) compress;
Index created.
SQL>
```

Check the BLEVEL and the number of leaf blocks in the index.

```
SQL> select num_rows,blevel,leaf_blocks from user_indexes
  2* where index_name='COMPRESS_IDX';
NUM_ROWS      BLEVEL       LEAF_BLOCKS
--------      ------       -----------
 2925312         2             4968
SQL>
```

109

Notice that compressing the index reduced the number of leaf blocks to 4,968 from 16,954. This reduction in the number of leaf blocks means range scans might perform better. In addition, due to the reduction in the number of leaf blocks, the index requires a much larger number of rows to be inserted into the index before the BLEVEL height grows to 3. As you know, the higher the BLEVEL height, the more blocks the database has to read to traverse from the root of the B-tree to the leaf nodes. Note that since the same number of index rows are now stored in fewer leaf blocks, each leaf block contains a much larger number of rows stored in it.

Obviously, reducing storage for a large index is the primary reason for compressing an index. Can you tell how much space you might save before you actually compress the index? Yes, you can do this by validating an index, as shown here:

```
SQL> create index nocompress_idx on objects(owner,object_name);

Index created.

SQL> validate index nocompress_idx;

Index analyzed.

SQL>

SQL> select opt_cmpr_count,opt_cmpr_pctsave from index_stats;
OPT_CMPR_COUNT      OPT_CMPR_PCTSAVE
--------------      ----------------
             2                    70
SQL>
```

The index_stats shows the optimal key compression length (opt_cmpr_count) is 2. The OPT_CMPR_PCTSAVE column value is 70 (percent), which is the corresponding space savings in the index after it is compressed. Yu can also use the DBA_SEGMENTS view to check the used space before and after the index compression, to estimate the storage space savings.

Advanced Index Compression

Oracle Database 12c introduced a new type of index compression called *advanced index compression*. Advanced index compression reduces the size of the index by working at the block level to enforce the best compression for each leaf block. A great feature of advanced index compression is that it automatically chooses the right compression for each block. You must license the Oracle Advanced Compression option to use advanced index compression.

You must specify the COMPRESS ADVANCED LOW clause for enabling advanced index compression during the creation of an index, as shown here:

```
SQL> create index emp_nmdp_idx on emp_test (manager_id, department_id) compress advanced low;
Index created.
SQL>
```

While compression is designed to reduce the size of an index, it's quite possible that you may end up increasing the size of an index by compressing it. This is true whenever the compressed indexes have very little repeated data. To choose to compress an index, you need to make several decisions regarding which indexes—and which columns in those indexes—are candidates for compression. Fortunately, Oracle's advanced index compression can help you replace guesswork with educated decisions. For example, it can decide not to compress indexes where the index leaf blocks don't have duplicate entries. If the leaf blocks do have repeated columns, the feature decides how to efficiently compress each and every individual index leaf block, depending on the number of repeated values in the columns.

Let's use some test cases to learn how this new feature can help you.

1. Create a test table.

```
SQL> create table test (id number, track_id number, name varchar2(30));
Table created.
SQL>
SQL> insert into test select rownum, rownum, 'SAM ALAPATI' from dual
  2  connect by level <=1000000;
1000000 rows created.
SQL>
```

2. Update the table so a small part (a third) of the table has repeated values in the TRACK_ID column.

```
SQL> update test set track_id = 999 where id between 300000 and 600000;
300001 rows updated.
SQL> commit;
Commit complete.
SQL>
```

Note that the other third of the table have unique values, based on the way we created the data set earlier.

3. Let's create a normal, uncompressed index on the TRACK_ID column.

```
SQL> create index test_idx2 on test(track_id);
Index created.
SQL>
SQL> select index_name, leaf_blocks, compression from user_indexes;
INDEX_NAME          LEAF_BLOCKS       COMPRESSION
----------          -----------       -----------
TEST_IDX2                 2186        DISABLED
SQL>
```

The preceding query shows that there are 2,186 leaf blocks in the index.

4. Next, compress the index using the alter index ...rebuild command.

```
SQL> alter index test_idx2 rebuild compress;
Index altered.
SQL>
  SQL> select index_name, leaf_blocks, compression from user_indexes;
    2  where index_name='TEST_IDX2';
INDEX_NAME          LEAF_BLOCKS       COMPRESSION
----------          -----------       -----------
TEST_IDX2                 2607        ENABLED
SQL>
```

Compression has increased the number of leaf blocks in the index from 2,186 to 2,607 leaf blocks. The compressed index is about 18 percent larger than the uncompressed index. The reason for this increase in the size of the index is that while Oracle compressed one-third of the data that consists of repeated values just fine, the problem is that a much larger portion of the table's data is unique. Compression results in an additional prefix section in the leaf blocks, and in the case of the unique data, this extra space usage isn't offset by a reduction in the space usage due to duplicated data.

5. Finally, let's again use the alter index ...rebuild command to compress the data, but this time by using the advanced index compression capability. The COMPRESS ADVANCED LOW clause is how you do tshis, as shown here:

```
SQL> alter index test_idx2 rebuild compress advanced low;
Index altered.
SQL>
SQL> select index_name, leaf_blocks, compression from user_indexes
  2  where index_name='TEST_IDX2';
INDEX_NAME          LEAF_BLOCKS          COMPRESSION
----------          -----------          -----------
TEST_IDX2                  2022          ADVANCED LOW
SQL>
```

The index size has been reduced to 2,022 leaf blocks from the original 2,186 leaf blocks. With the advanced index compression capability, Oracle ignores all leaf blocks where it determines that compressing the data isn't a sensible thing to do, due to unique values. Oracle instead focuses only on the portion of the index's data that's worth compressing, which happens to be roughly a third of the index's data, as you've seen. Oracle is able to reduce the index size significantly, even with just a third of the table containing repeated data. If a table has a higher percentage of repeated values in the indexed column, then the reduction in the index size is correspondingly higher.

To reiterate, a great feature of the advanced index compression capability is that you can simply turn it on for all indexes in your database, and let Oracle determine the best way to compress (or not) each leaf block in every index in the database. Obviously, if you have upgraded to Oracle Database 12c, you can simply write a short script to rebuild all your indexes to take advantage of this truly useful Oracle Database 12c new feature.

Composite Indexes

You can create an index on multiple columns in a table. If you want to create an index on the EMPLOYEE_ID and DEPARTMENT_ID columns in the employees table, for example, you can do so, and the result is called a composite or concatenated index. Here's an example:

```
SQL> create index test_idx1 on employees(employee_id,department_id);
Index created.

Index created.

SQL>
```

You can create composite B-tree indexes as well bitmap indexes. The optimizer takes into account a composite index when the WHERE clause in a query refers to all the columns in the index or even the leading column. The previous example showed a composite index with just two columns, but you can have even more columns if you wish. The following example shows a composite index created by using three columns (LAST_NAME, JOB_ID, SALARY) from the employees table in the HR schema. You do this when you have an application that frequently refers to these three columns.

```
SQL> create index employees_idx1
  2* on employees (last_name,job_id,salary)
SQL> /
Index created.
SQL>
```

Once you create this index, any query that refers to the LAST_NAME column, the LAST_NAME and JOB_ID columns, or all three columns, is likely to cause the optimizer to use the index. A query that doesn't include the leading column in a composite index (LAST_NAME, in this example) will ignore the index. At least, this was the traditional behavior. Oracle's use of index skip scans changes this default behavior.

Understanding Index Skip Scans and Composite Indexes

In early releases of Oracle Database, a SQL statement used a composite index only if the statement's constructs used a leading portion of the index. The leading portion of an index is one or more columns in the index that are specified first in the list of columns. For example, let's say that you have the following composite index:

```
SQL> create index mycomp_idx
on table mytable(a,b,c);
Index created.
```

In this index, a, ab, and abc are all considered leading portions of an index. The column or column combinations b, c, and bc aren't considering leading portions. However, Oracle's index skip scan feature eliminates or skips through a composite index by using logical subindexes.

An index skip scan eliminates or skips through a composite index by using logical subindexes. Logical subindexes mean just that: you don't create those indexes. The skip scanning feature assumes that the composite index is indeed composed of multiple subindexes. When does the database perform a skip scan? It may do so when your query predicate doesn't specify the leading column of a composite index.

If the leading portion of a composite index has a small number of distinct values and the non-leading portion of the index contains a large number of distinct values, skip scanning proves useful. Let's use a simple example to demonstrate how index skip scanning works. The test query is as follows:

```
SQL> select * from customers where cust_email='Sam@mycompany.com';
```

The customers table also has a column named GENDER, which takes only two values: M and F. Here's a sample of the composite index's entries from an index block:

```
F,Wolf@company.com,rowid
F,Wolsey@company.com,rowid
F,Wood@company.com,rowid
F,Woodman@company.com,rowid
F,Yang@company.com,rowid
F,Zimmerman@company.com,rowid
M,Abbassi@company.com,rowid
M,Alapati@company.com,rowid
```

Let's say that you issue a query that only specifies the CUST_MAIL column, and not the leading column GENDER, in its WHERE clause. Since the leading column gender has only two distinct values, it really doesn't matter if you don't specify it in the query. The database divides your composite index into two logical subindexes, one with the key M and the other with the key F. Even though you haven't specified the leading column gender, the database searches the two logical subindexes one after the other and gets you the results. In other words, the database treats the query as this:

```
SQL> select * from sh.customers where cust_gender = 'F'
  and cust_email = 'Alapati@company.com'
union all
select * from sh.customers WHERE cust_gender = 'M'
  and cust_email = 'Alapati@company.com';
```

Ordering the Columns in a Composite Index

When creating a composite index, a big question is how to order the columns in the multi-column index. Oracle recommends that you place the most commonly accessed column first in the index.

Traditionally, it was thought that you should avoid using a low-cardinality column (a column with few distinct values) as the leading column in a composite index. However, regardless of the index order, the database can navigate straight to the leaf block containing the indexed column values because the index leaf branch entries contain column entries based on all indexed columns.

In fact, a leading column with lower cardinality may have more advantages, as the optimizer is likely to at least consider using an index skip scan in these cases. It has also been suggested to use the clustering factor as a criterion when deciding which column should be the leading index column in a composite index. The clustering factor indicates how well ordered the table's rows are in comparison to the way the index entries are ordered in an index. For example, an arrangement that would "guarantee" the order of the table rows to match the order of the index entries (and therefore be reflected by the resulting clustering factor), would be if you loaded a table from a sorted set of input data in a single action. One of the most common reasons you use a composite index is when an important query refers to two or more columns, none of which have a high degree of selectivity. By constructing a composite index, you increase the odds of the optimizer choosing to use that composite index, whereas it would probably have bypassed any indexes you created separately on the two columns, both of which have a very low selectivity.

■ **Note**   Selectivity is a computation based on column statistics (particularly on the number of distinct values and high/low values). The optimizer computes selectivity for multiple columns in an "ANDed" predicate by computing the individual selectivity (1/number of distinct values) for each column and then multiplying those results together to get the overall selectivity. For example, if you have WHERE GENDER = 'F' AND STATUS = 'ACTIVE' where both gender and status have only 2 distinct values, each column has a selectivity of .5. The total predicate selectivity is then .5 * .5 or .25. If a composite index exists that has both columns, the optimizer will compute index selectivity using the .25 combined predicate selectivity along with the index stats (like the clustering factor) to make its final cost calculation for using the index.

A big advantage of using a composite index is that if all the columns required by a query are in the composite index itself, the database returns the values of the columns from the index without subsequently having to access the table. Thus, you'll see a reduced I/O when using composite indexes in most cases since you're avoiding the scan of the table itself using the ROWIDs, as is the case when you use an index on a single column.

A key criterion in deciding how to order keys in a composite index is to ensure that the leading portion of the index consists of keys used in WHERE clauses. If some of the keys are often specified in WHERE clauses, make sure that these keys make up the leading portion of the index. This ensures that queries that specify only these keys will use the index.

Choosing Keys for Composite Indexes

You can create a composite index with its columns in any order that you want, but your goal should be to create a composite index only when the different keys appear frequently together in an application's WHERE clauses and you're currently using an AND operator to combine the columns. A composite index would be a better choice in this case. The one thing you must do is get a rough estimate of the selectivity of the columns you want to include in a composite index. If the combined selectivity of the columns is better than the individual selectivity of the columns, the composite index is beneficial. You can also consider a composite index in cases where key queries do a select of the same set of keys based on multiple key values. Simply create a composite index with all the keys for better performance.

Let's use a couple of simple examples to drive home our point as to how a composite index will benefit you by reducing I/O when all the columns required to satisfy a query are in the index itself. In the first example, you create a single column index and check the explain plan.

```
SQL>  create table test_tab
  2*  (a number, b varchar2(10), c varchar2(10))
SQL> /xxxx

Table created.

SQL> create index single_idx1 on test_tab (a);

Index created.

SQL> set autotrace on explain;
SQL> select b,c,a from test_tab where b='pc-5895' and c='pc-2893' and a=564;

no rows selected

Execution Plan
----------------------------------------------------------
Plan hash value: 384229489

---------------------------------------------------------------------------------
--------------------

| Id  | Operation                           | Name         | Rows  | Bytes | Cost
 (%CPU)| Time      |

---------------------------------------------------------------------------------
--------------------

|   0 | SELECT STATEMENT                    |              |     1 |    27 |
1   (0)| 00:00:01 |

|*  1 |  TABLE ACCESS BY INDEX ROWID BATCHED| TEST_TAB     |     1 |    27 |
1   (0)| 00:00:01 |

|*  2 |   INDEX RANGE SCAN                  | SINGLE_IDX1  |     1 |       |
1   (0)| 00:00:01 |

---------------------------------------------------------------------------------
--------------------
```

```
    Predicate Information (identified by operation id):
    ------------------------------------------------------

       1 - filter("B"='pc-5895' AND "C"='pc-2893')
       2 - access("A"=564)

    Note
    -----
          - dynamic statistics used: dynamic sampling (level=2)
SQL>
```

The optimizer uses an index scan, but it also has to scan the table rows since all the required columns are not part of your single column index. This means more I/O and more time to complete the query in most cases. You now drop the index on the single column and create a composite index using all three columns this time.

```
SQL> drop index single_idx1;
Index dropped.

SQL> create index comp_idx1 on test_tab(a,b,c);

Index created.

SQL> select b,c,a from test_tab where b='pc-5895' and c='pc-2893' and a=564;

no rows selected

Execution Plan
------------------------------------------------------------
Plan hash value: 1685463053
```

Id	Operation	Name	Rows	Bytes	Cost (%CPU)	Time
0	SELECT STATEMENT		1	27	1 (0)	00:00:01
* 1	INDEX RANGE SCAN	COMP_IDX1	1	27	1 (0)	00:00:01

```
Predicate Information (identified by operation id):
------------------------------------------------------

   1 - access("A"=564 AND "B"='pc-5895' AND "C"='pc-2893')

Note
-----
   - dynamic statistics used: dynamic sampling (level=2)

SQL>
```

Since all the requisite data is found within the new composite index, the database doesn't have to perform the additional table scan.

Creating Virtual Indexes

Creating a virtual index is just what it sounds like: you create an index but it has no physical existence! A virtual index is also referred to as a nosegment index or even a fake index, and you create it by specifying the nosegment clause when creating an index, as shown here:

```
SQL> create index fake_idx on employees(last_name) nosegment;
Index created.
SQL>
```

You can issue the following query to confirm that the index is present:

```
SQL>  select index_name,column_name,table_name from user_ind_columns
  2*   where index_name like 'FAKE%';
```

INDEX_NAME	COLUMN_NAME	TABLE_NAME
FAKE_IDX	LAST_NAME	EMPLOYEES
```
SQL>
```

The virtual index that you've created doesn't take up any storage—and isn't available to the cost optimizer by default. If you query the DBA_INDEXES view, you won't see the fake indexes you've created, as shown here:

```
SQL> select index_name,table_name from dba_indexes
  2* where index_name like 'FAKE%'
SQL> /

no rows selected
SQL>
```

The reason this query returns no rows is that the DBA_INDEXES view shows information only about actual index segments, and since a fake index doesn't really use storage, it doesn't show up in this view.

You make the index visible to the optimizer by setting the following undocumented initialization parameter:

```
SQL> alter session set "_use_nosegment_indexes" = true;
Session altered.
SQL>
```

Setting the _use_nosegment_indexes parameter doesn't mean that the database will actually use the index; after all, the index doesn't really exist. You can use this parameter to check if an execution plan for a query will use the index or not, as shown in the following example.

■ **Tip**   Even after creating a virtual index on a column, you can create a regular index on the same column.

```
SQL> create  index virtual_idx
  2  on emp(ename) nosegment;

Index created.
```

117

```
SQL> set autotrace on explain
SQL> alter session set "_use_nosegment_indexes"=true
SQL> /

Session altered.
SQL> select ename from emp where ename='KING';
ENAME
----------
KING

Execution Plan
------------------------------------------------------------
Plan hash value: 1165707112

----------------------------------------------------------------------------
| Id  | Operation          | Name        | Rows  | Bytes | Cost (%CPU)| Time     |
----------------------------------------------------------------------------
|   0 | SELECT STATEMENT   |             |     1 |     5 |     2   (0)| 00:00:01 |
|*  1 |   INDEX RANGE SCAN | VIRTUAL_IDX |     1 |     5 |     2   (0)| 00:00:01 |
----------------------------------------------------------------------------

Predicate Information (identified by operation id):
---------------------------------------------------
   1 - access("ENAME"='KING')
SQL>
```

Once you have completed your testing with the virtual index in place, you can drop it in the following way:

```
SQL> drop index virtual_idx;
Index dropped.
SQL>
```

The preceding explain plan shows that the optimizer considers the virtual index virtual_idx. While the virtual or fake index feature seems enticing, especially in development environments, it's good to remember that the optimizer may or may not really use it because the index doesn't have as much information about the column data as a real index does.

The database doesn't collect optimizer statistics for an index while it's in the invisible state. The optimizer uses the same basic default optimizer statistics (such as index level, leaf blocks, distinct keys, and clustering factor) for a virtual index as it does for any normal index for which you haven't collected any statistics.

You can gather statistics on an invisible index by either converting the index into a "visible" index so the optimizer can "see" it, or set the optimizer_use_invisible_indexes parameter to true. We much prefer using an invisible index wherever possible when you want to test the efficacy of a potential index. The one place where we do see a use for the virtual index is when we're dealing with large tables and want to quickly find out if the optimizer will use a potential index on that table. Developers can then run an explain plan as if the index actually exists without having to wait for the creation of a large index.

You create a virtual index only when you want to explore what happens if you create an index—but don't want to go through the mechanics of actually creating an index. When you create a nosegment index, Oracle doesn't create an index segment as it does for a normal index; it simply creates an index definition. Also, you can't rebuild or alter the index as you can in the case of a real index. Note that when you create a nosegment index, the database populates only a few data dictionary tables and, of course, there's no index tree associated with the index.

Several Oracle tuning tools, such as the Oracle Tuning Pack and other third-party tools, make use of the hidden parameter _use_nosegment_indexes to simulate the presence of an index. The virtual indexes let you evaluate whether the cost-based optimizer will actually use the indexes in its execution plans. You can thus use the fake or virtual index to test whether an index may help performance without actually using up the space for the index on disk.

Reverse Key Indexes

You can create an index as a reverse key index for performance reasons; they're especially suited for Oracle RAC environments. A reverse key index stores the index entries with their bytes reversed. The ROWIDs are stored in the same format as a regular index. When you insert rows in a column where the database populates one of the columns using an increasing sequence, each new entry is inserted into the same index block. When each new key value in an index is greater than the previous value, it is said to be a *monotonically increasing value*. In a RAC database, when multiple sessions simultaneously insert data into monotonically increasing index nodes, it leads to contention for the same index block. A reverse key index prevents this contention because the database inserts the successive index entries into indexed blocks that are spread out. Although RAC environments usually use reverse key indexes, any high volume transaction processing system that is experiencing contention for index blocks could potentially benefit from this type of an index.

A reverse key index is actually simple: it simply reverses the index column values before inserting (storing) into the index.

In a normal B-tree index, the database inserts index values sequentially. If the next two primary key value generated by an Oracle sequence are 12345 and 12346, for example, the database stores both values in the same index block. While this makes for efficient index lookups and for faster index range scans, the key point is that each insert statement must be able to access the newest block in the index to do the insertion of the new values.

If index key values are being concurrently inserted into leaf blocks or branches of the B-tree, a leaf or branch block split could become a serialization point. A reverse key index, on the other hand, when faced with the same index values in this example, reverses them into 54321 and 64321 before inserting them into the index. Similarly, if a column value is ORACLE, the database stores it in the indexed in reverse order, as ELCARO. As you can see, while the index values 12345 and 12346 would have been stored next to each other, the values 54321 and 64321 are stored in different index leaf blocks that are spread throughout the index structure. Consequently, even in a busy database, the insertion of sequential key values won't result in contention for the rightmost index block (the index is also said to have a right growing tree in this case).

Instead of storing new values in the same "hot" index block, the database spreads around the new entries across a number of blocks, reducing contention for a busy block and thus, buffer contention (denoted by the buffer busy wait event).

You can see how an index that's populated with sequentially increasing values results in all values going to the rightmost index leaf block. Let's say that you create a primary key with the following values:

```
696900
696901
696902
696903
696904
...
```

In a regular B-tree index, these sequential index values are all stored in an identical rightmost index block, increasing contention for that block. In a reverse key index, Oracle inserts the same values in the following manner:

```
009696
109696
209696
309696
409696
...
```

As you can see, the index values aren't in sequential order, although the actual values of the primary key are. Oracle reverses the bytes in the data before inserting into the index. This reversing of the values naturally spreads the key values by storing them non-sequentially all through the index blocks instead of storing them in sequential order. During an insertion, the reverse key index distributes insertions across all the leaf keys in the index, thus avoiding hotspots and enhancing performance.

Using a reverse key index often speeds up data loads in an Oracle RAC environment during batch loads. While reverse key indexes are often mentioned in the context of an Oracle RAC environment, you can consider them even for a single instance databases if you notice contention for index blocks, shown by the buffer busy wait event. There are many applications where a primary key column is populated by an increasing sequence. Often, you'll notice a significant buffer busy wait time for the index segments. Consider a reverse key index for these kinds of situations. The reverse key index has the potential to dramatically reduce the buffer busy waits and speed up performance.

Disadvantages of a Reverse Key Index

A big disadvantage to using a reverse key index is that you can't perform range scans on these indexes. This is because the index entries are scattered all over instead of being stored sequentially. Reversing the index key values randomly distributes the index blocks across the index leaf nodes.

You can certainly use the index to fetch by specific index key values and for a full index scan, however. Use reverse key indexes when your queries have equality predicates. Note also that even though the database doesn't perform a range scan when you use a reverse key index, it can perform a fast full scan of the index. There could be a slight overhead in terms of CPU usage when the database searches on a reverse key index. The reason, of course, is that the database has to reverse the order of bytes in the values of the index so they represent the actual values stored in the table.

Remember that the main purpose of using a reverse key index is to eliminate contention caused when the database is inserting rows with index key values generated by a sequence. Other solutions are possible. For example, you can you can partition a hot index rather than make it into a reverse index, using the partitioning to mitigate the input/output hotspot that you otherwise would have.

You can make the decision whether to implement a reverse key index by comparing the benefits they provide (the faster insert rates due to the reduction in contention) with the biggest drawback (their inability to support range-based predicates). If your application uses a primary key that is always used through an equality predicate, a reverse key index is helpful, especially in an Oracle RAC environment. Reverse key indexes are very helpful if your application is suffering from a hot right-hand side index block. If the contention is due to a hot index root block, partitioning the index is potentially helpful because the index ends up with multiple index root blocks.

If you create a reverse key index and your query specifies WHERE ind_col = value, the database will certainly use the reverse key index. However, since the index values in a reverse key index aren't stored in their natural order, the optimizer sometimes has a problem with the index. For example, the index values 54321 and 64321are more likely to be in different index life blocks than they are to be together in the same block. The database thus has to search for the two values independently as the values are most likely stored in different data blocks. Thus, the database is unable to use a reverse index when handling a range predicate, such as BETWEEN, <=, <, <, and <=. Regardless of whether you use an index hint, when confronted with a reverse key index in the context of a range predicate, the database performs a full table scan, ignoring your index.

You can overcome the limitation described here by replacing the range predicate where possible with an IN clause. The database then transform each IN clause into an OR clause, which is compatible with a reverse key index. That is, instead of specifying BETWEEN (12345, 12346, 12347), you can specify IN (12345, 12346, 12347). The database changes this to 12345 OR 12346 OR 12347 and is able to use your reverse key index. An Oracle database can do this because reverse key indexes are fully compatible with an equality predicate.

There are a couple of exceptions to the technical fact that Oracle can't perform an index range scan when dealing with a reverse key index. The first is when you use a non-unique index rather than a unique index. Since duplicate values are stored in the index structure, the database performs an index range scan when it does an equality search with the non-unique reverse key index. However, this is an unlikely event anyway, since the primary reason for using reverse key indexes is to eliminate contention caused by insertions into a primary key that's populated using monotonically increasing sequence values. During batch inserts, a reverse key index usually helps make the insertion of data faster.

As explained earlier, a reverse key index is often considered an ideal solution in cases where a generated or sequential key causes severe contention on the index leaf blocks. Whenever you use a date or a sequence with values that increase monotonically, you are likely to encounter this contention, especially in a RAC environment. However, before you go in for a reverse key index, do consider alternatives such as a hash-partitioned global index. In a multi-user RAC environment, a hash-partitioned global index can improve the performance of inserts by spreading out the inserts. Oracle's hashing algorithm determines the location of the index values in each of the global index's partitions. The algorithm uses the index's keys to generate unique values that it places in different partitions. When your application is inserting frequently into segments with indexes that are right-growing, a hash-partitioned global index can reduce contention.

When to Use a Reverse Key Index

You can make the best case for using a reverse key index when you're facing index block contention, which reveals itself through the well-known "buffer busy" and "read by other session" wait events. This is usually due to a situation where you're dealing with an Oracle RAC OLTP environment and there are large numbers of concurrent inserts. If your application uses monotonically increasing indexes, such as when you use a primary key generated by an Oracle sequence, you often encounter these types of contention. In this context, inserts are said to contend for the rightmost index block because that where the highest values of the sequentially primary key are stored. In a RAC environment especially, this rightmost index leaf block contention leads to block transfers among the instances, leading to slow performance.

Using sequences to generate primary key values is often the cause of contention, especially in an Oracle RAC environment. Unlike table entries, index entries must be stored in order. Thus, entries are sequentially stored in the index structure, and if multiple uses are concurrently inserting into the same index block, you end up with high buffer busy waits.

In a RAC environment, Oracle recommends that you use the NOORDER and the CACHE options when creating a sequence in order to reduce index contention. The rowlock cache statistics from the V$SYSTEM_ EVENT view tells you if monotonically increasing sequences are causing contention in the database. You can examine the EQ_TYPE column in the GV$ENQUEUE_STAT view to determine if sequences are causing any index enqueue waits. If you see a value of SQ Enqueue for the EQ_TYPE column, it is usually an indication of contention for a sequence. If the index key values are derived from a sequence, you can increase the size of the sequence cache to reduce index contention. You can easily raise the cache size for a sequence with an alter sequence statement.

Creating a Reverse Key Index

It's easy to create a reverse key index. Simply add the reverse clause at the end of a regular index creation statement, as shown here:

```
SQL> create index dept_idx on emp(department_id) reverse;
Index created.
SQL>
```

You can also convert a normal index into a reverse key index by rebuilding it with the reverse clause, as shown by the following alter index statement:

```
SQL> alter index my_idx1 rebuild reverse;
Index altered.
SQL>
```

You can change a reverse key index into a regular index by specifying the noreverse clause in an alter index statement, like so:

```
SQL> alter index my_idx1 rebuild noreverse;
Index altered.
SQL>
```

Application Domain Indexes

Of all the specialized types of indexes discussed in this book, application domain indexes are the least known and the least used by most developers and DBAs. Application domain indexes let you create your own index structures in order to implement new index types that don't currently exist in the database. A good example of an application domain index is the way the database itself implements text indexes, which are commonly used to facilitate searching on large text items. To create a text index, you include the indextype clause in a create index statement, as shown here:

```
SQL> create index test_idx2 on test_tab(desc)
  2* indextype is ctxsys.context;

Index created.
SQL>
```

Once you create a text index, you can use text operators to query the text columns.

```
SQL>select * from test_tab where contains(desc,'word pattern') >0;
```

You can gather statistics on the text index just as you would with a regular index, by invoking the DBMS_STATS.GATHER_INDEX_STATS procedure. Although we discuss application domain indexes briefly here, for the most part, these indexes are of more interest to third-party solution providers that need to use innovative indexing solutions to access various types of non-traditional data, such as text and images. When you're using certain types of data such as video clips, for example, they may not fit very well into Oracle data types. In addition, these special types of data may need special kinds of operators, for example, to grade the colors in images. You can define these special types of operators using comparison operators that enable the grading of colors in an image.

Domain indexes are mostly relevant to applications you implement with Oracle's data cartridges. For more information on implementing domain indexes, check out the *Oracle Database Cartridge Developer's Guide*.

Summary

This chapter provided an introduction to various specialized indexes that you can create in an Oracle database to enhance performance and make index management simpler. You learned how to use invisible indexes to test the efficiency of indexes. This chapter showed you how to take advantage of function-based indexes to influence the optimizer's choice of indexes during the execution of queries where the predicates involve a function on a column. This chapter also explained the benefits of key compression and how and when to compress indexes. Composite indexes are very important in many applications and you learned the advantages of using composite indexes. This chapter showed you both how to create and manage indexes on virtual columns, as well as how to create a virtual or fake index that doesn't utilize any storage. Reverse keys are critical in avoiding contention on hot blocks, especially in an Oracle RAC environment. This chapter explained in detail when and how to create reverse key indexes. It also listed the disadvantages involved in the use of reverse key indexes.

CHAPTER 6

■ ■ ■

Partitioned Indexes

If you use partitioned tables as part of your application, it is likely, if not imperative, that you use partitioned indexes to complement the advantages gained by using table partitioning. Usually, having partitioned table and indexes go hand in hand—when there's one, there's usually both. This is common, but not essential. It is possible to have partitioned tables without partitioned indexes, and it is possible to have a non-partitioned table with partitioned indexes. There are several factors that affect the design of the database tables and indexes, including the following:

- Application data loading requirements (DML)
  - Is it an OLTP system?
  - Is it a data warehouse?
- Client query requirements
- Data volume
- Data purging requirements

Deciding on whether your indexes should be partitioned is largely based on the answers to the aforementioned factors. All of these factors are important, but often it boils down to data volume. The volume of your data affects load speed, query speed, and data purging speed. Obviously, as volume increases, design considerations must include factors to improve the speed of all these factors. All this said, the following are some key reasons to have partitioned indexes:

- You can perform maintenance on only a portion of the index based on activity in the table.
- You can rebuild only portions of an index.
- You can spread an index out evenly—that is, you can always have a balanced index.
- You can use partition pruning to limit the data accessed to a subset of the partitions of a given table.

Within this chapter are examples of how to create partitioned indexes. In addition, there are some examples of partitioned index usage, along with examples of operations that are performed on the database that can affect partitioned indexes.

© Darl Kuhn, Sam R. Alapati and Bill Padfield 2016
D. Kuhn et al., *Expert Oracle Indexing and Access Paths*, DOI 10.1007/978-1-4842-1984-3_6

Understanding Partitioned Indexes

Partitioned indexes offer many advantages over their non-partitioned counterparts. The following are some of the key advantages of using partitioned indexes:

- Performance benefits

    - Loading data via DML operations

    - Loading data via DDL operations

    - Querying data via SELECT statements

- Maintenance benefits

    - Rebuilding indexes

    - Setting indexes unusable at a partition level

You can create partitioned indexes either locally or globally. Local partitioned indexes can only exist on partitioned tables, while global partitioned indexes can be created on partitioned or non-partitioned tables. You can also create non-partitioned indexes on partitioned tables. As of Oracle 12c, you can create partial indexes, which are either local or global indexes on a subset of a table's partitions. The most common configuration for partitioned indexes is to create local partitioned indexes on a partitioned table, simply because the overall benefits and trade-offs of this configuration generally beat out both global partitioned and non-partitioned indexes on partitioned tables.

■ **Note** Creating non-partitioned indexes on partitioned tables is identical to creating non-partitioned indexes on non-partitioned tables. Refer to the "Maintaining Indexes on Partitioned Tables" section for more information on the use of non-partitioned indexes on partitioned tables.

Creating a Local Partitioned Index

The most common type of partitioned index is the local partitioned index. Local partitioned indexes can only be created on partitioned tables. As specified by the name, *local* means there is a direct relationship between entries for an index and the corresponding data. There is a one-to-one relationship between data partitions and index partitions. If you have a table partitioned by range based on dates and you have a partition for every month of the year, then for all the data for the January 2016 partition, you have, for each index created, the corresponding index entries in the January 2016 index partition(s). Figure 6-1 shows an example of the architecture between data and index partitions for a local partitioned index.

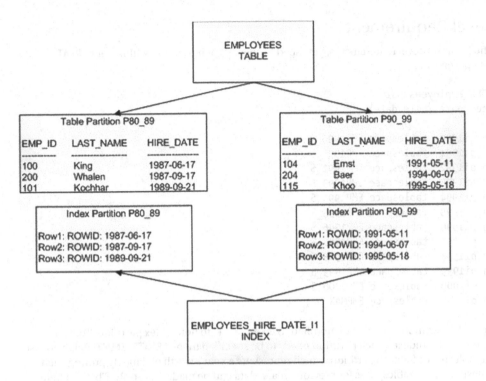

Figure 6-1. *Local partitioned index architecture*

The Simplest Form

Creating a local partitioned index is, at its most basic form, identical to creating a non-partitioned index—except for the LOCAL keyword.

```
SQL> CREATE INDEX employees_part_1i
  2  ON employees_part (hire_date)
  3  TABLESPACE empindex_s
  4  LOCAL;

Index created.
```

For this example, the partition names that Oracle creates have the same names as the data partitions. Furthermore, all partitions are created in the EMPINDEX_S tablespace.

Based on the requirements of your application, you may need to specify partition-specific information, such as the following:

- Partition name

- Tablespace name

- Storage parameters

Partition-Level Requirements

If you have specific partition-level requirements, you need to specify each partition within your CREATE INDEX DDL. Here's an example:

```
SQL> CREATE INDEX employees_part_i1
  2  ON employees_part (hire_date)
  3  LOCAL
  4  (partition pi1990   tablespace EMP1990_S
  5  ,partition pi1991   tablespace EMP1991_S
  6  ,partition pi1992   tablespace EMP1992_S
  7  ,partition pi1993   tablespace EMP1993_S
  8  ,partition pi1994   tablespace EMP1994_S
  9  ,partition pi1995   tablespace EMP1995_S
 10  ,partition pi1996   tablespace EMP1996_S
 11  ,partition pi1997   tablespace EMP1997_S
 12  ,partition pi1998   tablespace EMP1998_S
 13  ,partition pi1999   tablespace EMP1999_S
 14  ,partition pi2000   tablespace EMP2000_S
 15  ,partition pimax    tablespace EMPMAX_S);
```

In this example, the partition names were modified to insert an "I" to note index partition. To have different partition names for indexes, each partition needs to be specified in the CREATE INDEX DDL. You also specified different tablespaces for each partition, which represents a year's worth of data. By putting each year in its own tablespace, now tablespaces for previous years' data can be made read-only. This can help with both query speed and backup speed, because you won't need to back up read-only tablespaces with each backup of a database.

Again, to create a local partitioned index, it must be on top of a partitioned table. If not, you'll receive the following error:

```
SQL> CREATE INDEX EMPLOYEES_I1
ON EMPLOYEES (HIRE_DATE)
TABLESPACE EMPINDEX_S
LOCAL;
  2    3    4  ON EMPLOYEES (HIRE_DATE)
     *
ERROR at line 2:
ORA-14016: underlying table of a LOCAL partitioned index must be partitioned
```

Prefixed and Non-Prefixed Options

Local partitioned indexes can be created as prefixed or non-prefixed. When you create a prefixed local partitioned index, it means that the partitioning column(s) for the table are on the leading edge of the index. If the partitioning column(s) are not on the leading edge, it is regarded as a non-prefixed index. In earlier versions of Oracle, having a local index as prefixed offered performance advantages over its non-prefixed counterpart. With later versions of Oracle, including version 12c, the advantages of creating local indexes as prefixed have diminished. However, if your database environment is an OLTP system, it still benefits query performance to have local prefixed indexes over non-prefixed indexes, because the optimizer potentially scans fewer index partitions in order to retrieve the data for a query. Refer to the *Oracle Database VLDB and Partitioning Guide* for your specific database release to get more information on using prefixed and non-prefixed local partitioned indexes.

When creating a unique local partitioned index, the partitioning column(s) must be included as part of the index, or you will receive the following error:

```
SQL> CREATE UNIQUE INDEX employees_part_pk
  2  ON employees_part (employee_id)
  3  LOCAL
  4  /
ON employees_part (employee_id)
   *
ERROR at line 2:
ORA-14039: partitioning columns must form a subset of key columns of a UNIQUE
index
```

After adding the partitioning column (in this case, HIRE_DATE) to the unique index definition, you can now create the unique index on the EMPLOYEES_PART TABLE.

```
SQL> CREATE UNIQUE INDEX employees_part_pk
  2  ON employees_part (employee_id, hire_date)
  3  LOCAL
  4  /

Index created.
```

Managing Primary Keys and Unique Indexes

It is generally regarded as good practice when a primary key constraint is needed on a table to first create a unique index using the columns to be used for the primary key constraint, and then add the constraint after the index has been created. Here's an example:

```
CREATE UNIQUE INDEX employees_part_pk
ON employees_part (employee_id, hire_date)
LOCAL;

alter table employees_part add constraint employees_part_pk
primary key (employee_id, hire_date);
```

The advantage of doing this is it allows you to disable and re-enable the constraint when necessary without dropping the underlying index. For a large table, that ability can be a substantial time-saver when performing constraint management. Disabling and then re-enabling constraints is very common in data warehouse environments where a large volume of data is bulk loaded into tables. In this scenario, constraints are disabled prior to loading and re-enabled after loading. This can substantially save overall data processing time.

If you have created your UNIQUE INDEX first, and then enabled your primary key constraint, you can see in the following example that your constraint and index still exist in the database:

```
SQL> alter table employees_part disable constraint employees_part_pk;

Table altered.
```

129

```
SQL> select i.index_name, c.constraint_type, i.partitioned
  2  from user_indexes i left join user_constraints c
  3  on (i.index_name = c.constraint_name)
  4  where i.index_name = 'EMPLOYEES_PART_PK';


INDEX_NAME                         C PAR
------------------------------     - ---
EMPLOYEES_PART_PK                  P YES
```

If you created your primary key in-line with the CREATE TABLE statement or a single ALTER TABLE statement, this creates the underlying unique index. If you disable your primary key constraint in this case, you can see it drops the underlying index.

```
SQL> alter table employees_part disable constraint employees_part_pk;

Table altered.

SQL> select i.index_name, c.constraint_type, i.partitioned
  2  from user_indexes i left join user_constraints c
  3  on (i.index_name = c.constraint_name)
  4  where i.index_name = 'EMPLOYEES_PART_PK';

no rows selected
```

When this becomes very useful with local partitioned indexes is when you need to perform partition-level operations on your table, which would render the index for a partition UNUSABLE—such as performing a partition split on a table. In the case of your primary key, you could simply disable the primary key constraint (in which case the underlying index would remain intact), perform your partition-level operation, rebuild the index(es) for that partition, and then re-enable the primary key constraint. In this case, the only part of the index that would be rebuilt is the partition(s) affected by the operation.

Another common issue with the limitation of having the partitioning column as part of a unique index, which in turns becomes the primary key, is that sometimes the user requirements are such that the partitioning column is not desired as one of the primary key columns on a table. As shown in the following example, you can simply alter the EMPLOYEES table to create a primary key constraint using the unique index created previously:

```
SQL> alter table employees_part add constraint employees_part_pk
  2  primary key (employee_id);

Table altered.
```

If your client requirement states that the partitioning column, in this case HIRE_DATE, can't be part of the primary key, you can also simply create the constraint using the same syntax, which creates the constraint along with a non-partitioned underlying index. The following query demonstrates the result:

```
SQL>  select i.index_name, c.constraint_type, i.partitioned
  2   from user_indexes i join user_constraints c
  3   on (i.index_name = c.constraint_name)
  4*  where i.index_name = 'EMPLOYEES_PART_PK';


INDEX_NAME                         C PAR
------------------------------     - ---
EMPLOYEES_PART_PK                  P NO
```

An index did indeed get built for your table, but it is non-partitioned. The advantage of this is that the limitation of the partitioning column having to be part of a unique index has been lifted, and you can create the "natural" primary key constraint on the single EMPLOYEE_ID column. The disadvantage is that now you have a non-partitioned index on top of your partitioned EMPLOYEES table. If you need to perform any partition-level operations now on your table—such as truncating a partition, moving a partition, or splitting a partition, to name a few—the entire underlying non-partitioned index is marked UNUSABLE and must be rebuilt after any partition-level operation. Refer to the "Maintaining Indexes on Partitioned Tables" section for more information.

Creating a Global Partitioned Index

An index that is globally partitioned essentially means that the index is partitioned based on a different column or set of columns than the data. This is primarily done to increase the performance of queries against the data in the database. Based on user queries against a given table, it may lend itself to having a global partitioned index on a given queried column in order to improve query performance. Figure 6-2 shows an example of how a global partition is constructed based on the data in a given table.

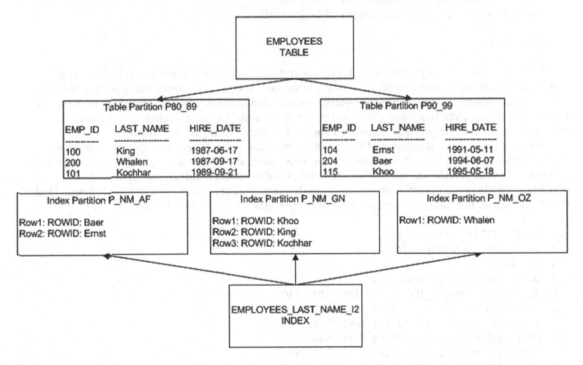

Figure 6-2. *Global partitioned index architecture*

You can create the following types of global partitioned indexes:

- Range
- Hash

To show an example for a range-based global partitioned index, for your EMPLOYEES table, you find out there are many requirements to query by MANAGER_ID, so you can therefore create a partitioned index on the MANAGER_ID column, with the partitioning being completely independent of the table. The following is an example of a range partitioned index:

```
SQL> CREATE INDEX employees_gi2
  2  ON employees (manager_id)
  3  GLOBAL
  4  partition by range(manager_id)
  5  (partition manager_100 values less than (100),
  6  partition manager_200 values less than (200),
  7  partition manager_300 values less than (300),
  8  partition manager_400 values less than (400),
  9  partition manager_500 values less than (500),
 10  partition manager_600 values less than (600),
 11  partition manager_700 values less than (700),
 12  partition manager_800 values less than (800),
 13  partition manager_900 values less than (900),
 14* partition manager_max values less than (maxvalue));

Index created.
```

You can create a global partitioned index on a partitioned table or a non-partitioned table. In other words, there is no requirement for the table to be partitioned in order to create a global partitioned index. Because of the maintenance considerations on global partitioned indexes on partitioned tables discussed later in the chapter, global partitioned indexes are not often used. They are therefore often underutilized or ignored as an option to improve query performance, especially on non-partitioned tables.

For range-based global partitioned indexes, there must always be a maximum specified for the index, with a high value of MAXVALUE. This assures that any new insertions into the corresponding table have a place in the global partitioned index. In other words, with a global partitioned index, you can never have an "out of bounds" condition on the index. If you don't specify a high-bound partition on a global partitioned index, Oracle will simply not allow you to create the index, and you will receive the following error:

```
SQL> CREATE INDEX employees_gi2
  2  ON employees (manager_id)
  3  GLOBAL
  4  partition by range(manager_id)
  5  (partition manager_100 values less than (100),
  6  partition manager_200 values less than (200),
  7  partition manager_300 values less than (300),
  8  partition manager_400 values less than (400),
  9  partition manager_500 values less than (500),
 10  partition manager_600 values less than (600),
 11  partition manager_700 values less than (700),
 12  partition manager_800 values less than (800),
 13* partition manager_900 values less than (900))
SQL> /
partition manager_900 values less than (900))
                                             *
ERROR at line 13:
ORA-14021: MAXVALUE must be specified for all columns
```

Because of having to have to include a high-bound partition within every global partitioned index, the only manner in which you can add a partition to a global partitioned index is with the ALTER INDEX ... SPLIT partition command. This is an example:

```
SQL> alter index employees_i2
  2   split partition manager_max at (1000)
  3   into (partition manager_max, partition manager_1000);

Index altered.
```

You can also drop partitions of a global partitioned index. However, when doing so, if the partition being dropped contains index entries, the higher adjacent partition is marked UNUSABLE. In the following code, you are querying the status of the index partitions prior to dropping the MANAGER_125 partition:

```
SQL> SELECT partition_name, status from user_ind_partitions
  2* WHERE index_name = 'EMPLOYEES_GI2';

PARTITION_NAME                     STATUS
------------------------------     --------
MANAGER_100                        USABLE
MANAGER_125                        USABLE
MANAGER_200                        USABLE
MANAGER_300                        USABLE
MANAGER_400                        USABLE
MANAGER_500                        USABLE
MANAGER_600                        USABLE
MANAGER_700                        USABLE
MANAGER_800                        USABLE
MANAGER_900                        USABLE
MANAGER_MAX                        USABLE
```

Then you drop partition MANAGER_125.

```
SQL> ALTER index employees_i2
  2   DROP partition manager_125;

Index altered.
```

When you query USER_IND_PARTITONS again, you can see it marked the higher partition UNUSABLE.

```
SQL> select partition_name, status from user_ind_partitions
  2* where index_name = 'EMPLOYEES_GI2';
PARTITION_NAME                     STATUS
------------------------------     --------
MANAGER_100                        USABLE
MANAGER_200                        USABLE
MANAGER_300                        UNUSABLE
MANAGER_400                        USABLE
MANAGER_500                        USABLE
MANAGER_600                        USABLE
MANAGER_700                        USABLE
MANAGER_800                        USABLE
MANAGER_900                        USABLE
MANAGER_MAX                        USABLE
```

Once you have already dropped the global index partition, you must issue an ALTER INDEX command to rebuild the partition that was marked UNUSABLE due to the DROP PARTITION operation.

```
SQL> ALTER INDEX employees_i2 rebuild partition manager_300;

Index altered.
```

Since it is a requirement to specify a partition with MAXVALUE on a global partitioned index, you can never drop the highest partition, as shown in this example:

```
SQL> ALTER INDEX employees_i2
  2  DROP PARTITION manager_max;
DROP PARTITION manager_max
               *
ERROR at line 2:
ORA-14078: you may not drop the highest partition of a GLOBAL index
```

Global partitioned indexes can be unique or non-unique. So far, you have only created a non-unique index. The following shows how to create a unique global partitioned index on a table:

```
SQL> create unique index employees_uk1
  2  on employees (manager_id, employee_id)
  3  global
  4  partition by range(manager_id)
  5  (partition manager_100 values less than (100),
  6  partition manager_200 values less than (200),
  7  partition manager_300 values less than (300),
  8  partition manager_400 values less than (400),
  9  partition manager_500 values less than (500),
 10  partition manager_600 values less than (600),
 11  partition manager_700 values less than (700),
 12  partition manager_800 values less than (800),
 13  partition manager_900 values less than (900),
 14* partition manager_max values less than (maxvalue));

Index created.
```

Unlike local partitioned indexes that can be defined as prefixed or non-prefixed, all global partitioned indexes must be created as prefixed; that is, the partitioning column must be on the leading edge of the index. If you try to create a non-prefixed global partitioned index, you will receive the following error:

```
SQL> create unique index employees_uk1
  2  on employees (employee_id)
  3  global
  4  partition by range(manager_id)
  5  (partition manager_100 values less than (100),
  6  partition manager_200 values less than (200),
  7  partition manager_300 values less than (300),
  8  partition manager_400 values less than (400),
  9  partition manager_500 values less than (500),
 10  partition manager_600 values less than (600),
 11  partition manager_700 values less than (700),
```

```
12  partition manager_800 values less than (800),
13  partition manager_900 values less than (900),
14* partition manager_max values less than (maxvalue));
partition by range(manager_id)
                              *
ERROR at line 4:
ORA-14038: GLOBAL partitioned index must be prefixed
```

The second type of global partitioned that can be created is the hash partitioned index. This is typically done for performance reasons and it keeps the index more evenly spread between the partitions. The following example creates a hash-based global partitioned index:

```
SQL> CREATE INDEX employees_ih1
  2  ON employees (department_id)
  3  GLOBAL
  4  PARTITION BY HASH(department_id) partitions 4;

Index created.
```

■ **Note**   Global partitioned indexes must be created on heap-organized tables. Also, you can't create global partitioned bitmap indexes.

Partial Indexes

New with Oracle 12c, partial indexes can now be created on partitioned tables, giving you the ability to create indexes on a subset of the partitions of a partitioned table. This can give your application a great deal of flexibility. Based on the user access patterns of your data, you can now customize indexes on a partitioned table to enable index usage on certain partitions when applicable, and allow full table scans on partitions that may not be accessed as frequently. An obvious additional benefit of partial indexes is simply saving storage. You no longer have to create an index on an entire partitioned table. You can now customize indexes at the partition-level. You can create partial indexes as local partitioned indexes, as well as global partitioned indexes, depending on what best suits your application.

First, here is an example of a CREATE TABLE statement for a partitioned table for which you want to use partial indexes:

```
CREATE TABLE employees_part
(
 EMPLOYEE_ID        NUMBER(6)        NOT NULL
,FIRST_NAME         VARCHAR2(20)
,LAST_NAME          VARCHAR2(25)     NOT NULL
,EMAIL              VARCHAR2(25)     NOT NULL
,PHONE_NUMBER       VARCHAR2(20)
,HIRE_DATE          DATE             NOT NULL
,JOB_ID             VARCHAR2(10)     NOT NULL
,SALARY             NUMBER(8,2)
,COMMISSION_PCT     NUMBER(2,2)
,MANAGER_ID         NUMBER(6)
,DEPARTMENT_ID      NUMBER(4)
```

```
,GENDER                  CHAR
,constraint employees_part_pk primary key (employee_id, hire_date)
)
indexing off
partition by range(hire_date)
(
partition p2013 values less than ('2014-01-01'),
partition p2014 values less than ('2015-01-01') indexing off,
partition p2015 values less than ('2016-01-01') indexing on,
partition p2016 values less than ('2017-01-01') indexing on,
partition p2017 values less than ('2018-01-01'),
partition p9999 values less than ('9999-12-31'),
partition pmax values less than (MAXVALUE)
);
```

The syntax for the aforementioned table DDL looks the same as any create table DDL, except for the INDEXING keyword. This tells the database what the default behavior for indexes is for a partitioned table. If INDEXING ON is specified, it means that when indexes are created on the table, the indexes are created for the partitions by default. If INDEXING OFF is specified, then by default, indexes are not created for the partitions.

In the previous example, you also note that the INDEXING clause can be specified at the partition-level. If you specify INDEXING at the partition-level, it overrides the default setting at the table level. For each partition, you can explicitly set the INDEXING clause depending on your requirements. In the example, partitions P2015 and P2016 are set with INDEXING ON. Because of the table default of INDEXING OFF, plus having partition P2014 as set with INDEXING OFF, the only partitions that would have segments built if partial indexes were created on this table would be the P2015 and P2016 partitions. To further clarify, some examples are shown in the following sections.

Creating Local Partial Indexes

Let's first create a partial local index on the previously created table, as follows:

```
CREATE INDEX ep_di_i on employees_part(department_id)
LOCAL INDEXING PARTIAL;

Index created.
```

Now, let's check the data dictionary to see the status of the index and corresponding segments:

```
select partition_name, status
from dba_ind_partitions
where index_name = 'EP_DI_I';

PARTITION_NAME          STATUS
--------------------    --------
PMAX                    UNUSABLE
P9999                   UNUSABLE
P2017                   UNUSABLE
P2016                   USABLE
P2015                   USABLE
P2014                   UNUSABLE
P2013                   UNUSABLE
```

```
select partition_name, bytes
from dba_segments
where segment_name = 'EP_DI_I';

PARTITION_NAME                          BYTES
------------------------------- ----------
P2016                              51380224
P2015                              51380224
```

As seen from the aforementioned query results, partitions created with INDEXING OFF are simply created as UNUSABLE. Only those actually created have a USABLE status. Moreover, only those partitions specified with INDEXING ON have segments created.

Let's say that for our table, which in the future, there was a need to do some heavy reporting for 2014, and you wanted the index segment built for that year of data, you simply need to rebuild that index partition as you would any unusable index partition, as follows:

```
ALTER INDEX ep_di_i rebuild partition p2014;
```

If you run the two queries against the data dictionary again to show index status and segment information, you can indeed see that the 2014 index partition was rebuilt:

```
INDEX_NAME          PARTITION_NAME                    STATUS
------------------- --------------------------------- --------------------
EP_DI_I             P2013                             UNUSABLE
EP_DI_I             P2014                             USABLE
EP_DI_I             P2015                             USABLE
EP_DI_I             P2016                             USABLE
EP_DI_I             P2017                             UNUSABLE
EP_DI_I             P9999                             UNUSABLE
EP_DI_I             PMAX                              UNUSABLE

PARTITION_NAME                          BYTES
------------------------------- ----------
P2016                              51380224
P2015                              51380224
P2014                              42991616
```

Creating Global Partial Indexes

Creating global partial indexes on a table is essentially creating one segment on a subset of partitions for a partitioned table. Let's create the same index on DEPARTMENT_ID as a global partial index:

```
CREATE INDEX ep_di_i on employees_part(department_id)
GLOBAL INDEXING PARTIAL;

Index created.
```

Again, let's check the data dictionary to see the status of the index and corresponding segment:

```
select index_name, status
from dba_indexes
where index_name = 'EP_DI_I';
```

```
INDEX_NAME          STATUS
------------------- --------------------
EP_DI_I             VALID
```

```
select segment_name, bytes
from dba_segments
where segment_name = 'EP_DI_I';
```

```
SEGMENT_NAME            BYTES
------------------- ----------
EP_DI_I               134217728
```

As you can see, there is only one segment created since this is a global partial index. As with any global index, if you needed to do a partition-level operation on any of the partitions that are included in the partial global index, the entire index becomes unusable, and need to be rebuilt. Let's truncate one of the partitions and then check the status of the index:

```
alter table employees_part truncate partition p2015;
```

```
Table truncated.
```

```
INDEX_NAME          STATUS
------------------- --------------------
EP_DI_I             UNUSABLE
```

Performance Implications of Partial Indexes

When running queries against tables with partial indexes, the behavior of the optimizer is fairly predictable. For partitions accessed within a query that are indexed, the optimizer may use those indexes. For partitions excluded from a partial index, the optimizer has no choice but a full partition scan. And finally, if you have a query that crosses partition boundaries of both—that is, partitions with indexes and those without indexes—the optimizer can use the index for indexed partitions and does partition scan operations for those that are not indexed.

To demonstrate, let's look at the explain plan when querying our table against partitions with the local partial index on DEPARTMENT_ID:

```
select * from employees_part
where hire_date between '2015-11-01' and '2016-05-01'
and department_id = 5;
```

```
--------------------------------------------------------------------------
| Id  | Operation                                  | Name            |
--------------------------------------------------------------------------
|   0 | SELECT STATEMENT                           |                 |
|   1 |  PARTITION RANGE ITERATOR                  |                 |
|   2 |   TABLE ACCESS BY LOCAL INDEX ROWID BATCHED| EMPLOYEES_PART  |
|   3 |    INDEX RANGE SCAN                        | EP_DI_I         |
--------------------------------------------------------------------------
```

If you then query against partitions without any local partial indexes, as expected, the optimizer performs a full partition scan:

```
select * from employees_part
where hire_date between '2013-11-01' and '2013-12-01'
and department_id = 5;
```

```
------------------------------------------------------------
| Id  | Operation             | Name            |
------------------------------------------------------------
|   0 | SELECT STATEMENT      |                 |
|   1 |  PARTITION RANGE SINGLE|                |
|   2 |   TABLE ACCESS FULL   | EMPLOYEES_PART  |
------------------------------------------------------------
```

Finally, if you query against partitions where some partitions are indexed, and some not, the explain plan reflects that, as shown here:

```
select * from employees_part
where hire_date between '2014-07-01' and '2015-06-01'
and department_id = 5;
```

```
---------------------------------------------------------------------------
| Id  | Operation                                   | Name            |
---------------------------------------------------------------------------
|   0 | SELECT STATEMENT                            |                 |
|   1 |  VIEW                                       | VW_TE_6         |
|   2 |   UNION-ALL                                 |                 |
|   3 |    PARTITION RANGE SINGLE                   |                 |
|   4 |     TABLE ACCESS BY LOCAL INDEX ROWID BATCHED| EMPLOYEES_PART  |
|   5 |      INDEX RANGE SCAN                       | EP_DI_I         |
|   6 |    PARTITION RANGE SINGLE                   |                 |
|   7 |     TABLE ACCESS FULL                       | EMPLOYEES_PART  |
---------------------------------------------------------------------------
```

If you re-create the index on DEPARTMENT_ID as a global partial index, and then run the query against those partitions that are indexed, you again see that the index is used:

```
select * from employees_part_pi
where hire_date between '2015-11-01' and '2016-05-01'
and department_id = 5;
```

```
----------------------------------------------------------------------------
| Id  | Operation                                    | Name             |
----------------------------------------------------------------------------
|   0 | SELECT STATEMENT                             |                  |
|   1 |  COUNT STOPKEY                               |                  |
|   2 |   TABLE ACCESS BY GLOBAL INDEX ROWID BATCHED | EMPLOYEES_PART_PI |
|   3 |    INDEX RANGE SCAN                          | EP_DI_I          |
----------------------------------------------------------------------------
```

If you query against partitions where some partitions are indexed, and some not, the explain plan still reflects that, as shown here:

```
select * from employees_part_pi
where hire_date between '2014-07-01' and '2015-06-01'
and department_id = 5;
```

```
------------------------------------------------------------
| Id | Operation              | Name              |
------------------------------------------------------------
|  0 | SELECT STATEMENT       |                   |
|  1 |  VIEW                  | VW_TE_6           |
|  2 |   UNION-ALL            |                   |
|  3 |    PARTITION RANGE SINGLE|                 |
|  4 |     TABLE ACCESS FULL  | EMPLOYEES_PART_PI |
|  5 |    PARTITION RANGE SINGLE|                 |
|  6 |     TABLE ACCESS FULL  | EMPLOYEES_PART_PI |
------------------------------------------------------------
```

■ **Note**   Partial indexes cannot be used on indexes that enforce constraints, and cannot be used for unique indexes. Also, partial indexes cannot be created on index-organized tables.

Choosing the Type of Index for Your Application

Using local partitioned indexes is the most popular implementation of indexes on partitioned tables, especially in the data warehouse environment. One of the primary reasons is that local partitioned indexes reduce the amount of index partition maintenance necessary overall when you perform table-level partition operations. Local partitioned indexes are easy to create and much easier to maintain than their counterparts, the non-partitioned index and the global partitioned index. While their use does reduce the amount of maintenance and time it takes to perform partition maintenance, using local partitioned indexes doesn't eliminate maintenance entirely. That said, implementing local partitioned indexes offer the strongest advantages over both global partitioned indexes and non-partitioned indexes.

One of the key drawbacks of global partitioned indexes is that performing table-level operations generally make the entire global partitioned index unusable. The same is true for non-partitioned indexes that exist on partitioned tables—that is, any partition-level operations at the table level marks the entire non-partitioned index unusable.

Space utilization may be a concern in your environment, and if so, partial indexes may be a good option. They are also a viable option based on the usage patterns of the data within your application. For example, you may use partial indexes to index partitions with newer, more frequently accessed data, and not for partitions with older, less frequently accessed data.

If you have partitioned tables, it is best to implement a guideline to simply use local partitioned indexes on all partitioned tables. Of course, there are always exceptions to any rule or guideline. When these exceptions occur, you simply need to weigh the advantages and disadvantages of implementing a certain kind of index. This can vary greatly based on the type of application. For instance, the answer for an OLTP system greatly varies from a data warehouse system.

It's hard to find reasons not to use local partitioned indexes, but the following are a couple of possible reasons to use non-partitioned indexes or global partitioned indexes:

- Global partitioned index scans may offer significant query performance benefits.

- During database design, your application team decides it's not possible to include the table-partitioning column as part of the table primary key (therefore, primary key index would need to be non-partitioned).

Table 6-1 is for a quick synopsis of the effect table-level partition operations have on the different types of indexes, whether it is non-partitioned, local partitioned, or global partitioned. You'll see clearly that local partitioned indexes are the easiest to maintain. One key caveat to Table 6-1 is if you use the UPDATE INDEXES clause on a partition-level operation, the indexes are updated and therefore marked USABLE.

Table 6-1. *Index Partition Maintenance Comparison on Table-Level Partition Operations*

Table-Level Partition Operation	Non-Partitioned Index	Local Partitioned Index	Global Partitioned Index
Add partition	Index is unaffected.	Index is unaffected.	Index is unaffected.
Split partition	Entire index marked UNUSABLE.	Index for affected partitions from split operation marked UNUSABLE.	All partitions of index marked UNUSABLE.
Move partition	Entire index marked UNUSABLE.	Index for partition being moved marked UNUSABLE.	All partitions of index marked UNUSABLE.
Exchange partition	Entire index marked UNUSABLE.	Index for partition being exchanged marked UNUSABLE.	All partitions of index marked UNUSABLE.
Merge partition	Entire index marked UNUSABLE.	Index for affected partitions from merge operation marked UNUSABLE.	All partitions of index marked UNUSABLE.
Truncate partition	Entire index marked UNUSABLE.	Index is unaffected.	All partitions of index marked UNUSABLE.
Drop partition	Entire index marked UNUSABLE.	Local index partition is dropped; remaining index partitions are unaffected.	All partitions of index marked UNUSABLE.
Making data read-only	Not possible unless entire table is static (no DML activity ever on table).	Can make partition-level index data read-only via tablespace isolation.	Conceptually possible to make partition-level index data read-only. Practically speaking, not possible unless entire table is static.

Maintaining Indexes on Partitioned Tables

Having partitioned tables and indexes offer many advantages, but there are maintenance implications when creating partitioned tables and indexes that must be considered and taken into account when designing your application. The maintenance activities vary based on the circumstances and your specific application design and database design. For your specific application, this includes the DML patterns of your application and the volume of data that is being inserted, updated, and deleted. DML activity is slowed by the presence of indexes. In some applications, particularly in the data warehouse arena, it is beneficial to perform partition-level operations in order to speed up the overall application processing time. Partition-level operations can have significant impact on indexes, depending on what type of indexes you are using within your application.

In the examples that follow, you can see the effect partition-level operations have on the different types of indexes. Each of the examples uses a test table containing employee data. On this table, there are three indexes: one non-partitioned index (EMPLOYEES_PART_I1), one local partitioned index (EMPLOYEES_PART_LI1), and one global partitioned index (EMPLOYEES_PARTTEST_GI1). You'll see the impact a partition-level operation on the table has on each index within the table.

■ **Note** If any of the following operations are performed on an empty partition, all associated indexes are unaffected. This is true regardless of whether they are local partitioned, global partitioned, or non-partitioned indexes.

Adding a Partition

Adding partitions to a table is the least intrusive to existing indexes on your table. In fact, regardless of the type of index you choose to use (be it local partitioned, global partitioned, or non-partitioned), none of the index partitions that exist are affected, and there are no specific index-level operations needed after the partition add operation. In the following example, you are adding a partition to the test employees table for historical 2010 data:

```
SQL> alter table employees_parttest add partition p2010
  2  values less than ('2011-01-01') tablespace users;

Table altered.
```

After adding the partition, you can run the following query to determine the impact the add partition operation had on the existing indexes on the table:

```
SQL> SELECT index_name, null partition_name, status
  2  FROM user_indexes
  3  WHERE table_name = 'EMPLOYEES_PARTTEST'
  4  AND partitioned = 'NO'
  5  UNION
  6  SELECT index_name, partition_name, status
  7  FROM user_ind_partitions
  8  WHERE index_name in
  9  (SELECT index_name from user_indexes
 10  WHERE table_name = 'EMPLOYEES_PARTTEST')
 11  ORDER BY 1,2,3;
```

INDEX_NAME	PARTITION_NAME	STATUS
EMPLOYEES_PARTTEST_GI1	MANAGER_100	USABLE
EMPLOYEES_PARTTEST_GI1	MANAGER_500	USABLE
EMPLOYEES_PARTTEST_GI1	MANAGER_900	USABLE

```
EMPLOYEES_PARTTEST_GI1          MANAGER_MAX                    USABLE
EMPLOYEES_PARTTEST_I1                                          VALID
EMPLOYEES_PART_LI1              P2010                          USABLE
EMPLOYEES_PART_LI1              PI1990                         USABLE
EMPLOYEES_PART_LI1             PI1995                          USABLE
EMPLOYEES_PART_LI1             PI2000                          USABLE
```

Truncating a Partition

Truncating a partition is a simple way to remove all the data for a table partition. And, for tables with local partitioned indexes, truncating a partition has no impact on the underlying index partitions, including the truncated partition. However, if you have either non-partitioned indexes or global partitioned indexes, truncating a partition makes it impossible for Oracle to be able to know which index entries have been affected by the truncate operation. Therefore, Oracle has no choice but to simply mark the entire index UNUSABLE. The following is an example:

```
SQL> ALTER TABLE employees_parttest truncate partition p1995;

Table truncated.

INDEX_NAME                     PARTITION_NAME                 STATUS
------------------------------ ------------------------------ --------
EMPLOYEES_PARTTEST_GI1         MANAGER_100                    UNUSABLE
EMPLOYEES_PARTTEST_GI1         MANAGER_500                    UNUSABLE
EMPLOYEES_PARTTEST_GI1         MANAGER_900                    UNUSABLE
EMPLOYEES_PARTTEST_GI1         MANAGER_MAX                    UNUSABLE
EMPLOYEES_PARTTEST_I1                                         UNUSABLE
EMPLOYEES_PART_LI1             PI1990                         USABLE
EMPLOYEES_PART_LI1             PI1995                         USABLE
EMPLOYEES_PART_LI1             PI2000                         USABLE
```

Moving a Partition

There are various reasons to move a table partition. You may need to move some tables or partitions to a different tablespace, you may decide to compress a partition's data, or you may need to reorganize the table's partition because rows have become migrated due to heavy update activity.

When doing partition move operations, you again see that local partitioned indexes are the least impacted. A key difference for a local partitioned index over a partition-level truncate operation is that the index for the partition being moved has been marked UNUSABLE. This needs to be done by Oracle because by moving each row in the partition, each row now has a different ROWID value; thus the index entries for that partition are now invalid because they now contain obsolete ROWID entries. The index partition needs to be rebuilt to reflect the new ROWID values.

As with the truncate example, Oracle has no knowledge of the table partition boundaries for the global partitioned and non-partitioned indexes on the table, and therefore needs to mark the entire index UNUSABLE, and the entire index needs to be rebuilt. For the local partitioned index, only the index partition of the partition being moved needs to be rebuilt.

In the following example, you're moving the older 1995 employee data to its own tablespace, presumably so it can be made read-only:

```
SQL> alter table employees_parttest move partition p1995 tablespace emp1995_s;
```

Table altered.

INDEX_NAME	NULL	STATUS
EMPLOYEES_PARTTEST_GI1	MANAGER_100	UNUSABLE
EMPLOYEES_PARTTEST_GI1	MANAGER_500	UNUSABLE
EMPLOYEES_PARTTEST_GI1	MANAGER_900	UNUSABLE
EMPLOYEES_PARTTEST_GI1	MANAGER_MAX	UNUSABLE
EMPLOYEES_PARTTEST_I1		UNUSABLE
EMPLOYEES_PART_LI1	PI1990	USABLE
EMPLOYEES_PART_LI1	PI1995	UNUSABLE
EMPLOYEES_PART_LI1	PI2000	USABLE

Splitting a Partition

Splitting a partition is usually done because a table's partition no longer meets the application requirements or needs to be split for maintenance reasons. One of the most common reasons is simply to add a partition to a table when it is not the high-end partition of a table, and because of that, it needs to be done via a split rather than a partition add operation.

The following example splits the MAXVALUE partition to add a partition for data older than January 2000. For your local partitioned index, since the split operation touches the PIMAX index partition and also creates a new one (P1999), the rows in the PMAX partition have been split between the two partitions. Therefore, the index entries for the PMAX partition are obsolete since some data presumably moved from the PMAX table partition to the new P1999 table partition. In the case of this split operation, then, both local index partitions have been marked UNUSABLE. Since the new partition previously did not exist, there really isn't an existing local index partition, so Oracle creates one and it is automatically marked UNUSABLE.

As with previous operations such as truncate and move, all global partitioned and non-partitioned indexes have been marked entirely UNUSABLE.

```
SQL> ALTER TABLE employees_parttest SPLIT PARTITION Pmax at ('2000-01-01') INTO
  2  (partition P1999 tablespace users,
  3  partition pmax tablespace users);
```

Table altered.

INDEX_NAME	NULL	STATUS
EMPLOYEES_PARTTEST_GI1	MANAGER_100	UNUSABLE
EMPLOYEES_PARTTEST_GI1	MANAGER_500	UNUSABLE
EMPLOYEES_PARTTEST_GI1	MANAGER_900	UNUSABLE
EMPLOYEES_PARTTEST_GI1	MANAGER_MAX	UNUSABLE
EMPLOYEES_PARTTEST_I1		UNUSABLE
EMPLOYEES_PART_LI1	PI1990	USABLE
EMPLOYEES_PART_LI1	PI1995	USABLE
EMPLOYEES_PART_LI1	P1999	UNUSABLE
EMPLOYEES_PART_LI1	PIMAX	UNUSABLE

An important note to stress is that if a partition split operation is necessary to essentially add partitions to a table because there is a need for high-end partition to hold default data of some kind, partition split operations just to add an empty partition can take quite a bit of time. Oracle needs to analyze every row in an existing partition to effectively perform the split correctly. In this case, for tables with a high-end value or one where MAXVALUE is specified, it may be beneficial to add an unused "dummy" partition below the high-end partition that is always empty. Then, if you add historical partitions to your table, you can always use the empty "dummy" partition to split the partition. This offers two key benefits. First, the partition split operation is fast because there is no data to analyze. Second, no indexes are marked as unusable because there is no data in either partition, the partition being split, or the new partition.

Take a look at the following CREATE TABLE DDL statement. For the EMPLOYEES_PART table, once employees left the company, their HIRE_DATE was altered to MAXVALUE and left in the table for historical purposes. In this case, you always have data in the PMAX partition. When you add partitions to the table for future years by doing a partition split on the PMAX partition, it always takes time to do, and the underlying index partitions are marked UNUSABLE. By creating the P9999 partition as a "dummy" partition, you never need to add any rows into this partition. Then, when you split the P9999 partition to add a partition for 2001 data and beyond, it is always split on an empty partition. Thus, the split operation is fast and all underlying local index partitions are usable because the split operation occurred on an empty partition.

```
CREATE TABLE employees_part
(
  EMPLOYEE_ID          NUMBER(6)         NOT NULL
  ,FIRST_NAME          VARCHAR2(20)
  ,LAST_NAME           VARCHAR2(25)      NOT NULL
  ,EMAIL               VARCHAR2(25)      NOT NULL
  ,PHONE_NUMBER        VARCHAR2(20)
  ,HIRE_DATE           DATE              NOT NULL
  ,JOB_ID              VARCHAR2(10)      NOT NULL
  ,SALARY              NUMBER(8,2)
  ,COMMISSION_PCT      NUMBER(2,2)
  ,MANAGER_ID          NUMBER(6)
  ,DEPARTMENT_ID       NUMBER(4)
  ,constraint employees_part_pk primary key (employee_id, hire_date)
)
partition by range(hire_date)
(
partition p1990 values less than ('1991-01-01'),
partition p1991 values less than ('1992-01-01'),
partition p1992 values less than ('1993-01-01'),
partition p1993 values less than ('1994-01-01'),
partition p1994 values less than ('1995-01-01'),
partition p1995 values less than ('1996-01-01'),
partition p1996 values less than ('1997-01-01'),
partition p1997 values less than ('1998-01-01'),
partition p1998 values less than ('1999-01-01'),
partition p1999 values less than ('2000-01-01'),
partition p2000 values less than ('2001-01-01'),
partition p9999 values less than ('9999-12-31'),
partition pmax values less than (MAXVALUE);
```

Exchanging a Partition

Especially in the data warehouse environment, partition exchanges are common for large batch loads. The loads are performed into a standalone table, so read operations are not affected during the load operation. Then a partition exchange is done, which is essentially a data dictionary change to repoint a standalone table segment to be part of a partitioned table and make the associated affected table partition a standalone table segment.

A partition exchange is similar to performing a partition move in that only the affected, exchanged partition of a local partitioned index is marked UNUSABLE.

For the global partitioned and non-partitioned indexes, you can see again that both entire indexes have been marked UNUSABLE.

```
SQL> ALTER TABLE employees_parttest EXCHANGE PARTITION p1995
  2  WITH TABLE employees_parttest_exch;

Table altered.
```

INDEX_NAME	NULL	STATUS
EMPLOYEES_PARTTEST_GI1	MANAGER_100	UNUSABLE
EMPLOYEES_PARTTEST_GI1	MANAGER_500	UNUSABLE
EMPLOYEES_PARTTEST_GI1	MANAGER_900	UNUSABLE
EMPLOYEES_PARTTEST_GI1	MANAGER_MAX	UNUSABLE
EMPLOYEES_PARTTEST_I1		UNUSABLE
EMPLOYEES_PART_LI1	PI1990	USABLE
EMPLOYEES_PART_LI1	PI1995	UNUSABLE
EMPLOYEES_PART_LI1	PIMAX	USABLE

Dropping a Partition

Dropping a partition usually occurs for date- or timestamp-based partitioned tables and occurs when the data is no longer needed because the data retention for the data has expired.

For local partitioned indexes, there is no impact on any of the remaining local index partitions. All local partitioned indexes remain in USABLE status. Once again, however, for the global partitioned and non-partitioned indexes, the entire indexes have been marked unusable, because Oracle can't determine for either of these indexes which rows have been dropped via the partition drop operation.

```
SQL> ALTER TABLE employees_parttest DROP PARTITION p1995;

Table altered.
```

INDEX_NAME	NULL	STATUS
EMPLOYEES_PARTTEST_GI1	MANAGER_100	UNUSABLE
EMPLOYEES_PARTTEST_GI1	MANAGER_500	UNUSABLE
EMPLOYEES_PARTTEST_GI1	MANAGER_900	UNUSABLE
EMPLOYEES_PARTTEST_GI1	MANAGER_MAX	UNUSABLE
EMPLOYEES_PARTTEST_I1		UNUSABLE
EMPLOYEES_PART_LI1	PI1990	USABLE
EMPLOYEES_PART_LI1	PIMAX	USABLE

In the following "Rebuilding Global Partitioned and Non-Partitioned Indexes" section, note that you have the option of updating indexes as part of the DROP operation, which can make it simpler to drop a partition and rebuild any indexes in one step. The drawback is it may take longer, because the rebuild process is done serially; whereas if you manually rebuild the unusable indexes, they can be parallelized, and the rebuild operations are faster.

Merging a Partition

The partition merge operation is essentially the opposite of a partition split, and like a partition split, is performed to meet some application requirement or is done for maintenance reasons.

The following example merges the P1995 and PMAX partitions into a single PMAX partition. In this scenario, all the rows for the two partitions are combined into one essentially new partition. For your local partitioned index, there is a matching PMAX index partition. Since the row makeup changed because of the merge, the local partitioned PMAX index partition has been marked UNUSABLE.

Because again, the global partitioned index and non-partitioned indexes have no knowledge of the table partition make-up, the entire indexes have been marked UNUSABLE.

```
SQL> ALTER TABLE employees_parttest MERGE PARTITIONS p1995 , pmax
  2  into PARTITION pmax;

Table altered.
```

INDEX_NAME	NULL	STATUS
EMPLOYEES_PARTTEST_GI1	MANAGER_100	UNUSABLE
EMPLOYEES_PARTTEST_GI1	MANAGER_500	UNUSABLE
EMPLOYEES_PARTTEST_GI1	MANAGER_900	UNUSABLE
EMPLOYEES_PARTTEST_GI1	MANAGER_MAX	UNUSABLE
EMPLOYEES_PARTTEST_I1		UNUSABLE
EMPLOYEES_PART_LI1	PI1990	USABLE
EMPLOYEES_PART_LI1	PIMAX	UNUSABLE

■ **Tip**   Most partition-level table operations will not affect any underlying indexes if the affected partition(s) are empty.

Rebuilding Global Partitioned and Non-Partitioned Indexes

Almost any partition-level operation on a table render any global partitioned or non-partitioned index unusable. Essentially, the indexes always must be rebuilt. One built-in feature in Oracle 11g is to allow you to rebuild the indexes as part of the partition-level table operation. Using the partition-level merge operation example in the previous "Merge Partition" section, you can see that you can add the UPDATE INDEXES clause as part of the ALTER TABLE...MERGE command. This instructs Oracle to rebuild any indexes marked unusable by the partition-level operation, as shown in the following example:

```
SQL> ALTER TABLE employees_parttest merge PARTITIONS p1995 , pmax
  2  INTO PARTITION pmax
  3  UPDATE INDEXES;

Table altered.
```

Using the same query to see index partition status information, you can see that the global partitioned index and the non-partitioned index are now usable, even after the merge operation.

```
INDEX_NAME·                          NULL                              STATUS
---------------------------------    --------------------------------  --------
EMPLOYEES_PARTTEST_GI1               MANAGER_100                       USABLE
EMPLOYEES_PARTTEST_GI1               MANAGER_500                       USABLE
EMPLOYEES_PARTTEST_GI1               MANAGER_900                       USABLE
EMPLOYEES_PARTTEST_GI1               MANAGER_MAX                       USABLE
EMPLOYEES_PARTTEST_I1                                                  VALID
EMPLOYEES_PART_LI1                   PI1990                            USABLE
EMPLOYEES_PART_LI1                   PIMAX                             USABLE
```

A key advantage to using the UPDATE INDEXES clause when rebuilding an index is that it remains online and available during the rebuild operation. While the aforementioned example is extremely simple, one drawback of using the UPDATE INDEXES clause is that by packaging the partition-level operation with the index rebuild operation, you lose some flexibility in how you rebuild your indexes. For instance, if you have multiple indexes to rebuild, it may be faster to issue each index rebuild separately. By doing this, you can run multiple ALTER INDEX...REBUILD commands concurrently. This is a more complex method, but it may be necessary simply for speed.

For non-partitioned indexes, you simply need to issue an ALTER INDEX...REBUILD command.

```
SQL> ALTER INDEX EMPLOYEES_PARTTEST_I1 REBUILD;

Index altered.
```

Also, for each index, you can optionally decide to use parallelism, as shown in the following example:

```
SQL> alter index EMPLOYEES_PARTTEST_I1  rebuild parallel(degree 4);

Index altered.
```

As always, you need to use judgment and common sense using this approach. If you have many indexes to rebuild at once, and you want to also use parallelism at the same time, there comes a point of diminishing returns with concurrent operations. This decision needs to be made based on your specific environment. Initially, it's best to use a cautious approach to start. Operations can be submitted slowly at first to ensure concurrent operations don't become an I/O or CPU bottleneck, as well as a temporary tablespace bottleneck. If not, you can then run more rebuild commands concurrently.

You also always have the option of simply dropping the non-partitioned unusable indexes and re-creating the index(es) using the CREATE INDEX command.

To rebuild global partitioned indexes, you can also just drop and re-create the index as a whole by using the CREATE INDEX command, or you can rebuild each global partition one at a time. Note the following example:

```
  1  ALTER INDEX employees_parttest_gi1
  2* rebuild partition MANAGER_MAX
SQL> /

Index altered.
```

You would need to execute this statement for every global index partition using the ALTER INDEX... REBUILD command.

You can't rebuild a global partitioned index as a whole. Look at the following example:

```
SQL> ALTER INDEX EMPLOYEES_PARTTEST_GI1 REBUILD;
ALTER INDEX EMPLOYEES_PARTTEST_GI1  REBUILD
            *
ERROR at line 1:
ORA-14086: a partitioned index may not be rebuilt as a whole
```

Because of this, when an entire global partitioned index has been marked UNUSABLE, it may be simpler to drop and re-create the index using the CREATE INDEX command.

In Oracle 12c, if you have performed a DROP PARTITION operation with a table that contains global partitioned indexes or partial global indexes, there is different behavior from previous versions of Oracle that needs to be mentioned. The new functionality is called asynchronous global index maintenance. Using Oracle 11g as a baseline example, when you issued a DROP PARTITION with UPDATE INDEXES or UPDATE GLOBAL INDEXES clause, the index was rebuilt as part of the DROP PARTITION operation. In Oracle 12c, the associated index is essentially not maintained during the DROP operation. In turn, the DROP PARTITION operation is very fast.

To illustrate, see the following table partition, which contains over 2 million rows, and has a global partitioned index:

```
select partition_name, num_rows
from user_tab_partitions
where table_name = 'EMPLOYEES_PART'
and partition_name = 'P2014';

PARTITION_NAME    NUM_ROWS
--------------- ----------
P2014              2621440
```

The same table was created in an 11g database and a 12c database on the same server and with a similar database configuration. When dropping the partition within the 11g database, it did take time to both drop the partition and rebuild the associated global index:

```
alter table employees_part drop partition p2014 update global indexes;

Table altered.

Elapsed: 00:00:09.58
```

When running the same command in the 12c database, the DROP is instantaneous:

```
alter table employees_part_pi drop partition p2014 update global indexes;

Table altered.

Elapsed: 00:00:00.03
```

Let's validate the index structure, so it'll be apparent that the index now has orphaned rows:

```
analyze index ep_di_i validate structure;

Index analyzed.
```

At the end of the DROP operation, the index shows as usable in the data dictionary. You also notice that there are now orphaned entries in the index:

```
select index_name, status, orphaned_entries
from dba_indexes
where index_name = 'EP_DI_I';
```

```
INDEX_NAME                           STATUS    ORP
------------------------------       --------  ---
EP_DI_I                              VALID     YES
```

If you query the INDEX_STATS view, you can see how many deleted leaf blocks are now in the index:

```
select name, lf_rows, del_lf_rows from index_stats;
```

```
NAME        LF_ROWS  DEL_LF_ROWS
----------  -------  -----------
EP_DI_I     8912912      2621440
```

Under the covers, Oracle simply orphans the index entries for the given dropped partition. Any queries against the table that crosses the boundaries of the dropped partition simply ignore the associated index entries. Later, the index can be rebuilt, at which time these index entries are no longer present in the newly rebuilt index.

The key advantage of asynchronous global index maintenance is that dropping a partition can now be accomplished very fast. The trade-off is it may slow future DML and queries, simply because more blocks need to be traversed.

You must decide whether this feature is a benefit or detriment to you application. If it is deemed a detriment, the alternative is to simply rebuild the index after the DROP PARTITION operation.

Setting Index Partitions as Unusable and then Rebuilding

In a data warehouse environment, when loading large volumes of data, the speed of bulk DML operations can be slowed tremendously by the presence of indexes. One of the key advantages of the partitioned index is the ability to set portions of the index UNUSABLE prior to a bulk data load, and then simply rebuild on the portion of the index after the load based on the partitions impacted.

At its most basic, it is fairly simple to mark an index unusable and then rebuild an index, as shown in this example:

```
SQL> alter table employees_parttest
  2  modify partition pmax
  3  unusable local indexes;
```

Then, after the bulk load operation, you can issue the following command to rebuild the indexes for the given partition(s) affected by the bulk load operation:

```
SQL> alter table employees_parttest
  2  modify partition pmax
  3  rebuild unusable local indexes;
```

One significant drawback of rebuilding indexes using this command is that if you have many indexes on your table, the index partitions are built serially—one index partition at a time. This can slow the rebuild process and can become prohibitive if this operation occurs as part of a regular process. One way to alleviate the serial limitation of the ALTER INDEX...REBUILD UNUSABLE LOCAL INDEXES command is to parallelize the rebuild of each affected partition.

There are several ways to accomplish the parallelization of the rebuild operations. For example, this may be especially useful if you have a subpartitioned table with local subpartitioned indexes. One example, shown next, is a Korn shell script, which submits many index partition rebuild operations in the background. The following specific shell script is an example of rebuilding many subpartitioned index partitions for many indexes:

```
#!/bin/ksh

typeset -Z4 YEAR=${1:-2011}
typeset -Z2 MM=${2:-08}
YY=`echo $YEAR|cut -c3-4`

LOGDIR=$HOME/logs
DT=`date +%Y%m%d.%H%M`
LOG="$LOGDIR/`echo \`basename $0\`|cut -d'.' -f1`_${YEAR}${MM}_${DT}"

IDXFILE=/tmp/bf_i.$$.out
PARTFILE=/tmp/bf_p.$$.out

# Get list of subpartitions for an index

sqlplus -s $CONNECT_STRING@$ORACLE_SID <<EOT > /dev/null
set echo off
set pages 0
set head off
set feedback off
spool $PARTFILE

select subpartition_name from user_ind_subpartitions
where index_name = 'BILLING_FACT_PK'
and subpartition_name like '%${YY}_${MM}%'
order by 1;

quit;
EOT

# Get list of indexes for a table

sqlplus -s $CONNECT_STRING@$ORACLE_SID <<EOT > /dev/null
set echo off
set pages 0
set head off
set feedback off
spool $IDXFILE
```

```
select index_name
from user_ind_columns
where table_name = 'BILLING_FACT'
and index_name != 'BILLING_FACT_PK'
order by 1;

quit;
EOT

DT=`date +%Y%m%d.%H%M`
echo "Starting index rebuilds at $DT" >> $LOG

# Loop through each subpartition of every index and rebuild the index subpartitions.
#    All indexes for table are done all at once, subpartition at a time (in the background)

for p in `cat $PARTFILE`
do
  for i in `cat $IDXFILE`
  do
    DT=`date +%Y%m%d.%H%M`
    sqlplus -s $CONNECT_STRING@$ORACLE_SID <<EOT >> $LOG &
    prompt Rebuilding index $i, subpartition $p at $DT
    $PROMPT alter index $i rebuild subpartition $p;
    quit;
    EOT
  done
  wait
done

DT=`date +%Y%m%d.%H%M`
echo "Completed index rebuilds at $DT" >> $LOG
```

Index Implications for Interval Partitioning

Interval partitioning, which is available as of Oracle 11g, is a wonderful feature that has Oracle automatically create partitions on a table when incoming data doesn't match the partition boundaries on a table. In early versions of Oracle, trying to insert new data would have generated an Oracle error and the DML operation fail. With interval partitioning, Oracle now simply adds new partitions as needed to match the incoming data.

In regards to indexes on interval-based table partitioning, similar rules apply as if you were using other partitioning methods, such as local partitioned indexes. On your interval-based partitioned local indexes, if you want your new index partitions to be placed in a specific tablespace, you need to make sure that each index points to that tablespace. As with table partitions, you can also modify the default attributes for an index to accomplish the same task.

```
SQL> alter index test_i3 modify default attributes tablespace test09index_s;
```

If you then insert a row in the table that is outside the existing partition boundaries, a new local index partition is generated in the desired tablespace.

```
SQL> insert into testtab values (1,'2009-05-01');

SQL> select partition_name, tablespace_name from user_ind_partitions;
```

PARTITION_NAME	TABLESPACE_NAME
SYS_P74	TEST08INDEX_S
TEST307_11P	TEST08INDEX_S
TEST307_12P	TEST08INDEX_S
SYS_P75	TEST08INDEX_S
SYS_P76	TEST09INDEX_S

Making Older Data Read-Only

Especially within the data warehouse environment, it is important to be able to make older data read-only because it speeds up query time. It can also assist in reducing the backup times on very large databases (VLDBs), because data and indexes that reside in read-only tablespaces only have to be backed up occasionally.

If you are using date- or timestamp-based partitioning on your tables and indexes, it is important to segregate both the data and index partitions into tablespaces based on that date-based interval. Once data becomes static and no longer updated, you can then make those tablespaces read-only. So, during physical database design, the DBA needs to consider whether making data read-only is a necessity for the environment based on the size of the database. If so, it is important to isolate local data and index partitions into date-based tablespaces.

Reporting on Partitioned Indexes

There are many things you can glean from the data dictionary regarding index partitions, including the following:

- Partition names

- Type of index

- Status of index partitions (need to query appropriate view)

- Size of the index partitions

In the following example, you simply want to get a list of the index name, partition names, and status for your EMPLOYEES_PARTTEST table. On this table, since you have both partitioned and non-partitioned indexes, you UNION two queries together.

```
SQL> select table_name, index_name, partition_name, p.status
  2  from user_ind_partitions p join user_indexes i using(index_name)
  3  where table_name = 'EMPLOYEES_PARTTEST'
  4  union
  5  select table_name, index_name, null, status
  6  from user_indexes
  7  where table_name = 'EMPLOYEES_PARTTEST'
  8* order by 2,3;
```

TABLE_NAME	INDEX_NAME	PARTITION_NAME	STATUS
EMPLOYEES_PARTTEST	EMPLOYEES_PARTTEST_GI1	MANAGER_100	USABLE
EMPLOYEES_PARTTEST	EMPLOYEES_PARTTEST_GI1	MANAGER_500	USABLE
EMPLOYEES_PARTTEST	EMPLOYEES_PARTTEST_GI1	MANAGER_900	USABLE

EMPLOYEES_PARTTEST	EMPLOYEES_PARTTEST_GI1	MANAGER_MAX	USABLE
EMPLOYEES_PARTTEST	EMPLOYEES_PARTTEST_GI1		N/A
EMPLOYEES_PARTTEST	EMPLOYEES_PARTTEST_I1		VALID
EMPLOYEES_PARTTEST	EMPLOYEES_PART_LI1	PI1990	USABLE
EMPLOYEES_PARTTEST	EMPLOYEES_PART_LI1	PIMAX	USABLE
EMPLOYEES_PARTTEST	EMPLOYEES_PART_LI1		N/A

Note that the STATUS column shows N/A on partitioned indexes when querying the USER_INDEXES view. The status column is only populated on the most granular data dictionary view based on partitioning of the index. That is, for partitioned indexes, the STATUS column is populated on the USER_IND_PARTITIONS view. If you had any subpartitioned indexes, the STATUS column would only be populated on the USER_IND_SUBPARTITIONS view, and the status column of USER_INDEXES and USER_IND_PARTITIONS would be N/A.

Next, you want to issue a query to determine each type of index partition that you have on your tables.

```
  1  select table_name, index_name, partitioning_type, locality, alignment
  2* from user_part_indexes
00:37:56 SQL> /
```

TABLE_NAME	INDEX_NAME	PARTITION	LOCALI	ALIGNMENT
EMPLOYEES	EMPLOYEES_UK1	RANGE	GLOBAL	PREFIXED
EMPLOYEES	EMPLOYEES_IH1	HASH	GLOBAL	PREFIXED
EMPLOYEES	EMPLOYEES_I2	RANGE	GLOBAL	PREFIXED
EMPLOYEES_PART	EMPLOYEES_PART_PK	RANGE	LOCAL	NON_PREFIXED
EMPLOYEES_PART	EMPLOYEES_PART_LI1	RANGE	LOCAL	PREFIXED
EMPLOYEES_PARTTEST	EMPLOYEES_PART_LI1	RANGE	LOCAL	PREFIXED
EMPLOYEES_PARTTEST	EMPLOYEES_PARTTEST_GI1	RANGE	GLOBAL	PREFIXED

A distinction needs to be noted for subpartitioned indexes when querying for segment information. In subpartitioned indexes, there is a subpartition column on most data dictionary views that gets information on subpartitions. One exception to that is when you want to get segment information from a view such as DBA_SEGMENTS; only the actual PARTITION_NAME or the SUBPARTITION_NAME that is an actual segment is represented in DBA_SEGMENTS. In other words, for subpartitioned indexes, the subpartition_name appears as the PARTITION_NAME in the DBA_SEGMENTS column. In the following example, you want to get the BILLING_FACT table index subpartitions that are greater than 8GB in size. You perform a subquery against USER_IND_SUBPARTITIONS, which demonstrates that the PARTITION_NAME column in DBA_SEGMENTS actually represents the SUBPARTITION_NAME in USER_IND_SUBPARTITIONS.

```
 1  select segment_name, partition_name, round(bytes/1048576) meg
 2  from dba_segments
 3  where (segment_name, partition_name) in
 4  (select index_name, subpartition_name
 5  from user_ind_subpartitions
 6  where index_name in
 7  (select index_name from user_indexes
 8  where table_name = 'BILLING_FACT'))
 9  and bytes > 1048576*8192
10* order by 3 desc;
```

```
SEGMENT_NAME                    PARTITION_NAME                       MEG
------------------------------  ------------------------------  ----------
BILLING_FACT_PK                 BILLING_FACT11_08P_EAST               9687
BILLING_FACT_PK                 BILLING_FACT11_09P_EAST               9591
BILLING_FACT_PK                 BILLING_FACT11_07P_EAST               8951
```

For partitioned indexes, the partition names between DBA_SEGMENTS and USER_IND_PARTITIONS match.

Summary

As a guideline, partitioned indexes should be used on partitioned tables. More specifically, local partitioned indexes should be used whenever possible. You can also use partial indexes, which can save storage while still getting advantages of indexing partitions that are often used. Index maintenance on partitioned tables is far easier when using local partitioned indexes, as noted in Table 6-1. That said, with the new Oracle 12c feature asynchronous global index maintenance, dropping partitions on tables with global indexes can now be accomplished very quickly. There are, of course, exceptions based on application requirements. For instance, application requirements may dictate that the partitioning column(s) can't be part of a unique index that becomes the primary key. In cases such as these, you may simply have to implement a non-partitioned index. Alternatively, query performance using a global partitioned index may be beneficial to warrant their use in certain circumstances.

As with many aspects of software development, the trade-offs between the different types of indexes need to be analyzed before making a final determination. During application and database design, it is important to understand all the ramifications and impacts of using each type of index. This includes weighing the following factors:

- Data model requirements

- Data access requirements

- Data volume

- Time needed to perform index maintenance operations

- Available maintenance windows

Once you take all the aforementioned items into consideration, you can make an informed decision as to what is best for your application.

CHAPTER 7

■ ■ ■

Tuning Index Usage

To tune index usage, it's important to understand the various types of index access paths available to the cost optimizer. This chapter summarizes the most important index access paths available to the optimizer. Often, Oracle database administrators are bewildered when the optimizer chooses not to use what they believe is a very useful index, but does a full table scan instead. This chapter devotes attention to exploring some reasons why the optimizer might prefer a full table scan to using an index. You'll also learn how to force the optimizer to use (or not to use) an index. Oracle provides a large number of index-related hints to enable you to control the behavior of the optimizer regarding index usage. You'll find descriptions of the key index-related hints in this chapter.

Before we plunge into the various ways you can direct the optimizer to access (or not to access) an index, let's review the different access paths the optimizer can choose from.

Optimizer Access Paths

An access path is the path chosen by the optimizer to retrieve data from the database. There are two basic types of access paths: index access paths and a full table scan. A full table scan is simply a scan of all the rows in a table, and the optimizer uses it mostly when a query requests a large portion of a table's blocks. Sometimes the percentage of rows retrieved by a query is relatively small, but due the way the table's data is distributed among the blocks in the table segment, rows that satisfy the query are present in the majority of blocks. Oracle reads blocks, and block selectivity is critical to access path selection. Index scans, on the other hand, are typically used to retrieve a small set of a table's rows, and thus the query needs to access fewer index (if all the data is present in the index itself) or data blocks (if the query needs to access the table as well to retrieve all the data).

■ **Note** The optimizer is often concerned with blocks rather than rows. It's really when a query must touch the larger portion of the *blocks* assigned to a table and below the high water mark that a table scan is often used.

Generally, the optimizer prefers a full table scan under the following conditions, even in the presence of an index on the table:

- The table being accessed is small, consisting of few blocks.

- A large amount of data is requested from a table.

- Very few distinct values exist in an indexed column being referenced in the WHERE clause.

- There is a high degree of parallelism defined for the table.

© Darl Kuhn, Sam R. Alapati and Bill Padfield 2016
D. Kuhn et al., *Expert Oracle Indexing and Access Paths*, DOI 10.1007/978-1-4842-1984-3_7

Of course, absence of an index on a table guarantees a full table scan, and so does the specifying of the FULL hint in the query in most cases.

ROWIDS

While a full table scan requires reading all the data in a table, specifying the ROWID of a row is the fastest way to retrieve a single row from a table. The ROWID specifies the exact location of the row and the database goes straight to the row to fetch it. However, you rarely specify a ROWID directly in a query. Instead, the database gets ROWID(s) from an index scan of a table's index.

Index Scans

An index on a column contains two types of data: the indexed column value and the ROWID of the row. Each leaf block of a B-tree index contains the indexed data value and the corresponding ROWID that is used to locate the actual row in the table. The optimizer sorts the index entries by (key, ROWID). An index scan occurs whenever the database retrieves column values from an index for a specific column or columns. If your SQL statement refers only to the indexed columns, the database retrieves the column values from the index itself and it doesn't need to access the table. If the query refers to columns other than the indexed column(s), the database accesses the table as well in the next step, using the ROWIDs it reads during the index access.

Index Unique Scan

If a query requires only a single row from a table, the database performs an index unique scan. The database uses an index unique scan when the query contains only columns from a unique index. It also does so when the query specifies an equality condition along with a primary key constraint.

In the following example, there's a primary key constraint on column A. Therefore, the query guarantees that only a single row is accessed via the predicate "where A=2000".

```
SQL> select * from testtab where a=99;
Execution Plan
-----------------------------------------------------------
Plan hash value: 3966921780
-----------------------------------------------------------
```

Id	Operation	Name	Rows	Bytes	Cost (%CPU)	Time
0	SELECT STATEMENT		1	26	1 (0)	00:00:01
1	TABLE ACCESS BY INDEX ROWID	TESTTAB	1	26	1 (0)	00:00:01
* 2	INDEX UNIQUE SCAN	SYS_C0010248	1		0 (0)	00:00:01

```
Predicate Information (identified by operation id):
-----------------------------------------------------------
   2 - access("A"=99)
SQL>
```

In this example, the database uses the primary key on column A (TEST_PK1). Note that the database is likely to perform an index unique scan when you specify all columns of a unique index as well.

Index Range Scan

The database performs an index range scan when it needs to access highly selective data. The database returns the values of the indexed column in ascending order. If the indexed column is identical for all rows, the output is ordered according to ROWID.

The optimizer chooses an index range scan when dealing with the following types of conditions, where col1 is the leading column for an index:

```
col1 =:b1
col1 < :b1
col1 > :b1
```

Additionally, any AND combinations of these three conditions involving a leading column in an index results in an index range scan.

Index data is stored in ascending order. If the database needs to return data in descending order, as when it needs to return the latest data first or when it needs to retrieve values less than a specific value, the database uses an index range scan descending.

The following example shows how the database will use an index range scan when you specify a "less than" condition such as "a > 10000":

```
SQL> select * from testtab where a > 10000;
no rows selected
Execution Plan
----------------------------------------------------
Plan hash value: 4152566211
--------------------------------------------------------------------
| Id | Operation                         | Name         | Rows | Bytes | Cos
t (%CPU)| Time     |
--------------------------------------------------------------------
|  0 | SELECT STATEMENT                  |              |   1  |  26  |
 0   (0)| 00:00:01 |
|  1 |  TABLE ACCESS BY INDEX ROWID BATCHED| TESTTAB    |   1  |  26  |
 0   (0)| 00:00:01 |
|* 2 |   INDEX RANGE SCAN                | TESTTAB_IDX1 |   1  |      |
 0   (0)| 00:00:01 |

Predicate Information (identified by operation id):
---------------------------------------------------
   2 - access("A">10000)
   - dynamic statistics used: dynamic sampling (level=2)
SQL>
```

Reading from the bottom, the explain plan shows that the optimizer performs an index range scan first and uses the ROWIDs from the index range scan to perform the table access (table access by index rowid batched operation).

The database also performs an index range scan when you use the BETWEEN operator, as shown in the following example:

```
SQL> select * from testtab where col1 between 1000 and 2000;
no rows selected
Execution Plan
----------------------------------------------------------------
Plan hash value: 4152566211

---------------------------------------------------------------------------------
| Id | Operation                          | Name         | Rows | Bytes | Cos
t (%CPU)| Time        |
---------------------------------------------------------------------------------
|  0 | SELECT STATEMENT                   |              |    1 |    26 |
 0   (0)| 00:00:01 |
|  1 |  TABLE ACCESS BY INDEX ROWID BATCHED| TESTTAB     |    1 |    26 |
 0   (0)| 00:00:01 |
|* 2 |   INDEX RANGE SCAN                 | TESTTAB_IDX1 |    1 |       |
 0   (0)| 00:00:01 |
---------------------------------------------------------------------------------
Predicate Information (identified by operation id):
---------------------------------------------------
   2 - access("COL1">=1000 AND "COL1"<=2000)
   - dynamic statistics used: dynamic sampling (level=2)
SQL>
```

Note that while the database uses an index range scan when you specify the WHERE a < 50 condition as well as the WHERE a > 9000 condition, it reverts to a full table scan when you modify the query predicate to WHERE a < 2000. The reason is simple: there are far fewer values for the database to scan when you specify the a < 50 and a > 9000 conditions as compared to when you specify the a < 2000 condition. It is more likely that there are a far larger number of values that satisfy the a < 2000 condition, and consequently, the database performs a full table scan to retrieve the data when you specify this condition, as shown in the following example:

```
SQL> select * from testtab where col1 < 2000;
100 rows selected.
Execution Plan
----------------------------------------------------------
Plan hash value: 2692415588

-----------------------------------------------------------------------
| Id | Operation          | Name    | Rows | Bytes | Cost (%CPU)| Time     |
-----------------------------------------------------------------------
|  0 | SELECT STATEMENT   |         |  100 |  2600 |    2   (0)| 00:00:01 |
|* 1 |  TABLE ACCESS FULL | TESTTAB |  100 |  2600 |    2   (0)| 00:00:01 |
-----------------------------------------------------------------------
Predicate Information (identified by operation id):
---------------------------------------------------
   1 - filter("COL1"<2000)
Note
-----
   - dynamic statistics used: dynamic sampling (level=2)
SQL>
```

An INDEX RANGE SCAN DESCENDING operation is very similar to an index range scan; the difference is that the database engine reads the results in descending order. One reason the optimizer might make that choice is to avoid a sort down the road. The cost optimizer will use an index range scan descending operation when you specify the ORDER BY <column_name> DESC clause and the index can satisfy the clause, thereby avoiding a descending sort operation. An INDEX RANGE SCAN DESCENDING operation reads the index backward to avoid having to read it in its normal order (ascending) and then execute a sort operation.

```
SQL>
SQL> select * from testtab where col1 between 1000 and 2000 order by col1 desc;
no rows selected

Execution Plan
----------------------------------------------------------
Plan hash value: 3967923105

--------------------------------------------------------------------------
| Id  | Operation                    | Name         | Rows  | Bytes | Cost (%CPU)| Time     |
--------------------------------------------------------------------------
|   0 | SELECT STATEMENT             |              |     1 |    26 |     0   (0)| 00:00:01 |
|   1 |  TABLE ACCESS BY INDEX ROWID | TESTTAB      |     1 |    26 |     0   (0)| 00:00:01 |
|*  2 |   INDEX RANGE SCAN DESCENDING| TESTTAB_IDX1 |     1 |       |     0   (0)| 00:00:01 |
--------------------------------------------------------------------------

Predicate Information (identified by operation id):
---------------------------------------------------
   2 - access("COL1">=1000 AND "COL1"<=2000)
Note
-----
   - dynamic statistics used: dynamic sampling (level=2)
SQL>
```

Index Skip Scan

An index skip scan occurs when a query "skips" the leading column of a composite index when a query doesn't specify that column in, say, a WHERE clause predicate. The database splits the composite index into logical subindexes. The fewer the distinct values in the leading column of a composite index and the larger the distinct values in the other keys that are part of the composite index, the better the performance of an index skip scan. For example, if the leading column has just three distinct values, the database divides the composite index into three logical subindexes and searches for the values of the non-leading indexed columns. Chapter 5 explains the index skip scan in detail in the context of a composite index.

In the following example, the database uses the composite index test_idx1, which was created on columns (b,e). The query specifies the e=10 condition. The query's WHERE clause doesn't use the leading column of the composite index, thus skipping that column.

```
SQL> select b,e from test where e=10;

Execution Plan
----------------------------------------------------------
Plan hash value: 3001938079
```

161

```
-----------------------------------------------------------------------
| Id  | Operation        | Name      | Rows | Bytes | Cost (%CPU)| Time     |
-----------------------------------------------------------------------
|  0  | SELECT STATEMENT |           |   1  |    7  |    3   (0)| 00:00:01 |
|* 1  | INDEX SKIP SCAN  | TEST_IDX1 |   1  |    7  |    3   (0)| 00:00:01 |
-----------------------------------------------------------------------
Predicate Information (identified by operation id):
---------------------------------------------------
   1 - access("E"=10)
       filter("E"=10)
SQL>
```

The number of logical subindexes into which the database splits the composite index will depend on the number of distinct values of the leading column. In this example, the leading column B of the composite index has very few distinct values:

```
SQL> select distinct b from test;

        B
----------
        1
        2
SQL>
```

As the output shows, there are only two distinct values for the leading column of your composite index. The database splits the composite index on (b,e) into two subindexes: the first with the key "1" and the second with the key "2". The database searches the first subindex with the key "1" and then searches the second subindex with the key "2". The nonleading column of the index, E, on the other hand, has 10,000 distinct values (same as the number of rows in the table). In cases such as this, the database finds that it is cheaper to perform an index skip scan due to the low number of distinct values in the leading column of the composite index.

Index Full Scan

An index full scan is the operation of reading *all* the entries in a given index. In that sense, an index full scan is analogous to a full table scan. An index full scan is a good alternative to doing a full table scan first and sorting the data afterward. An Oracle database is likely to use a full index scan in any of the following conditions:

- *A query requires a sort merge join.* All columns referenced by the query must exist in the index and the order of the leading index columns must be identical to the columns specified in the query.

- *The query contains an* ORDER BY *clause.* All the columns in the clause must be present in the index.

- *The query contains a* GROUP BY *clause.* The index and the GROUP BY clause must contain the same columns, although not necessarily in the same order.

The following is an example that shows how the database utilizes an index full scan operation to retrieve the data without performing a sort. The full index scan avoids a sort operation because the index is already sorted. Full index scans read single data blocks and don't perform a multiblock read operation.

```
SQL> select * from test order by a;

Execution Plan
-------------------------------------------------------------
Plan hash value: 3311708430
----------------------------------------------------------------------
| Id|Operation                      |Name    |Rows|Bytes|Cost (%CPU)|Time     |
----------------------------------------------------------------------
|  0|SELECT STATEMENT               |        |9433|1040K|  79   (0)|00:00:03|
|  1| TABLE ACCESS BY INDEX ROWID|TEST    |9433|1040K|  79   (0)|00:00:03|
|  2|  INDEX FULL SCAN              |TEST_PK1|9433|     |  21   (0)|00:00:01|
----------------------------------------------------------------------
SQL>
```

In this query, the database performs an index full scan first and then performs a table access by index ROWID operation. This is so because the query requests columns besides the indexed column (SELECT * FROM ...). However, if a query requests just the indexed column along with an ORDER BY clause, the database skips the table access and gets the data back by accessing the index alone, without having to read the table values.

Index Fast Full Scan

An Oracle database performs an index full scan as an alternative to a full table scan, when the index itself contains all the columns that you specify in the query. In the following example, notice that there's only an index full scan operation to retrieve the data and that the table itself isn't accessed at all:

```
SQL> select b,e from test where e > 100;
Execution Plan
-------------------------------------------------------------
Plan hash value: 703934364
----------------------------------------------------------------------
| Id  | Operation            | Name      | Rows  | Bytes | Cost (%CPU)| Time     |
----------------------------------------------------------------------
|   0 | SELECT STATEMENT     |           | 9901  | 69307 |    7   (0)|00:00:01|
|*  1 |  INDEX FAST FULL SCAN| TEST_IDX1 | 9901  | 69307 |    7   (0)|00:00:01|
----------------------------------------------------------------------
Predicate Information (identified by operation id):
-------------------------------------------------------
   1 - filter("E">100)
SQL>
```

Note that unlike in the case of a full index scan, an index full scan uses a multiblock read operation to read the index. Thus, this type of scan tends to be faster due to the multiblock I/O and due to the fact that this type of scan can run in parallel, just as a full table scan.

Determining Whether a Query Uses an Index

DBAs and developers often wonder if the database is using a certain index. Your explain plans may indicate the use of the index, but you may want to make sure that the database is actually using the index. You can easily track the usage of an index by enabling the monitoring of index usage in your database. By default, an Oracle database doesn't monitor index usage. You can make the database monitor an index by altering the index that you're interested in with the MONITORING USAGE clause, as shown here:

```
SQL> alter index employees_idx1 monitoring usage;
Index altered.

SQL>
```

Once you turn on index monitoring, the database tracks the usage of the EMPLOYEES_IDX1 index. You can query the new DBA_OBJECT_USAGE view display statistics about an index's usage, thus helping you monitor the index usage. You can monitor any index that has been used at least once.

```
SQL> select index_name,monitoring,used from dba_object_usage;
INDEX_NAME                      MONITORING           USED
-------------------             ------------------   ------------
TESTTAB_IDX1                    YES                  YES

SQL>
```

Both the MONITORING and the USED columns take either of two possible values: YES and NO. You can monitor all indexes that the database has used by querying the V$OBJECT_USAGE view.

Once you're done examining the index usage, you can turn off the monitoring.

```
SQL> alter index employees_idx1 nomonitoring  usage;

Index altered.

SQL>
```

While monitoring indexes in the way shown here works well for the most part, index monitoring only tells you whether the *optimizer* has planned the use of an index. It doesn't tell you whether the query execution has actually used the index! Therefore, be very cautious before you drop an index after a cursory glance at the V$OBJECT_USAGE view after turning on index monitoring.

■ **Note**   The database refreshes the V$OBJECT_USAGE view each time you turn on monitoring for a specific index. Each time you turn on index monitoring for a specific index, the database removes the current usage information and records a new start time for the monitoring.

You can also use the DBA_HIST_SQL_PLAN and the DBA_HIST_SQLSTAT views to find out the number of times the database has accessed an index, as well as the type of index access, such as an index range scan or a unique index scan. Here's an example:

```
SQL> select
  2      d.object_name,
  3      d.operation,
  4      d.options,
  5      count(1)
  6  from
  7      dba_hist_sql_plan d,
  8      dba_hist_sqlstat h
  9  where
 10      d.object_owner <> 'SYS'
```

```
11  and
12      d.operation like '%INDEX%'
13  and
14      d.sql_id = h.sql_id
15  group by
16      d.object_name,
17      d.operation,
18      d.options
19  order by
20*     1,2,3;
```

```
object_name              operation          options        count
-----------------------  -----------------  -------------  -----
ACHTRANSACTION_NU1       INDEX              RANGE SCAN       209
ACHTRANSACTION_NU2                          FULL SCAN          6
ACHTRANSACTION_NU2                          RANGE SCAN        38
ACH_DETAIL_NU1           INDEX              RANGE SCAN         4
ACH_DETAIL_NU2                              FAST FULL SCAN    10
ACH_DETAIL_NU2                              RANGE SCAN         9
ACH_DETAIL_PK            INDEX              RANGE SCAN        19
ACH_DETAIL_PK                               UNIQUE SCAN        6
...
SQL>
```

Avoiding an Index

It is much more likely that you'll be looking for ways for the cost optimizer to use the indexes that you've created, rather than for it to ignore existing indexes. However, there are times when you want to do exactly this: you want to keep the optimizer from using an index.

Avoiding All Use of an Index

You may want to avoid an index, for example, when you are dealing with an unselective index. That's because if an index is not selective enough, it can sometimes be more efficient to scan the entire underlying table.

If a SQL statement contains a construct such as a WHERE clause that includes an indexed column, the optimizer is likely to use the index on that column. To preclude that from happening, you can specify the NO_INDEX hint to let the optimizer disallow the use of a certain index, as shown in this example:

```
SQL> select /*+ NO_INDEX(employees emp_emp_id) */employee_id
     from employees
     where employee_id >200;
```

This example lists a specific index that you want the optimizer to ignore. If there are other indexes on the table, the optimizer still considers the use of those indexes.

Instead of specifying a single index, you can also list a set of indexes that the optimizer must ignore. If you just specify the NO_INDEX hint without listing any indexes, the optimizer will ignore all indexes on the table you specify. As with the INDEX hint that you'll encounter later in this chapter, the NO_INDEX hint applies to B-tree, function-based, cluster, or domain indexes.

Avoiding Only the Fast Full Scan

You can use the NO_INDEX_FFS hint to direct the optimizer to avoid a fast full index scan of an index. Note that you must specify the name of a specific index along with this hint, as in the case of an INDEX hint; for example:

```
SQL> select /*+ no_index_ffs (items item_order_ix) +/ order_id from order_items;
```

Similarly, you can include the NO_INDEX_SS hint to tell the optimizer to exclude a skip scan of a specific index on a table.

Forcing a Table Scan

Another way to avoid index usage is to come at the problem from the opposite direction by demanding a table scan. Use the FULL hint to instruct the optimizer to choose a full table scan instead of an index scan. Here is an example of how you specify the FULL hint:

```
SQL> select /*+ FULL(e) */ employee_id, last_name
          from employees
          where last_name like :b1;
```

■ **Caution**   Hints change across Oracle releases, so be sure to review the applicable hints when you get a new Oracle release!

Choosing Between an Index and a Table Scan

Users are often bewildered as to why the optimizer chooses a full table scan when they believe it ought to be using an index. In a later section, this chapter explains several scenarios where the optimizer prefers a full table scan to an index. Before we delve into these scenarios, however, let's understand the essentials of how the cost-based optimizer works.

The job of the cost-based optimizer is to select the best or optimal execution plan from among a set of possible plans. The cost-based optimizer uses information such as the number of rows in a table or index, the number of distinct values for each column, and much more to estimate the cost of alternative execution plans. It then picks the execution plan with the lowest cost.

For demonstration purposes, let's focus on one of the most important factors in determining the cost of a query: the number of rows in a table and the number of rows the optimizer needs to read from that table. It's all but certain that the optimizer will fully read a table if its size is very small. Let's say that your table contains 10,000,000 rows and that the table uses 100,000 table blocks because each block holds on the average about 100 rows. Now, create an index on this table with the index requiring roughly 20,000 leaf blocks to store the index entries for each indexed column.

The index requires fewer blocks than the table because it holds just one column value (and the ROWID for the associated table column). Assume that this index has a height of 3, meaning it has a BLEVEL of 2, and that there are 100 distinct values in each indexed column, with those values evenly distributed. Thus, the index will contain 100,000 occurrences number of rows divided by the average number of rows in a block of each index value. Let's use a test query such as the following to demonstrate how the optimizer decides among multiple execution plans:

```
SQL> select * from test_table where test_code='ABCDE';
```

Does the optimizer choose an index or a full table scan, and why? Let's analyze the cost of the index access first. Since the index on the `test_code` column is evenly distributed among all possible values, the optimizer needs to select one out of the 100 distinct values in the index on the `test_code` column. This works out to one percent of the data in the index. To do this, the database needs to first read the root and the branch block (`BLEVEL = 2` in this example). Therefore, the optimizer starts with the cost of these two block reads. Next, the database has to read 1 percent of the index leaf blocks, which amounts to 200 (20,000 × 0.01) leaf blocks. You thus have 202 index block accesses for the index reads.

Since the query asks for the values of all the columns in the table, the database must next read the table rows itself. Here, the crucial variable is the clustering factor of the index; that is, how well clustered the index column values are in the table.

The more well clustered the index column values are, the fewer block accesses it will take to read all the necessary table rows. Let's say that the clustering factor is the worst possible, meaning that it's almost the same as the number of rows in the table (10,000,000). With each of the table's 100,000 data blocks containing 100 rows, the database selects 10 rows, or 1 percent from each data block. Thus, the total cost of accessing the table data is going to be the selectivity times the clustering factor, which is 100,000 (0.1 × 10,000,000). So the approximate cost of the index-based read is 202 index block accesses plus 100,000 table block accesses, for a grand-total cost of 100,202 blocks.

When it comes to the full table scan costs, remember that unlike an index read, which is always done in single block I/Os, a full table scan uses multiblock reads. Since this example assumes that each table block contains 100 rows, the database needs to scan roughly 100,000 data blocks during a full table scan. Let's assume the `multi_block_read_count` value is set at 10. The database then has to perform a total of 10,000 (100,000 ÷ 10) reads. If you want to be more precise, you can also add the read of the segment header block to the total, making it 10,001.

Clearly the full table scan in this case is much cheaper (10,001 block reads compared to 100,202 block reads for the index access), even after assuming the worst possible index clustering factor. In addition, you can parallelize this full table scan, making it perform even faster.

In the previous example, the query is fetching only 1 percent of the data in a large table, yet the full table scan is much cheaper. This is a simple demonstration to show that the choice of the index or full table scan by the optimizer doesn't always depend on the percentage of rows a query must retrieve. Rather, it depends on critical factors such as the data distribution, the number of table and leaf blocks, the average number of rows in a table block, the average number of leaf entries in an index leaf block, the index clustering factor, and the size of the multiblock read count, There simply is no magic percentage of rows that a query must retrieve, such as 1, 5, 10, 25, or 50 percent, that by itself tells the optimizer it must use an index or a full table scan. This simple example here shows that the optimizer is likely to go for a full table scan even when a query retrieves a very small percent (1 percent) of a table's rows.

Why the Optimizer May Ignore Indexes

Creating an index is never a guarantee that the optimizer will use the index when evaluating an execution plan. If a query is selecting a high percentage of rows from a table, the optimizer might determine that it can get the results faster through a full table scan instead of an index scan. Remember that when the database uses an index first, it looks up the index to obtain the ROWIDs and then uses those ROWIDs to retrieve the requested rows. If a query selects a large percentage of rows from a table, leading to a large percentage of the table's blocks being read, the database might perform a full table scan to avoid reading both the index and the table, which could end up being more expensive than just scanning the table once.

Many factors determine the usage of an index by the optimizer, as the following sections in this chapter explain.

Number of Distinct Rows

A crucial factor that determines the choice between a full table scan and an index scan is the number of distinct rows in a table matching a given query predicate vis-à-vis the number of total rows in the table. You can find the number of rows in a table by querying the NUM_ROWS column in the DBA_TABLES view. You can similarly find the number of distinct values in any column by querying the NUM_DISTINCT column from the DBA_TAB_COLUMNS view. The closer the value of the NUM_DISTINCT column to the NUM_ROWS column, the more likely it is for the optimizer to prefer accessing an index on that column to performing a full table scan; in other words, the more selective an index, the more likely the database is to use it.

The selectivity of an index has probably the biggest impact on whether the database will use an index or not. Selectivity refers to how many distinct values there are for each column value. If an index is very selective, it has few rows for each index entry. If an index is unselective, on the other hand, there are many rows for each index entry.

Do remember that the optimizer multiplies the selectivity of the column with the leaf block statistics to get an estimate of the index blocks the database must access during an index read. While it's true that most of the time highly selective columns will indeed use an index, it isn't always the case since the ultimate deciding factor in the choice of an index vs. full table scans is block selectivity.

Index Clustering Factor

You can find the value of an index's clustering factor by querying the CLUSTERING_FACTOR column from the DBA_INDEXES view. The clustering factor tells you how well ordered a table's rows are in comparison with an index's rows. If the clustering factor is close to the number of rows in a table, the rows are likely to be more randomly ordered and it's less likely that the index entries in an index block are located in the same data block.

The table's selectivity (with filtering) multiplied by the index clustering factor determines the cost of the table access by index. This is actually the table selectivity used in this portion of the calculation. Although most of the time, the index selectivity (multiplied by leaf blocks; discussed in the previous section) and table selectivity are the same, it is actually a computation intended to determine how many table data blocks will need to be accessed.

Often, the index clustering factor is assumed to be a guarantee of randomness, but it isn't. For example, what about the case where each row in the index refers to only two distinct blocks, but the entries are ROWID ordered as block 1, block 2, block 1, block 2, and so on? If there were 10,000 entries in the index, the clustering factor would be 10,000 but in reality, only two blocks would be accessed. Therefore, the computation for the clustering factor isn't guaranteed to prove randomness in quite the same way that most people may think of it.

In an index with a "good" clustering factor, the index values in a specific index leaf block point to rows distributed in the same data blocks. On the other hand, in an index with a "bad" clustering factor, index values in a specific leaf block point to multiple data blocks. A well-organized index structure has a good clustering factor and it can read data with fewer I/Os.

A poorly organized index with the same amount of data requires a much larger number of I/Os to read the data from a larger set of data blocks. In this context, it's crucial to note that only one index per table is likely to be ideally organized and that is actually only true if the table data was loaded in a specific order. For instance, perhaps the table was loaded by a column such as order_date. In that case, the clustering factor for the index on order_date is almost identical to the number of blocks in the table. But, since the table can only be present in one order, all other indexes will be less optimally ordered. So, in the end, "good" and "bad" become more relative and less absolute. This is probably one of the reasons why the cost calculation for an index use is comprised of multiple elements that include both table and index selectivity, so that one component doesn't get an extremely heavy weighting.

A rule of thumb is that a good clustering factor is closer to the number of *blocks* in a table and a poor clustering factor is closer to the number or *rows* in a table.

In addition to the two factors discussed here, the value of the multiblock read count has a bearing on the usage of indexes. The higher the value of the multiblock read count (DB_FILE_MULTIBLOCK_READ_COUNT), the lower the cost of a full table scan from the optimizer's point of view.

The following sections describe the most common scenarios that can potentially lead to the optimizer ignoring an index. First, here's a short explanation of how index access paths can change without new optimizer statistics.

How Index Access Paths Can Change Without New Statistics

In a production environment, an execution path for queries often changes, even in the absence of any related changes. You confirm that no new statistics were collected (in fact, you might even have locked the statistics to prevent changes in execution plans). Prior to Oracle Database 11g and the cardinality feedback feature and automatic query tuning capabilities, if nothing truly changed (i.e., stats, instance parameters, etc.), and something such as bind peeking with histograms present wasn't in play, then plans pretty much stayed the same. However, even if you're absolutely positive that the optimizer shouldn't change any execution plans, it does. How's this possible? Well, most databases are living organisms with a continual change in data due to ongoing transactions. In fact, if the underlying data undergoes significant modifications and if you don't collect fresh statistics to reflect those changes, it's quite likely that execution plans will change because the optimizer bases its decisions on the cost of various access paths, and the cost may change because of the changes made to the data.

If you don't update optimizer statistics in tune with the changes in the data, in some cases it's quite possible that the optimizer will have wrong estimates of the cardinality, which is the expected number of rows that will be returned by the query. If your applications are adding large amounts of data to the tables and you don't collect new statistics, you may think that since the optimizer isn't aware of the new data, it'll go on using the same execution plans (the plans that are currently efficient).

The cost-based optimizer can sometimes change its execution plans over time if it miscalculates the true selectivity and cardinality of a query. To execute the same query after a very large infusion of new data, the optimizer may use a different plan because it underestimates the number of rows that the query will retrieve now. If a full table scan was the optimal strategy before the adding of the massive amounts of data, after the addition of the data, the optimizer may wrongly assume that an index will work better, whereas the full table scan is probably still is the best way to go. You can find an interesting example that illustrates this possibility at richardfoote.wordpress.com/category/index-access-path. If you think that by not collecting fresh statistics on a table, you are forcing the optimizer to continue to use current execution plans in the future as well, think again!

Using the NOT EQUAL Condition

Using a condition such as NOT EQUAL, such as in the statement select * from mytable where last_name <>'ALAPATI' may sometimes result in the optimizer not using an index. The reason is that the optimizer tends not to use an index if it surmises that the query will select a high percentage of values from a table. Doing a full table scan of the table is likely to be more efficient if this is the case. Normally, the optimizer estimates the cardinality as (1 - (1/num_distinct)) * num_rows. In other words, if the column had 4 distinct values and 1,000 rows, the cardinality would be 750. Let's assume that a huge percentage of rows in the table do satisfy the value you specify for the NOT EQUAL condition. In such a case, you'd think that the optimizer is likely to go in for an index scan because, after all, you're asking to retrieve all rows that don't have the value you specified with the NOT EQUAL condition. However, when you specify the <> operator, the optimizer simply ignores any index you may have, even if the data is distributed unevenly and the <> condition will result in the retrieval of a very small percentage of rows from the table. In such a case, the optimizer simply prefers to do a full table scan instead of preferring to choose choosing the index.

Take the query in this example, which is as follows:

```
SQL> select id from mytab where last_name <> 'ALAPATI';
Execution Plan
---------------------------------------------------------------
Plan hash value: 1357081020


---------------------------------------------------------------------
| Id  | Operation          | Name | Rows  | Bytes | Cost (%CPU)| Time     |
---------------------------------------------------------------------
|   0 | SELECT STATEMENT   |      |  848K |  16M  | 2414   (1)| 00:00:01 |
|*  1 |  TABLE ACCESS FULL | MYTAB|  848K |  16M  | 2414   (1)| 00:00:01 |
---------------------------------------------------------------------

Predicate Information (identified by operation id):
---------------------------------------------------

   1 - filter("LAST_NAME"<>'ALAPATI')
SQL>
```

The NOT EQUAL clause here results in the optimizer skipping the index on the last_name column. You may try an index hint, as shown here:

```
SQL> select /*+ index (mytab name_idx) */ id from mytab where name <> 'ALAPATI'
Execution Plan
-----------------------------------------------------------------
Plan hash value: 332134091
-----------------------------------------------------------------------------
| Id|Operation                    |Name      | Rows | Bytes|Cost (%CPU)| Time     |
-----------------------------------------------------------------------------
|  0|SELECT STATEMENT             |          | 1739 | 19129|  12    (0)| 00:00:01 |
|  1| TABLE ACCESS BY INDEX ROWID | MYTAB    | 1739 | 19129|  12    (0)| 00:00:01 |
|* 2|  INDEX FULL SCAN            | NAME_IDX | 1739 |      |   8    (0)| 00:00:01 |
-----------------------------------------------------------------------------
Predicate Information (identified by operation id):
---------------------------------------------------

   2 - filter("NAME"<>'ALAPATI')
```

The index hint made the optimizer replace a full table scan with an index full scan, which is better, but not as good as an index range scan. An index full scan must read all the leaf nodes that contain the value you specified with the <> operator, and thus is not a very efficient approach. However, in other cases, it may be possible for the optimizer to perform an index range scan as a result of your specifying the INDEX hint.

The problem with specifying the <> condition is that the optimizer is likely to skip the index even if the query returns a very small percentage of the rows in a table—it simply ignores any indexes on the column in the WHERE predicate. Ignoring the index means that the optimizer will not even calculate the costs of the index scan before producing the "optimal" plan; it figures it'll save all the overhead involved in doing so because it assumes that the <> condition will result in the retrieval of a large percentage of rows from the table. In cases such as this, you can try to rewrite the query to avoid the <> operator.

■ **Note**   You can't force the database to perform a parallel index range scan. However, the database does perform a parallel index lookup when it performs a parallel nested loop join.

Your only option here is to rewrite your query to eliminate the NOT EQUAL clause. This is more true if you have multiple predicates and less so when you're dealing with a single predicate. Remember that the optimizer's behavior is the same when you specify the NOT IN clause as well. Another good solution in some cases is to replace the NOT EQUAL predicate with a CASE construct. Remember that if you use a CASE construct, you'd need a function-based index to match it.

Querying with Wild Characters

If you issue a query that includes a leading wildcard-based search, the optimizer is likely to ignore the index and perform a full table scan. Take, for example, the following query:

```
SQL> select * from employees where last_name like'%lapati';
```

The optimizer is more likely to use an index when the leading character in the pattern is not % or _. Using a % or _ wildcard for the initial character with the LIKE operator means that the database may have to read a significant proportion of a table's rows. If it were to use an index, it would need to access every index block, and after the index reads were completed, it might also need to scan a majority of the table blocks as well. A full table scan is potentially more efficient in this case. The optimizer skips the index on the last_name column because it has to check each value in the column to determine if it ends with the lapati value. It ends up choosing a full table scan instead, as shown by the following explain plan for this statement:

```
SQL> set autotrace on explain
SQL> select * from employees
  2  where last_name like '%lapati';
no rows selected

Execution Plan
----------------------------------------------------------
Plan hash value: 1445457117

---------------------------------------------------------------------------
| Id  | Operation         | Name      | Rows  | Bytes | Cost (%CPU)| Time     |
---------------------------------------------------------------------------
|   0 | SELECT STATEMENT  |           |     5 |   310 |     3   (0)| 00:00:01 |
|*  1 |  TABLE ACCESS FULL| EMPLOYEES |     5 |   310 |     3   (0)| 00:00:01 |
---------------------------------------------------------------------------

Predicate Information (identified by operation id):
---------------------------------------------------

   1 - filter("LAST_NAME" LIKE '%lapati')

SQL>
```

If you modify the statement as shown next, the optimizer chooses an index scan:

```
SQL> select * from employees where last_name like 'Alapati%';

no rows selected
```

```
Execution Plan
------------------------------------------------------------
Plan hash value: 116555896

--------------------------------------------------------------------------
----------------------

| Id | Operation                           | Name          | Rows | Bytes | C
ost (%CPU)| Time       |

--------------------------------------------------------------------------
----------------------

|  0 | SELECT STATEMENT                    |               |   1 |    62 |
   2   (0)| 00:00:01 |

|  1 |   TABLE ACCESS BY INDEX ROWID BATCHED| EMPLOYEES     |   1 |    62 |
   2   (0)| 00:00:01 |

|* 2 |    INDEX RANGE SCAN                 | EMPLOYEES_IDX1 |   1 |       |
   1   (0)| 00:00:01 |

--------------------------------------------------------------------------
----------------------

Predicate Information (identified by operation id):
---------------------------------------------------

   2 - access("LAST_NAME" LIKE 'Alapati%')
       filter("LAST_NAME" LIKE 'Alapati%')
SQL>
```

Note that the first example uses a leading wildcard-based search. In fact, to force the use of an index, moving the wildcard (%) from the leading position by even one space (select * from employees where last_name like 'A%lapati%) makes the optimizer use the EMPLOYEES_IDX1 index on the EMPLOYEES table in the example. The use of wildcards later in the search string doesn't inhibit index use as frequently as this example demonstrates. So how many characters before the % allows the index to be used? As additional characters are added to the search string prior to the specification of the wildcard (%,_), the optimizer naturally expects the database to read fewer index and table rows and it's more likely to choose the index. Thus, if you're searching for "ABC%" instead of "%ABC", the database is more likely to use an index range scan, so long as it figures that a full table scan is more expensive.

Referencing Null Values in Predicates

Suppose that you have a table with two columns, both of which are allowed to have NULL values. Let's also assume that there are, in fact, several rows in the table that do have NULLs in both rows. Let's say that you issue the following statement:

```
SQL> select * from mytable where a is null;
```

The optimizer won't use a unique index on this table because anytime you have NULL values for all columns of a unique index, the database lets you add the row to the table, but doesn't include it in the index. In fact, you can add multiple rows with NULL values for all the columns, even if you have a unique index on the table, because the database considers two rows with all NULL values as different so far as uniqueness is considered. The result is that the table has more values than the index, because the rows with all NULL values for its columns weren't inserted into the index. When you issue the previous query, the database ignores the index since that index doesn't include the rows with all NULL values. To avoid giving you a wrong answer, the database ignores the index.

The only way you can get the database to use the index in this case is to make sure that at least one of the two columns in this table is defined as NOT NULL, as shown here:

```
SQL>create table mytab1 (a int, b int NOT NULL);

Table created.

SQL> create unique index mytab1_idx on mytab1(a,b);

Index created.

SQL>
```

If all index columns are NULL, the database doesn't include rows into an index. However, you can actually index NULL values by simply adding another column to the index, like so:

```
SQL> create index with_null on employees(nullable_column, '1');
```

Writing Functions in a Query

If a query contains a function on an indexed column in the WHERE clause, the optimizer skips the index. Note that the optimizer ignores an index if you explicitly apply a function, or if the database applies a function implicitly without your knowledge. Let's discuss the use of explicit functions first. For example, let's say that you issue the following query:

```
SQL> select * from testtab where UPPER(LAST_NAME)='ALAPATI';
```

In this case, the optimizer skips the index on the LAST_NAME column due to the presence of the UPPER function. (Chapter 5 explains how to use function-based indexes to get around this problem). If your applications need to frequently apply a function to an indexed column, you're better off creating a function-based index to allow the use of an index.

Note that even if a query doesn't explicitly apply a function to a column, it may be implicitly doing so under some conditions. For example, if you define a number column in a table and then query the column's values by specifying a character instead of a number, the optimizer ignores the index. That is, if you issue the statement select * from mytab where emp_id='999' instead of select * from mytab where emp_id=999, the optimizer needs to apply the TO_NUMBER function behind the scenes to get you the answer. Again, the use of a function means that the optimizer will not use the index. Even if you specify the INDEX hint in such a case, the optimizer might perform an index full scan, but not an index unique scan. An index full scan has to scan the entire index, so it is much slower than an index unique scan.

Dates present many opportunities for implicit conversions to inhibit index use. It's very common to see expressions such as the following:

```
SQL> select * from employees where trunc(start_date) = trunc(sysdate);
```

The use of the TRUNC function is often subconscious in writing statements like this. We truncate our dates to eliminate time-of-day components, often without thinking of the consequences to query execution. However, as far as the database is concerned, it only notices that you haven't actually indexed the expression TRUNC (START_DATE); you have only indexed the START_DATE column. Therefore, the database ignores the index.

A function-based index on the TRUNC (SYSDATE) column makes the optimizer choose the index, but there's a simpler way to get around this problem without having to create the function-based index. Just use the TRUNC function for the SYSDATE values and replace the equality operator with a range comparison operator such a GREATER THAN or LESS THAN to eliminate the need to apply the TRUNC function on the START_DATE column. That is, instead of this statement:

```
select * from employees where trunc(start_date) = trunc(sysdate);
```

Use this statement:

```
select * from employees where start_date >= trunc(sysdate)
and start_date < trunc(sysdate+1);
```

The removal of the TRUNC function on the START_DATE indexed column makes the optimizer use the index on that column.

Skipping the Leading Portion of an Index

If you have a composite index on two or more columns and you don't use the leading portion of the index in your query, the optimizer is very likely to ignore the index on the table and do a full a table scan. Let's say that you have an index on the columns A, B in the mytab table, with A the leading column. If you then issue a SQL statement such as select * from mytable where b=999, the database ignores the index on the columns A, B because it has to check every single index entry in the table for all possible values of A.

Note that if you issue a query such as select A, B from mytable, the optimizer is more likely to use the index on A, B because it realizes that both columns are part of the index. An index is much more compact than the table, and because the database can get all the values that are requested by the query from the index itself, the optimizer is likely to perform a fast full scan of the index.

Even if a query leaves out the leading portion of the index, the database can still use the index, provided the leading column in a composite index has very few distinct values. In such a case, the database performs an index skip scan, as explained in Chapter 5.

There can be multiple leading columns in the index prior to the column used in the predicate when the optimizer chooses a skip scan. We've seen cases where as many as six columns preceded the predicate column and the optimizer still used a skip scan. DBAs tend to think of skip scans as only being feasible when the number of values in the leading columns is small; but "small" is a relative thing. If the optimizer deems a skip scan to be a lower cost than a full table scan, then the optimizer will choose the skip scan. In the end, it's the cost estimate that matters and that drives the choice.

Forcing the Optimizer to Use an Index

You can force the optimizer to use an index by using several techniques. You can use an INDEX hint (there are several of these, as explained later) to tell the optimizer to use a specific index or even any index the optimizer finds best. You can also adjust the `optimizer_index_cost_adj` initialization parameter, which, by making a direct adjustment to the computed cost of the index access, makes it very likely to cause the database to use an index instead of doing a full table scan.

■ **Note**   The effect of adjusting `optimizer_index_cost_adj` parameter is not really to *force* an index use per se. Rather, it forces an adjustment to the query cost, which makes it *more likely* that the resulting cost will be such that the optimizer chooses to use an index.

A note of caution is appropriate here: it's our experience that in the overwhelming majority of cases, the cost optimizer does know best. If you create primary and unique keys on all tables, and index all foreign keys as well as any non-unique columns that are likely to figure in your SQL queries, you've already provided the optimizer all the information that it needs. Of course, you must ensure that you gather timely optimizer statistics with the correct settings. If you follow the recommendations here, chances are that the cost optimizer will produce optimal plans just about all the time. You may occasionally find the need to intervene and override the optimizer's choices, but it'll be somewhat of a rare event.

Applying the INDEX Hint

Sometimes, the optimizer won't use an index, although you're certain the index will really help performance. The cost-based optimizer isn't perfect; it doesn't always have an accurate understanding of the nature and distribution of data. Developers and DBAs often possess a better understanding of their application and the nature of their data. In cases where you think the optimizer ought to use an index, you can force it to use an index by specifying an INDEX hint in the query.

An INDEX hint instructs the optimizer to use an index scan for a specific table. The optimizer respects the hint for all types of indexes, such as normal B-tree indexes and function-based, bitmap, bitmap join, and domain indexes.

You specify an INDEX hint in the following way:

```
SQL> select /*+ index (employees emp_dept_idx) +/
     employee_id, department_id from employees;
     where department_id > 50;
```

When you specify that the optimizer must use a specific index, remember that the optimizer honors your instruction and does not perform a full table scan, but it also ignores other potential indexes that it may have considered. Thus, specifying the INDEX hint forces the optimizer to use only the index that you specify with the hint.

You can also specify the INDEX hint without specifying an index, as shown here:

```
SQL> select /*+ index (employees) +/
     employee_id, department_id from employees;
     where department_id > 50;
```

Since the INDEX hint in this example doesn't specify an index to use, the optimizer has the leeway to select the best index—the index resulting in the least cost. The optimizer may also decide to use multiple indexes and merge the results. The optimizer is unlikely to use a full table scan, however, though it will use one if no indexes exist to be used.

If you have multiple indexes on a table and you just specify the index hint, hoping that the query will perform better because the optimizer might use one of the indexes, you may be in for a surprise. There is the possibility that the optimizer may choose the wrong index if you've got multiple indexes and just specify the INDEX hint without specifying an index. In fact, the optimizer sometimes chooses a far superior full table scan if you don't specify any index hints whatsoever. Specifying the INDEX hint without telling the optimizer which index you want to use may only force the usage of an inefficient index.

If you want to specify more than one index within the INDEX hint, Oracle recommends that you specify the INDEX_COMBINE hint rather than the INDEX hint. You specify the INDEX_COMBINE hint in the following way:

```
SQL> select /*+ index_combine(e emp_manager_ix emp_department_ix) */ *
     from employees e
     where manager_id = 108
     or department_id=110;
```

In this case, the optimizer uses the combination of the two indexes that has the lowest cost. If you specify the INDEX_COMBINE hint without providing a list of indexes, the optimizer will use the best combination of indexes based on its cost estimates.

Applying Related Hints

INDEX and INDEX_COMBINE aren't the only hints to instruct the optimizer to use an index. The database allows you to use a number of index-related hints, which are briefly described in the following sections.

In addition to the hints discussed here, there are additional index-related hints, such as the INDEX_FFS hint, which tells the optimizer to perform a fast full index scan instead of a full table scan. If an index contains all the columns necessary to satisfy a query, a fast full index scan is a good alternative to a full table scan.

The fast full index scan needs to access just the index and not both the index and the table together, as is the case with a normal index range scan. The database scans the entire index using multiblock reads. In most cases, a fast full index scan runs faster than a full index scan because it can use multiblock I/O. You can also parallelize this type of scan just as a table scan. The INDEX_FFS_DESC hint instructs the optimizer to do the fast full scan in descending order.

Sometimes you may want to the optimizer to perform an index range scan (by specifying the INDEX hint), but it goes ahead and does a full scan. Oracle offers you the two hints—INDEX_RS_ASC and INDEX_RS_DESC—to explicitly direct the optimizer to perform an index range scan in ascending or descending order. The cost optimizer uses the value of the DB_FILE_MULTIBLOCK_READ_COUNT initialization parameter to determine the relative costs of full table scans and index fast full scans. A large value for this parameter can influence the optimizer to choose a full table scan in preference to an index scan.

The following is a brief explanation of some additional index-related hints.

INDEX_ASC Hint

By default, the database scans indexes in ascending order of the index entries during an index range scan. If you created a descending index, the database scans the index in descending order. You can use the INDEX_ASC hint to explicitly specify an ascending range scan.

INDEX_DESC Hint

If a SQL statement performs an index range scan, specifying the INDEX_DESC hint makes the database scan an ascending order index in descending order of the indexed values. Note that if you specify this hint for an index sorted in descending order, the database scans the index entries in ascending order.

■ **Tip**   Don't rush to add a hint to your queries just because you can! See if you have the correct optimizer statistics for the objects and also check the way your SQL statement is framed before resorting to the use of a hint. Hints should be a last-ditch alternative.

INDEX_JOIN Hint

If two indexes contain all the columns required to return a query's results, you can specify that the database use an index join. The index join is simply a hash join of the individual indexes that together returns all the columns requested by the query. The database doesn't need to access the table data in this case, as all data is returned from the indexes themselves. You specify the index join with the INDEX_JOIN hint, as in this example:

```
SQL> select /*+ INDEX_JOIN(e emp_manager_ix emp_department_ix) */ department_id
     from employees e
     where manager_id < 110
     and department_id < 50;
```

Make sure that you have indexes on both the manager_id and the department_id columns before incorporating the INDEX_JOIN hint. The indexes that you specify must contain all the columns required to satisfy the query. The preceding SELECT statement results in two index range scans: one on the emp_manager_ix index and the other on the emp_department_ix index.

INDEX_SS Hint

The INDEX_SS hint tells the optimizer to perform an index skip scan. By default, the database scans the index in the ascending order of the index values.

Troubleshooting a Failed INDEX Hint

You must be aware that specifying an INDEX hint doesn't guarantee that Oracle will definitely use an index or indexes. Remember that that the choice of the access path (index or full table scan, for example) is only part of what the optimizer takes into account when deciding upon an optimal execution plan for a query. Besides the access path (along with any alternative paths), the optimizer also must evaluate join methods. In some cases, based on the join methods the optimizer selects, it may decide not to use any index. Another reason why the database still ends up performing a full table scan even after you specify the INDEX hint is when you're dealing with a unique index, which has many NULL values. The optimizer realizes that it might end up with wrong results because there may be some rows that don't appear in the index. To avoid this, the database simply ignores the INDEX hint that you provide.

There is a way to get around this inability of the optimizer to honor your index hint. You do so by adding more hints to the query. You must endeavor to specify a full set of hints to make sure that the optimizer has no choice but to use the index. The additional hints that you specify control things such as the precise join order between the tables and the exact join methods as well. The following example illustrates this:

```
SQL> select /*+ leading(e2 e1) use_nl(e1) index(e1 emp_emp_id_pk)
     use_merge(j) full(j) */
     e1.first_name, e1.last_name, j.job_id, sum(e2.salary) total_sal
     from employees e1, employees e2, job_history j
     where e1.employee_id = e2.manager_id
```

```
      and e1.employee_id = j.employee_id
      and e1.hire_date = j.start_date
      group by e1.first_name, e1.last_name, j.job_id
      order by total_sal;
```

And here's the execution plan for the previous statement:

```
FIRST_NAME              LAST_NAME                     JOB_ID      TOTAL_SAL
-------------------     -------------------------     ----------  ---------
Michael                 Hartstein                     MK_REP           6000
Lex                     De Haan                       IT_PROG          9000
Execution Plan
-----------------------------------------------------------------
Plan hash value: 4097587549
-----------------------------------------------------------------------
| Id| Operation                   |Name              |Rows|Bytes|Cost(%CPU)|Time      |
-----------------------------------------------------------------------
|  0|SELECT STATEMENT             |                  | 105| 5880|117   (5) |00:00:04|
|  1| SORT ORDER BY               |                  | 105| 5880|117   (5) |00:00:04|
|  2|  HASH GROUP BY              |                  | 105| 5880|117   (5) |00:00:04|
|  3|   MERGE JOIN                |                  | 105| 5880|115   (3) |00:00:03|
|  4|    SORT JOIN                |                  | 105| 3675|111   (2) |00:00:03|
|  5|     NESTED LOOPS            |                  |    |     |         |          |
|  6|      NESTED LOOPS           |                  | 105| 3675|110   (1) |00:00:03|
|  7|       VIEW                  |index$_join$_002  | 107|  856|  3  (34) |00:00:01|
|* 8|        HASH JOIN            |                  |    |     |         |          |
|  9|         INDEX FAST FULL SCAN|EMP_MANAGER_IX    | 107|  856|  1   (0) |00:00:01|
| 10|INDEX FAST FULL SCAN         |EMPLOYEES_IDX1    | 107|  856|  1   (0) |00:00:01|
|*11|         INDEX UNIQUE SCAN   |EMP_EMP_ID_PK     |   1|     |  0   (0) |00:00:01|
| 12|       TABLE ACCESS BY INDEX ROWID|EMPLOYEES    |   1|   27|      (0) |00:00:01|
|*13|    SORT JOIN                |                  |  10|  210|  4  (25) |00:00:01|
| 14|     TABLE ACCESS FULL       |JOB_HISTORY       |  10|  210|  3   (0) |00:00:01|
-----------------------------------------------------------------------
Predicate Information (identified by operation id):
---------------------------------------------------
   8 - access(ROWID=ROWID)
  11 - access("E1"."EMPLOYEE_ID"="E2"."MANAGER_ID")
  13 - access("E1"."EMPLOYEE_ID"="J"."EMPLOYEE_ID" AND "E1"."HIRE_DATE"="J"."STA
RT_DATE")
       filter("E1"."HIRE_DATE"="J"."START_DATE" AND "E1"."EMPLOYEE_ID"="J"."EMPL
OYEE_ID")
SQL>
```

In this example, the query includes hints in addition to the INDEX hint that specifies an index on the EMPLOYEES table that you'd like the optimizer to use. The query also includes the LEADING hint to specify the exact join order. The USE_NL and USE_MERGE hints specify the join method that the database must use.

Adjusting the optimizer_index_cost_adj Parameter

You can influence the optimizer to use an index by adjusting the value of the `optimizer_index_cost_adj` initialization parameter. You can set this parameter at the system or session level. Here's an example that shows how to set this parameter at the session level:

```
SQL> alter session set optimizer_index_cost_adj=50;

Session altered.
SQL>
```

The default value for the `optimizer_index_cost_adj` parameter is 100, and you can set the parameter to a value between 0 and 10,000. The lower the value of the parameter, the more likely it is for the optimizer to use an index.

The `optimizer_index_cost_adj` parameter lets you adjust the cost of an index access. The optimizer uses a default value of 100 for this parameter, which means that it evaluates an indexed access path based on the normal costing model. Based on the optimizer's estimate of the cost of performing an indexed read, it makes the decision as to whether to use the index. Usually this works fine. However, in some cases, the optimizer doesn't use an index, even if it leads to a better execution plan, because the optimizer's estimates of the cost of the indexed access path may be off.

The optimizer uses a default value of 100 for the `optimizer_index_cost_adj` parameter, so you make the index cost seem lower to the optimizer by setting this parameter to a smaller value. Any value less than 100 makes the use of an index look cheaper (in terms of the cost of an indexed read) to the optimizer. Often when you do this, the optimizer starts using the index you want it to use. In this example, you set the `optimizer_index_cost_adj` parameter to 50, making the cost of an index access path appear half as expensive as its normal cost of 100. The lower you set the value of this parameter, the cheaper an index cost access path appears to the optimizer, and the more likely it is to prefer an index access path to a full table scan.

We recommend that you set the `optimizer_index_cost_adj` parameter only at the session level for a specific query because the parameter has the potential to change the execution plans for many queries if you set it at the database level. By default, if you set the `ALL_ROWS` optimizer goal, there's a built-in preference for full table scans on part of the optimizer. By setting the `optimizer_index_cost_adj` parameter to a value less than 100, you're inducing the optimizer to prefer an index scan over a full table scan. Use the `optimizer_index_cost_adj` parameter with confidence, especially in an OLTP environment, where you can experiment with low values such as 5 or 10 for the parameter to force the optimizer to use an index.

By default, the optimizer assumes that the cost of a multiblock read I/O associated with a full table scan and the single block read cost associated with an indexed read are identical. However, a single block read is likely to be less expensive than a multiblock read. The `optimizer_index_cost_adj` parameter lets you adjust the cost of a single block read associated with an index read more accurately to reflect the true cost of an index read relative to the cost of a full table scan. The default value of 100 means that a single block read is 100% of a multiblock read—so the default value is telling the optimizer to treat the cost of an indexed read as identical to the cost of a multiblock I/O full table scan. When you set the parameter to a value of 50, as in this example, you're telling the optimizer that the cost of a single block I/O (index read) is only half the cost of a multiblock I/O. This is likely to make the optimizer choose the index read over a full table scan.

Accurate system statistics (`mbrc`, `mreadtim`, `sreadtim`, etc.) have a bearing on the use of indexes vs. full table scans. Ideally, you should collect workload system statistics and leave the `optimizer_index_cost_adj` parameter alone. You can also calculate the relative costs of a single block read and a multiblock read, and set the `optimizer_index_cost_adj` parameter value based on those calculations. However, the best strategy is to simply use the parameter at the session level for a specific statement and not at the database level. Simply experiment with various levels of the parameter until the optimizer starts using the index.

You can also use a more "scientific" way to figure out the correct setting for the optimizer_index_
cost_adj parameter by setting it to a value that reflects the "true" difference between single and multiblock
reads. You can compare the average wait times for the db file sequential read wait event (represents a
single block I/O) and the db file scattered read wait event (represents multiblock I/O) to arrive at an
approximate value for the optimizer_index_cost_adj parameter. Issue the following query to view the
average wait times for both of the wait events:

```
SQL> select event, average_wait from v$system_event
     where event like 'db file s%read';
EVENT                                          AVERAGE_WAIT
-------------------------------                --------------
db file sequential read                            1.14
db file scattered read                             2.28

SQL>
```

Based on the output of this query, single block sequential reads take roughly 75 percent of the time
that it takes to perform a multiblock (scattered) read. This indicates that the optimizer_index_cost_adj
parameter should be set to somewhere around 75. However, as mentioned earlier, setting the parameter
at the database level isn't recommended—instead, use this parameter sparingly for specific statements
where you want to force the use of an index. Note that setting the parameter at the session level requires the
DBA to grant user privileges to issue the ALTER SESSION command (or you must do it through some other
procedural mechanism). A good alternative to having to issue the alter session statement is to specify the
OPT_PARAM hint to change the parameter for a specific query, such as /*+ opt_param('optimizer_index_
cost_adj',50) */. That way, it is only for the specific query and doesn't require any special privileges.
Note that an OPT_PARAM hint allows you to set the value of an initialization parameter for just the duration of
the current query, and you can use it to set values for a handful of initialization parameters, including the
optimizer_index_cost_adj parameter.

Collecting Accurate Statistics for an Index

Gathering accurate statistics is probably the single biggest factor that influences the optimizer's selection of
an index scan. You collect optimizer statistics for an index just as you do for a table. Note that unlike in the
case of a table, an Oracle database automatically collects an index's statistics when you create the index, as
shown here:

```
SQL> create index test_idx on mytab2(employee_id,first_name);
Index created.

SQL> select index_name,last_analyzed, num_rows, sample_size from user_indexes
     where table_name='MYTAB2';

INDEX_NAME              LAST_ANAL      NUM_ROWS      SAMPLE_SIZE
--------------------    ----------     ----------    -------------
TEST_IDX                06-MAR-16      107           107

SQL>
```

When dealing with optimizer statistics, you must ensure that the scheduling of your statistics gathering
jobs is in tune with the amount of changes in a table's data. The frequency of statistics gathering should
depend on the frequency and amount of changes in your data. When you collect optimizer statistics for

a table with the DBMS_STATS procedure GATHER_TABLE_STATS, the cascade parameter determines if the database gathers statistics for the indexes as well. The default value for this parameter is the DBMS_STATS. AUTO_CASCADE constant, which means that the database determines if it should collect index statistics when it collects the table's statistics. Specify cascade=>true to ensure that the database collects statistics on the indexes along with the table statistics or change the value of the AUTO_CASCADE constant with the help of the SET_PARAM procedure.

You can also gather index statistics by themselves without collecting the table statistics by executing the DBMS_STATS.GATHER_INDEX_STATS procedure, as shown here:

```
SQL> execute dbms_stats.gather_index_stats(USER,'EMPLOYEES_IDX1',
        estimate_percent=>100, degree=>12);

PL/SQL procedure successfully completed.

SQL>
```

You can get index-related optimizer statistics information by querying the DBMS_STATS.GET_INDEX_ STATS procedure. You can also set index-related information by using the SET_INDEX _STATS procedure from the DBMS_STATS package.

Parallelizing Index Access

When dealing with partitioned indexes, you can direct the optimizer to use multiple concurrent parallel servers to parallelize several types of index operations. The operations you can parallelize include index range scans, full index scans, and fast full scans.

Here's an example that shows how you can specify the PARALLEL_INDEX hint to specify a parallel scan operation on a partitioned index:

```
SQL> select /*+parallel_index (employees, employee_id_idx, 4) */ last_name,
          employee_id
          from employees;
```

The integer 4 specifies the degree of parallelism for the index scan.

There is also a NOPARALLEL hint that overrides the degree of parallelism that you specified for an index. You can specify the degree of parallelism for a statement level PARALLEL hint in various ways, as explained through the following examples. Note that if you don't specify the degree of parallelism, the optimizer calculates its own degree of parallelism:

```
SQL>select /*+ parallel */ last_name from employees;
```

If you specify the PARALLEL (AUTO) hint, the database calculates the degree of parallelism, which could end up being just 1 (serial execution).

```
SQL> select /*+ PARALLEL (AUTO) */ last_name from employees;
```

If you specify the PARALLEL (MANUAL) hint, the optimizer uses the degree of parallelism in force for the object. If you specify PARALLEL (integer), the optimizer uses the degree of parallelism that you specify. If you're using the PARALLEL_INDEX hint, the database will not adjust the cost of a parallel index full scan by the degree of parallelism you specify unless you've also declared the table as parallel.

You can execute DDL statements in parallel for both partitioned and nonpartitioned indexes. For a partitioned index, the parallel DDL statements can be used for the following operations:

```
CREATE INDEX
ALTER INDEX ...[REBUILD|SPLIT] PARTITION
```

By default, an Oracle database uses a degree of parallelism of 1, as you can see in the following example:

```
SQL> create table testtab (x int, y int);
Table created.

SQL> create index testtab_idx1 on testtab(x,y);

Index created.

SQL> select degree from user_indexes where index_name='TESTTAB_IDX1';

DEGREE
----------------------------------------
1
SQL>
```

You can parallelize an index access by altering an index with the PARALLEL clause, as shown here:

```
SQL> alter index testtab_idx1 parallel;
Index altered.
SQL>
```

Since you didn't specify the degree of parallelism, the database uses the default degree of parallelism, as shown here:

```
SQL>select degree from user_indexes where index_name='TESTTAB_IDX1';
DEGREE
----------------------------------------
DEFAULT

SQL>
```

You can specify a non-default degree of parallelism by specifying the degree, as follows:

```
SQL> alter index testtab_idx1 parallel 12;
Index altered.
SQL>
```

You can specify the degree of parallelism for an index when you create one, as shown in the following example:

```
SQL> create index testtab_idx2 on testtab(x)
 2   parallel (degree 8);

Index created.
SQL>
```

You can disable a parallel degree setting by doing the following:

```
SQL>alter index testtab_idx2 noparallel;
```

You can also specify the parallel degree when you rebuild an index.

Summary

This chapter started off with a discussion of the various types of index access paths, such as a fast full scan and an index range scan, and their implications. You also learned under what conditions the optimizer might select various index access paths. On occasion, it may better to force a full table scan for some queries and this chapter showed you how to do that. This chapter discussed several reasons why the optimizer may not choose to use an index and how you can use various strategies to influence the optimizer's choice of an index. Finally, this chapter showed you how to parallelize index access and how to specify the parallel option when creating an index.

CHAPTER 8

■ ■ ■

Maintaining Indexes

Maintaining indexes is a big part of an Oracle DBA's workload. There are many aspects to maintaining indexes, and often there are multiple ways to achieve the same goals. This chapter explains several key aspects of index maintenance to help you improve the performance of your indexes and to efficiently manage index space usage.

Collecting optimal index statistics is, of course, a crucial part of index maintenance, and so we start with the collection of index statistics. The database sometimes makes an index unusable, following certain index maintenance operations or some error conditions. The chapter explains the implications of unusable indexes and shows how to deal with them. Often Oracle DBAs wonder if index fragmentation is something that affects performance and space usage, and if so, how to deal with it. The chapter explains the various techniques that Oracle offers—such as the ability to rebuild, coalesce, and shrink indexes—and when each of them is appropriate.

The chapter briefly explains the various ways in which you can create indexes faster, as well as how you can conserve index space usage. Finally, you'll learn how to efficiently extract complex index creation statements from the database when you need to re-create indexes in other environments.

Gathering Statistics for Indexes

The optimizer not only needs statistics about tables, but also about indexes to create the best query plans. Optimizer statistics for indexes include things such as statistics relating to the number of rows, the number of leaf blocks in the index, the number of levels in the B-tree, and the clustering factor of the index. Use the DBMS_STATS package to collect statistics for your indexes. As with tables, the frequency of statistics collection depends on the amount of changes your data is going through.

The DBMS_STATS Package

You can specify the collection of index statistics by specifying the CASCADE option with the GATHER_DATABASE_STATS, GATHER_SCHEMA_STATS, and GATHER_TABLE_STATS procedures, as shown in the following examples.

This is when collecting schema statistics:

```
SQL> execute dbms_stats.gather_schema_stats('HR', cascade=>TRUE);

PL/SQL procedure successfully completed.

SQL>
```

© Darl Kuhn, Sam R. Alapati and Bill Padfield 2016
D. Kuhn et al., *Expert Oracle Indexing and Access Paths*, DOI 10.1007/978-1-4842-1984-3_8

This is when collecting table statistics:

```
SQL> execute dbms_stats.gather_table_stats(ownname=>'HR', tabname=>'EMPLOYEES', -
    cascade=>TRUE);

PL/SQL procedure successfully completed.

SQL>
```

Specifying cascade=>true results in the database always collecting statistics for all indexes on a table. If you don't specify cascade=>true, Oracle may or may not collect statistics for the indexes. By default, the constant DBMS_STATS.AUTO_CASCADE determines whether the database must collect index statistics. Of course, you can change the default value of the CASCADE parameter at the table, schema, or database level. Here's an example of how to do so at the database level:

```
SQL> exec dbms_stats.set_database_prefs('CASCADE','TRUE');

PL/SQL procedure successfully completed.

SQL>
```

Setting the CASCADE parameter to TRUE gathers the index statistics as it would if you execute the GATHER_INDEX_STATS procedure. You can just run the GATHER_INDEX_STATS procedure to gather index statistics, as shown here:

```
SQL>  execute dbms_stats.gather_index_stats ('HR','EMP_EMP_ID_PK');

PL/SQL procedure successfully completed.

SQL>
```

The following is a simple script that lets you generate the necessary statistics collection commands for all indexes in a schema:

```
set serveroutput on
begin
for ind in
(select object_name
from user_objects
where object_type='INDEX')
  loop
    dbms_output.put_line(
      'Gathering Index Statistics for '||ind.object_name||'.....');
    dbms_stats.gather_index_stats(user, ind.object_name
      , estimate_percent=>100);
    dbms_output.put_line('Gathering Index Statistics for '
      ||ind.object_name||' is Complete!');
  end loop;
end;
/
```

If for some reason the script can't gather the statistics on an index, the script fails and stops. If this is a concern, you can add error-handling logic within the script to continue on to the next index.

GATHERING STATISTICS DURING A REBUILD

You can gather statistics on an index while rebuilding the index, as the following example shows:

```
SQL> alter index hr.emp_emp_id_pk rebuild compute statistics;
Index altered.
```

You save time by having the database gather statistics while it's rebuilding the index.

The METHOD_OPT Parameter

A parameter named METHOD_OPT gives you control over statistics collection as it relates to columns. You specify the METHOD_OPT parameter of the DBMS_STATS package in order to tell the database two things:

- The columns for which it should collect statistics.

- If it should collect a histogram for any column, and if so, the number of buckets that should be in the histogram.

Often, DBAs specify the for all indexed columns size auto value for the METHOD_OPT parameter when collecting table statistics. Greg Rahn shows why this may be really a bad idea in most cases in his interesting article on the use of this parameter (http://structureddata.org/2008/10/14/dbms-stats-method_opt-and-for-all-indexed_columns/).

Specifying the value for all indexed columns size auto for the METHOD_OPT parameter has the following implications:

- It tells the database to collect statistics only for those columns that are indexed.

- It lets the database determine if it should collect histograms, as well as the number of buckets it should allocate for a histogram.

When you specify the for all indexed columns size auto option, the database collects no statistics on the unindexed columns; it simply uses default values for the number of default values and cardinality. As a result, it may often end up with a vastly underestimated number of rows. When you get an explain plan with the help of the DBMS_XPLAN.DISPLAY_CURSOR procedure (run with the ALLSTATS LAST option), it shows that the number of estimated rows (E-rows) is often underestimated when compared to the number of actual rows (A-rows). The wrong cardinality estimates are very likely to play havoc with the selection of the access paths, join methods, and join order, leading to poor SQL execution times. The whole idea behind collecting optimizer statistics is to collect representative statistics. The database doesn't really *know* your data—you do! (If you *really* want to understand how to collect good statistics, please read the excellent article on the use of the DBMS_STATS package by Karen Morton titled "Managing Statistics for Optimal Query Performance," available on the method-r.com web site.)

The cost optimizer is very likely to produce suboptimal execution plans when it isn't fed accurate statistics. Inaccurate cardinality estimates are a good example of the consequences of the database collecting non-representative statistics. For example, a wrong cardinality estimate can lead to the optimizer selecting the wrong driving table. Alternatively, the optimizer may decide that a NL join is better when a hash join would be more appropriate, especially when dealing with large data sets.

The bottom line is that you must collect statistics on all columns, not just the indexed columns, and specifying the for all indexed columns size auto option makes this impossible. Data warehouses use fewer indexes in general compared to OLTP systems, so specifying the for all indexed columns size auto option in those environments is especially likely to lead to poor execution plans. The default value for the METHOD_OPT parameter starting with Oracle Database 11g is FOR ALL COLUMNS SIZE AUTO. Use this default value wherever possible.

■ **Note** Regardless of the value that you assign to the METHOD_OPT parameter, if you specify cascade=>true, the database collects statistics on all indexes.

Working with Unusable Indexes

The database may mark an index unusable in various situations, including when an index creation or rebuild fails midway. For example, when the table data becomes more up-to-date than the indexes on that table, SQL*Loader leaves the index in an unusable state. A direct path load may leave an index in an unusable state when any of the following occur:

- The instance fails during the building of the index.

- A unique key has duplicate values.

- An index isn't in the same order as that specified by a sorted indexes clause.

- SQL*Loader fails to update the index because the index runs out of space.

In addition to these reasons, an index can also acquire a status of UNUSABLE following various maintenance operations. For example, all of the following will result in an index becoming unusable:

- Moving a table or a table partition (alter table move and alter table move partition).

- Performing an online redefinition of a table.

- Truncating a table partition (alter table truncate partition).

- Importing a partition.

- Dropping a table partition.

- Splitting a table partition or a subpartition (alter table split partition).

- Maintenance operation on a partitioned index (alter index split partition).

Any time that you move a table or reorganize a table, internally the database uses a different set of ROWIDs to point to the rows on disk, and this makes the indexes unusable since they're still pointing to the old ROWIDs. A ROWID is an Oracle pseudo column that uniquely identifies a row in a table. You must make the index usable by rebuilding the index, which makes the index entries use the new set of ROWIDs for the table rows.

Unlike in the case of a valid index, the database doesn't maintain an unusable index when DML operations occur. When you create an unusable index, the database doesn't allocate a segment for the index.

■ **Note** The database drops the index segment when its status is marked UNUSABLE.

While the database marks an index as UNUSABLE following some events, you can also make an index unusable. You can either mark an existing index UNUSABLE or create an index in the UNUSABLE state. A reason for making an index unusable is to make a bulk load go faster, since the database doesn't need to maintain the indexes while inserting data into the table. You can make the index unusable and re-create it after the bulk load completes. Note that when dealing with partitioned indexes, even though a partition may be marked UNUSABLE, the remaining partitions of the index continue to be usable. That is, you can issue SQL statements that require the use of the index with an unusable partition, so long as the statement doesn't access an unusable partition.

Once the database marks an index as UNUSABLE, the optimizer ignores the index and the database no longer maintains the indexes following DML changes in the table. An index must have an USABLE status in order for the database to use it. In order to "use" an unusable index, you must take the index out of the UNUSABLE mode; you can rebuild the index or drop and re-create the index before you can use the index.

■ **Tip** Truncating a table makes an unusable index usable again.

Making an Index Unusable

Oracle gives you the ability to change an index status to UNUSABLE, obviously, because there may be times when it's advantageous to do so. One of the best reasons for making an index unusable is in a data warehouse environment when you have to perform a huge data load into a table with indexes. Leaving the indexes in place makes the data load extremely slowly. To avoid this, it's common to set the indexes to UNUSABLE, load the data, and make the indexes usable again by rebuilding them. In effect, you're re-creating the index, but it beats dropping and re-creating an index because the storage is already allocated to the index and you don't have to specify the index creation statement when you do this. Making the index unusable also "hides" the index from the optimizer until you rebuild it.

You can change the status of an existing index to that of an unusable index by specifying the UNUSABLE keyword, as shown here:

```
SQL> alter index hr.emp_email_uk unusable;

Index altered.
SQL>
```

The following example shows how to make a partition of an index unusable:

```
SQL> alter index sh.costs_PROD_BIX modify partition costs_1995 unusable;

Index altered.
```

In Oracle Database 12c, you can specify the ONLINE clause when making an index unusable, as in ALTER INDEX <index_name> UNUSABLE ONLINE.

The following is an example that shows how to specify one of the partitions of a local index as UNUSABLE when you're creating the index.

```
SQL> create index i_emp_ename ON employees_part (employee_id)
          local (partition p1_i_emp_ename UNUSABLE, partition
           p2_i_emp_ename);

Index created.
SQL>
```

189

In this example, the database creates a locally partitioned index with two partitions: p1-_i_empname and p2_i_empname. However, the index creation statement creates the second partition (p2_i_empname) as unusable. You can confirm the status of the two index partitions by executing the following query:

```
SQL> select index_name as "INDEX OR PARTITION NAME", status
  2  from user_indexes
  3  where index_name = 'I_EMP_ENAME'
  4  union all
  5  select partition_name as "INDEX OR PARTITION NAME", status
  6  from user_ind_partitions
  7  where partition_name like '%I_EMP_ENAME%';

INDEX OR PARTITION NAME          STATUS
------------------------         -------
I_EMP_ENAME                      N/A
P1_I_EMP_ENAME                   UNUSABLE
P2_I_EMP_ENAME                   USABLE
SQL>
```

The following query shows how the database allocates storage only for the usable index:

```
SQL> select p.partition_name, p.status as "part_status",
  2  p.segment_created as "seg_created"
  3  from user_ind_partitions p, user_segments s
  4  where s.segment_name = 'P1_I_EMP_ENAME';

PARTITION_NAME        PART_STA    SEG_CREATED
---------------       --------    -----------
P2_I_EMP_ENAME        USABLE      YES
P1_I_EMP_ENAME        UNUSABLE    NO
SQL>
```

Regardless of whether the index is partitioned or not, once you make an index or part of a partitioned index unusable, the segment that the index occupied no longer exists. The following query confirms this:

```
SQL> select segment_name,bytes from dba_segments
        where segment_name in ('HR.I_EMP_ENAME','HR.EMP_EMAIL_UK');

no rows selected
SQL>
```

Once you mark an index UNUSABLE, you must rebuild it in order to mark it usable again, as shown in the following examples:

```
SQL> alter index EMP_GLOBAL_HASH_IDX modify partition P2 unusable;

Index altered.

SQL> alter index sh.costs_PROD_BIX rebuild partition costs_2016;

Index altered.

SQL>
```

Specifying the SKIP_UNUSABLE_INDEXES Parameter

How the database handles an unusable index depends on the setting of the SKIP_UNUSABLE_INDEXES parameter. By default, the SKIP_UNUSABLE_INDEXES parameter is set to TRUE, meaning that when the database encounters an unusable index, it simply ignores it and doesn't issue an error. The SKIP_UNUSABLE_INDEXES parameter, when set to TRUE, allows you perform inserts, deletes, updates, and selects on a table with an unusable index or an index partition(s). Any DML statements that you issue against the unusable index will work fine, but the database stops maintaining the index. You can check the SKIP_UNUSABLE_INDEXES parameter's value thus:

```
SQL> show parameter skip_unusable_indexes

NAME                          TYPE     VALUE
--------------------------    -----    -------
skip_unusable_indexes         boolean  TRUE
SQL>
```

The following example shows how the database performs a full table scan and ignores the index when its status becomes unusable. First, let's make the index unusable by issuing the following alter index statement:

```
SQL> create index emp_idx1 on newemp(employee_id);

Index created.

SQL> alter index emp_idx1 unusable;

Index altered.

SQL> set autotrace on explain
SQL> select * from newemp
  2  where employee_id > 999;

no rows selected

Execution Plan
----------------------------------------------------------
Plan hash value: 3847232031

---------------------------------------------------------------------------
| Id  | Operation          | Name   | Rows  | Bytes | Cost (%CPU)| Time     |
---------------------------------------------------------------------------
|   0 | SELECT STATEMENT   |        |   391 | 52003 |  9643   (1)| 00:00:01 |
|*  1 |  TABLE ACCESS FULL | NEWEMP |   391 | 52003 |  9643   (1)| 00:00:01 |
---------------------------------------------------------------------------

Predicate Information (identified by operation id):
---------------------------------------------------

   1 - filter("EMPLOYEE_ID">999)

Note
-----
   - dynamic statistics used: dynamic sampling (level=2)

SQL>
```

Now rebuild the index and recheck the query's explain plan.

```
SQL> set autotrace off
SQL> alter index emp_idx1 rebuild;

Index altered.

SQL> set autotrace on explain
SQL> select * from newemp
  2  where employee_id > 999;
no rows selected
Execution Plan
-------------------------------------------------------------
Plan hash value: 428046832


| Id  | Operation                            | Name      | Rows  | Bytes | Cost (%
CPU)| Time       |
----------------------------------------------------------------------------------
|   0 | SELECT STATEMENT                     |           |     1 |   133 |     2
 (0)| 00:00:01 |
|   1 |   TABLE ACCESS BY INDEX ROWID BATCHED| NEWEMP    |     1 |   133 |     2
 (0)| 00:00:01 |
|*  2 |    INDEX RANGE SCAN                  | EMP_IDX1  |     1 |       |     2
 (0)| 00:00:01 |
----------------------------------------------------------------------------------

Predicate Information (identified by operation id):
---------------------------------------------------
   2 - access("EMPLOYEE_ID">999)


Note
-----
   - dynamic statistics used: dynamic sampling (level=2)
SQL>
```

Once the index is usable again, the database uses the index. As the two previous examples show, when dealing with a nonpartitioned index, the optimizer ignores an unusable index. In the case of a partitioned index, the database ignores the index if the optimizer can't determine at query compile time that any of the index partitions can be pruned. However, you can override the default behavior of the database where it ignores an unusable index by specifying an INDEX hint in the query.

Asynchronous Global Index Maintenance

Prior to Oracle Database 12c, when you had to drop or truncate a partition of a table with global indexes, you faced a tough choice: you could choose to make this a fast operation, which meant that the global indexes would be unusable, or you could keep the global indexes usable, but that meant a much longer time to complete the execution of the drop/truncate operation.

In Oracle Database 12c, you don't have to make this either/or choice: when you specify to update global indexes, the index remains usable through the drop/truncate operation. Just one caveat here: the database needs to perform extra work to ensure whether the entries belong to an existing or a deleted partition, when a query accesses the index entries as part of the update operation.

The entries belonging to the dropped partition ("orphaned entries") are asynchronously cleaned up by one of the following operations:

- A maintenance job

- A call to DBMS_PART.CLEANUP_GIDX

- An alter index rebuild statement

- An alter index coalesce cleanup statement

The Role of the INDEX_STATS View in Index Rebuilds

The INDEX_STATS view, by default, has no rows. You populate this view by executing the analyze index... validate structure command. Once you do this, the INDEX_STATS supposedly has the necessary data to guide your index rebuild decisions.

Benefits of the INDEX_STATS View

Once you have the view populated, you can use it to look at and compute a number of useful items of information that can help you stay on top of indexing in your database. The following are key columns that you need to pay attention to:

- HEIGHT: Height of the index, which begins at 1 for root only index.

- BLOCKS: Number of blocks allocated to the index.

- LF_ROWS: Number of leaf row entries (includes deleted row entries).

- DEL_LF_ROWS: Number of deleted leaf row entries not yet cleaned out.

- USED_SPACE: Total space used within the index (includes deleted entries).

- PCT_USED: Percentage of space used within the index (includes deleted entries). This is derived from using the following formula: (USED_SPACE/BTREE_SPACE)*100.

- BTREE_SPACE: Total size of the index (includes deleted entries).

You can estimate the non-deleted rows in an index by subtracting the DEL_LF_ROWS value from the LF_ROWS value. You can estimate the percentage of space used by the non-deleted rows of an indexed by using the following formula:

```
((USED_SPACE - DEL_LF_ROWS_LEN)/BTREE_SPACE) * 100
```

The following example shows how the optimizer is always aware of the deleted rows in a table and makes the correct choice, even when you delete a large percentage of a table's rows. Let's create a simple table with 100,000 rows and then create an index on it.

```
SQL> create table test as select rownum id, 'Sam' text from dual
  2* connect by level <=100000
SQL> /

Table created.

SQL> create index test_idx1 on test(id);
```

```
Index created.
SQL>
```

Run the analyze index validate structure statement to check the number of lf_rows and lf_blks.

```
SQL> analyze index test_idx1 validate structure
SQL> /

Index analyzed.
```

Query the INDEX_STATS view to check the number of deleted leaf rows.

```
SQL> select lf_rows, lf_blks, del_lf_rows from index_stats;

LF_ROWS      LF_BLKS      DEL_LF_ROWS
-------      -------      -----------
 100000          222                0
SQL>
```

Delete a large number of rows from the table and run the analyze index validate structure command again.

```
SQL> delete test where id <=99999;

99999 rows deleted.

SQL> commit;

Commit complete.

SQL> analyze index test_idx1 validate structure;

Index analyzed.

SQL> select lf_rows, lf_blks, del_lf_rows from index_stats;
LF_ROWS      LF_BLKS      DEL_LF_ROWS
-------      -------      -----------
 100000          222            99999
SQL>
```

Gather statistics on both the table and the index.

```
SQL> execute dbms_stats.gather_table_stats(ownname=>'HR',tabname=>'TEST',
cascade=>TRUE);

PL/SQL procedure successfully completed.

SQL>
```

Query the DBA_INDEXES view.

```
SQL> select index_name, num_rows, leaf_blocks from dba_indexes where
     index_name = 'TEST_IDX1'
SQL> /

OWNER    INDEX_NAME        NUM_ROWS    LEAF_BLOCKS
-----    ----------        --------    -----------
HR       TEST_IDX1                1              1
SH       TEST_IDX1                0              0

SQL>
```

The DBA_INDEXES view shows that only one leaf block is being utilized by the index to host the single column value that remains in the table. The optimizer correctly chooses the index, as expected.

```
SQL> set autotrace traceonly explain
SQL> select * from test where id > 10;

Execution Plan
----------------------------------------------------------
Plan hash value: 2624864549
-------------------------------------------------------------------------------
| Id  | Operation                    | Name      | Rows | Bytes | Cost (%CPU)| Time     |
-------------------------------------------------------------------------------
|   0 | SELECT STATEMENT             |           |    1 |     7 |     3  (0)| 00:00:01 |
|   1 |  TABLE ACCESS BY INDEX ROWID | TEST      |    1 |     7 |     3  (0)| 00:00:01 |
|*  2 |   INDEX RANGE SCAN           | TEST_IDX1 |    1 |       |     2  (0)| 00:00:01 |
-------------------------------------------------------------------------------

Predicate Information (identified by operation id):
---------------------------------------------------
   2 - access("ID">10)

SQL>
```

Once you rebuild and analyze the index (validate structure), this is what you get:

```
SQL> select lf_rows, lf_blks, del_lf_rows from index_stats;


LF_ROWS          LF_BLKS          DEL_LF_ROWS
-------          -------          -----------
      1                1                    0
SQL>
```

Problems with the INDEX_STATS View

There are several problems with the ANALYZE INDEX ...VALIDATE STRUCTURE command, including the fact that the command locks the table until the index is analyzed. The real problem with using the ANALYZE INDEX ...VALIDATE STRUCTURE command to determine whether you should rebuild an index is that Oracle automatically reuses deleted space in an index in most cases. The following is a simple example that illustrates this fact.

Create a test table.

```
SQL> create table reb_test (cust_id number, cust_code number, cust_name varchar2(20));

Table created.
SQL>
```

Insert a few test rows (nine rows in this example).

```
SQL> insert into reb_test select rownum, rownum, 'Groucho Marx' from dual
  2  connect by level < 10;

9 rows created.

SQL> commit;

Commit complete.
SQL>
```

Create an index on the CUST_ID column.

```
SQL> create index reb_test_cust_id_idx on reb_test(cust_id);

Index created.
SQL>
```

Delete four of the nine rows from the table.

```
SQL> delete from reb_test where cust_id in (1,2,3,4);

4 rows deleted.

SQL> commit;

Commit complete.
SQL>
```

Analyze the index with the analyze index ...validate structure command.

```
SQL> analyze index reb_test_cust_id_idx validate structure;

Index analyzed.
SQL>
```

Query the INDEX_STATS view to find the value of the DEL_PCT column, which shows the percentage of the deleted leaf rows in the index.

```
SQL> select lf_rows,del_lf_rows,del_lf_rows/lf_rows*100 del_pct from index_stats;
```

```
    LF_ROWS        DEL_LF_ROWS           DEL_PCT
    -------        -----------           --------
          9                  4           44.4444444
SQL>
```

As expected, the DEL_PCT column has a value of a little over 44%. Insert a single row into the table.

```
SQL> insert into reb_test values (999,1,'Franco Marx');

1 row created.

SQL> commit;

Commit complete.
SQL>
```

Analyze the index again.

```
SQL> analyze index reb_test_cust_id_idx validate structure;

Index analyzed.
SQL>
```

Check the percentage of the deleted rows now.

```
SQL> select lf_rows,del_lf_rows,del_lf_rows/lf_rows*100 del_pct from index_stats;

    LF_ROWS        DEL_LF_ROWS           DEL_PCT
    -------        -----------           -------
          6                  0                 0

SQL>
```

As you can see, the deleted percentage of rows, which was about 44%, is now zero. The reason for this is that although you've inserted a single row, it is still a quarter of the four rows initially deleted. If you insert a small number of rows into a large table after deleting a high percentage of rows, don't expect to see Oracle immediately reclaim the deleted space.

The real point that we're trying to make here is that, in most cases, the Oracle database utilizes the space left free by deleted rows for inserting fresh rows; the space doesn't necessarily end up as deadwood.

If you're rebuilding indexes simply based on an arbitrary cutoff point for the percentage of deleted space in an index, you may not see any real gains over time, since the index itself may very well reuse all of the so-called wasted space. The final size of the index may very well grow back to its "natural" state anyway. In addition, depending on the percentage of rows currently marked as deleted based on the DEL_IF_ROWS statistic from the INDEX_STATS view, you may actually miss potential opportunities for a valid rebuild. This is because, under some circumstances, the DEL_IF_ROWS statistic vastly underestimates the actual percentage of deleted rows in an index.

Blindly using the DEL_IF_ROWS statistic as an index-rebuilding criterion means that you may be both rebuilding indexes that don't need a rebuild *and* missing out on real opportunities to gain from rebuilding an index. You really must make the rebuild decision based on the nature of the data in a column (sequence based, for example) and the pattern of deletes and inserts. We also recommend that you actually test the performance before and after a rebuild to see if it proves beneficial to you.

Index Rebuilding: The Debate

There's a fair bit of debate over the question of whether to rebuild indexes, especially on a routine basis. There are many reasons why DBAs rebuild. Some are valid; some are based upon myth or misunderstanding.

Arguments for Rebuilding

In this section, we summarize the arguments traditionally advanced to support the regular rebuilding of indexes.

- *Oracle B-tree indexes become unbalanced over time.* One of the most common reasons advanced by proponents of frequent rebuilds is that Oracle B-tree indexes become unbalanced over time if they're subject to a heavy amount of updates and deletes. This is not true because the height between the root block and all the leaf blocks is always consistent.

- *Deleted space in an index is deadwood.* A common misconception is that deleted space in an index is wasted space that the database can't reuse. This is a false conception; in most cases, the database automatically cleans up the empty blocks for reuse without your having to perform an index rebuild. We presented a simple example in the previous section to demonstrate this point.

- *Indexes that reach a set number of levels are inefficient.* Another argument is that indexes that reach a certain number of levels somehow are inefficient. There's no valid reasoning behind this argument. If the index is performing well, it really doesn't matter how many levels there are in the index tree. Since Oracle keeps the index balanced, B-tree levels are simply a result of having lots of entries in the index. You'd likely expect there to be more levels in a 200-billion-entry index than in a 200-thousand-entry index. The levels in an index tree simply depend on the number of index entries that are present and the number of branch blocks that are necessary to contain the ranges of entries that lead to the leaf blocks.

- *Indexes with a poor clustering factor can be fixed by a rebuild.* Some people have put forth the argument that indexes with a poor clustering factor are "obvious" candidates for a rebuild. However, when you rebuild an index, it doesn't change the table or the index order; therefore, the clustering factor is completely unaffected by your index rebuild. If you want to improve the clustering factor, you must actually rebuild (and thus reorder) the table.

■ **Caution**   If you rebuild the table to "fix" the clustering factor for one index, you may mess up the clustering factor for another index. Since the table can only be rebuilt in one order, any index that doesn't match that order will have a less than perfect clustering factor. In our opinion, you need a really good reason (backed with proof) to rebuild a table to try to achieve a "good" clustering factor.

Arguments Against Rebuilding

This section summarizes the most important reasons why you should not be doing automatic index rebuilds based on the deleted percentage of index entries.

- *Locking issues during rebuilds.* The analyze index ...validate structure command could result in massive locking issues, so this is something to keep in mind if you're using the DEL_IF_ROWS statistics as your criterion for rebuilding indexes. In previous releases, even an online rebuild meant that the database applied locks, thus blocking users from doing their work until the index rebuilds were completed. Starting with Oracle 10g, an online rebuild of an index doesn't involve locking of the index.

- *Excessive redo generation.* Index rebuilds generate massive amounts of redo. If you use the nologging option, however, this is a non-issue.

We can see several specific situations where a DBA may rightly rebuild an index, however. Here are some of the most common scenarios:

- If an index or an index partition is damaged by media failure, index building may be the only alternative in some cases.

- Rebuild index partitions that have been marked UNUSABLE.

- Rebuild indexes if you want to quickly move them to a different tablespace, or if you want to change certain storage parameters.

- Rebuild an index partition following a data load of the table partition with SQL*Loader utility.

- Rebuild an index to enable key compression.

- Unlike B-tree indexes, a bitmap index can grow very large very quickly and may benefit from a rebuild.

Instead of rebuilding an index, you can shrink the space used by an index by coalescing or shrinking an index. Using the alter index ...shrink space compact command gets you the same results as when you execute the alter index...coalesce command. Both the shrink and coalesce commands are alternative ways to compact an index segment. Both operations achieve the same purpose and, in essence, are identical, but the shrink command offers more options, as explained in the following sections.

Coalescing Indexes to Reduce Fragmentation

The COALESCE command tells the database to merge the contents of the index blocks to free blocks for reuse later, where it is possible to do so. Here's an example:

```
SQL> alter index test_idx1 coalesce;

Index altered.

SQL>
```

Coalescing an index doesn't release space back to the database. The purpose of the COALESCE command is to reduce fragmentation in an index. It doesn't deallocate space that has been allocated to an index segment. Coalescing an index performs an in-place reorganization of the index data. It combines adjacent leaf blocks into a single leaf block and puts the newly empty leaf blocks on the free list of the index segment.

The freed up index leaf blocks are reused by the database during subsequent block splits. The goal here is to reduce the free space within the leaf blocks of an index. The database scans the index leaf blocks to compare the free space in neighboring index blocks. If there's free space in a block, the block's contents are merged with the contents of another block, thus freeing up index leaf blocks where possible. The database removes any freed index blocks from the index structure and places them on the free list of index blocks.

Coalescing an index keeps the space you allocated for the index intact; it doesn't return the unused space to the database. If you have a case where you're dealing with an index with monotonically increasing values, such as on a sequence or a date, and you delete a lot of the old values, coalescing might be helpful. Many shops regularly purge older data based on the sequence number or a data range. Coalescing indexes in such cases helps you reclaim the unused space, which is not going to be reused by the indexes anyway. If you're performing a select of all the rows in a table with such an index and are ordering the results by the indexed column, the database has to read the mostly empty index leaf blocks. Queries might perform better when you coalesce, such an index. Coalescing rather than rebuilding the index is the right action to take here. Unlike in the case of an index rebuild, coalescing an index doesn't require additional disk space; rebuilding an index requires space for both the original and the new index structures until the index is rebuilt. Coalesce also runs much faster than an index rebuild in most cases, freeing up unused leaf blocks for reuse.

■ **Note** Both the `coalesce` and the `shrink` commands result in the same number of leaf blocks in the index. The index height remains unchanged, unlike in the case of an index rebuild where the index height is sometimes shortened.

Shrinking Indexes to Reduce Fragmentation

Instead of coalescing an index, you can shrink an index segment by specifying the SHRINK SPACE clause, as shown here:

```
SQL> alter index test_idx1 shrink space;

Index altered.
SQL>
```

Shrinking an index compacts the index segment, and the database immediately releases any space that has been freed up. You can specify the SHRINK SPACE clause to reduce space usage in not only an index or an index partition/subpartition, but also in a table. For the primary keys of an index-organized table, you must use the ALTER TABLE statement instead and specify the COALESCE clause.

For a large index, the database may take quite a bit of time to complete the shrink operation. Therefore, Oracle lets you perform a shrink operation in two steps. If you specify the COMPACT clause with the SHRINK SPACE command, the database only performs a defragmentation of the segment space. It compacts the index but doesn't immediately release the free space. You must issue a separate ALTER INDEX ...SHRINK SPACE command to make the index release the free space. Since compacting an index segment may require the database to perform row movement, you must first enable row movement for a table before you specify the COMPACT clause.

When you shrink an index, the database returns all the freed up space to the tablespace holding the index—if you specified AUTOALLOCATE for the tablespace. If you specified UNIFORM extent allocation, on the other hand, the database won't return any extent that contains even a single block of index data.

During an index shrink operation, in the first phase, the database scans the index segment from the back to locate the position of the last row. Next, the database scans the index segment from the beginning to locate the position of the first free slot in an index block. If the two positions are identical, there's no need to do anything further. As long as the database finds that the two positions are different, it continues to remove rows from the back of the index and insert them into the free blocks at the front of the index segment. The SHRINK SPACE command is inherently more expensive than a coalesce operation because the command actually deallocates empty index blocks and places them on the free list. It must empty all index blocks from the physical end of the index segment for this deallocation to occur, and all this requires more work on the part of the database, as well as the generation of more redo. Use the SHRINK SPACE command only if you want to permanently reduce the size of the index segment, let's say because of a large number of permanent deletions from a large table. You won't need that space ever, so you can shrink the index segment. If your goal is merely to defragment an index, coalesce the index instead of shrinking it. You'll have all the freed up index blocks for subsequent use by the index and the operation requires far fewer resources.

Although both the COALESCE and SHRINK commands achieve the same purpose of defragmenting an index by rearranging existing index entries to reduce the number of blocks in an index structure, you use the two commands for different purposes. Whether you must coalesce or shrink an index depends on what is happening with the index. If you think the index is unlikely to grow much and has a lot of free space, you may want to shrink the index to reclaim the free space. However, if you think the index will probably need the free space in the future, you may want to just coalesce the index. Coalescing has an advantage over shrinking an index because the database never locks the index during the index coalescing operation (coalesce is *always* an online operation), although it does lock the table briefly during a shrink operation to release the free space.

Large indexes sometimes get fragmented over time and you may have a valid reason to reduce the fragmentation. Whether you employ the coalesce operation or the rebuild operation depends on exactly how the index is getting fragmented.

If you have an index on a sequence, for example, and the rows are deleted from an older part of the index, then you may have a case where the deleted space does become deadwood in the sense that it can't be used by new index entries that are being inserted into the newer, rightmost part of the index. In a case such as this, where the deletions are all occurring from a small portion of the index, a rebuild is overkill in general; you're better off with a coalesce (or shrink operation). The coalesce operation just goes through the small portion of the index that's fragmented and leaves the rest of the index alone; it takes far less time and resources to get the job down via coalescing the index in this case.

However, if there are numerous deletions through the index, and not from a specific part of the index structure, you are better off rebuilding the index completely. Rebuilding is far more efficient because, unlike a coalesce operation, it has to perform only a single scan of the index structure to create a new structure. Since the deletions are large and are all over the index structure, coalescing an index is far less efficient, as it has to keep moving the same index blocks through multiple leaf blocks to defragment them.

The choice between rebuilding and coalescing an index can also depend on whether you need to avoid downtime. If you can't have downtime, then you've got to coalesce since coalescing is always an online operation.

Moving Tables and Indexes

Whenever you move a table to a different tablespace (or perform any one of several table maintenance procedures), any indexes that depend on the table are rendered unusable. Here is an example:

```
SQL> alter table test move tablespace dev_oim;

Table altered.
```

```
SQL> select index_name, status from dba_indexes where table_name='TEST';

INDEX_NAME                         STATUS
-------------------------------    ----------------
TEST_IDX1                          UNUSABLE
SQL>
```

Once you rebuild the index, it becomes usable again.

```
SQL> alter index test_idx1 rebuild
  2   parallel 12
  3   nologging;

Index altered.

SQL> select index_name, status from dba_indexes where table_name='TEST';

INDEX_NAME                         STATUS
-------------------------------    ----------------
TEST_IDX1                          VALID

SQL>
```

Unlike in the case of a table, you can't move an index by using a "move index" command. You move an index to a different tablespace by rebuilding the index. So, if you want to move the index test_idx1 from the USERS tablespace to a different tablespace (DEV_OIM in the example), here is what you need to do:

```
SQL> alter index test_idx1 rebuild
  2   parallel 12
  3   nologging
  4*  tablespace dev_oim
SQL> /

Index altered.
```

Improving Index Creation Efficiency

The speed with which you can create an index is always critical when you're creating indexes on large tables. You can adopt several strategies to minimize the index creation time, as summarized in the following sections. Often, you can combine several of these strategies to cut short the time for creating an index.

Parallelizing Index Creation

Using the parallel option during index creation helps speed up the creation of a large index. In order to create an index, the database needs to perform a full table scan. Specifying the parallel clause makes the database perform the full table scan in parallel, thus making the index creation finish much faster. There is no hard-and-fast rule, of course, as to the appropriate degree of parallelism; it depends on the number of CPUs on your system. Here's an example that shows how to specify the parallel option:

```
SQL> create index text_idx1
     on employees (last_name,first_name)
     parallel 12;
```

You can also specify the `parallel` option when rebuilding an index, as shown here:

```
SQL> alter index text_idx1 rebuild parallel 12;
Index altered.

SQL>
```

Specifying parallelism during the creation or rebuilding of an index definitely makes the index creation/rebuild process finish much faster than otherwise, provided that you have the necessary I/O bandwidth and CPU resources to handle the demands of the parallel processes. A word of caution, however: the parallelism you specify during the creation or rebuilding of an index doesn't end there! Such a parallel operation *persists* the parallelism degree of the index, as shown in the following query.

```
SQL> select index_name,degree from user_indexes where degree > 1;

INDEX_NAME      DEGREE
----------      ------
TEXT_IDX1           12

SQL>
```

This query's output is telling you that even though you had merely intended to speed up your index creation or rebuild with the parallel option (`parallel 12`), the database has permanently modified the parallelism degree of the `text_index1` index to 12 from its default value of 1. Any query operations involving that index will begin defaulting to parallel execution. This is not always a good thing!

By the way, the same is also true with tables. If you specify the `parallel` option during an ALTER TABLE ...MOVE or a CREATE TABLE ... AS operation, the database will *permanently* modify the existing parallelism of the table (default is 1) to the degree that you specify for the operation on the table.

■ **Tip** Creating or rebuilding an index in parallel will change the degree of parallelism for that index. The optimizer takes into account this fact when it calculates the cost of alternative execution paths.

If you really intend to use parallelism in the database when dealing with your index, then you're fine. However, if you don't intend to use parallelism during query execution, disable parallelism on an index after any parallel maintenance operation, such as a `create index` or a `alter index rebuild` operation, as shown here:

```
SQL> alter index text_idx1 noparallel;

Index altered.

SQL>
```

If you forget to put the degree of parallelism of an index back to its default value of 1 (no parallelism), you may get bit you when you least expect it, especially in an OLTP application. All of a sudden, you may be confronted with heavy contention and a slowdown in processing due to the totally unintended use of parallelism.

When you encounter this situation, a check of the tables involved in the query may show that the degree of parallelism is at the default of 1. However, when you check the parallelism of all the *indexes* involved in the query, you'll find the culprit: the index that you've created or rebuilt with a parallel option has its parallel degree set to greater than 1. Even the presence of a single object in a query with a parallel degree greater than 1 means that the optimizer may choose to parallelize all operations on the query. So be careful: don't leave a degree of parallelism set unless you mean for it to be set.

Avoiding Redo Generation During Index Creation

You can achieve dramatic reductions in index creation times by choosing not to write the index creation entries to the redo log. Since you can always rebuild an index with the table data, you're not risking anything by creating indexes with the NOLOGGING option. The NOLOGGING option is especially helpful when creating very large indexes during short windows of time.

Simply specify the NOLOGGING option when creating an index to speed up the index creation process, as shown here:

```
SQL> create index hr.emp_name_idx on hr.employees (last_name, first_name)
  2  nologging
  3* tablespace example
SQL> /

Index created.
SQL>
```

When used for creating large indexes, the NOLOGGING option not only dramatically increases performance, but also saves space by not filling up several redo log files. Some redo is still generated, and you may possibly need to rebuild some indexes, depending on the situation.

Using Larger Block Sizes

According to Oracle (MOSC Note 46757.1), a large block size can save disk space for indexes. To create an index with a non-standard block size, first create a tablespace with the block size that you need. For example, if you want to create the index with a block size of 32KB when the database block size is 8KB, use the block size 32KB option when creating the tablespace. Once you do this, create the index by specifying the tablespace with the large block size, as shown here:

```
SQL> create index cust_idx1 on customer (cust_id)
       tablespace large_ts;
```

Using larger block sizes for indexes may offer some storage benefits because large block sizes provide more space for storing index keys in the branch node of a B-tree index. This certainly reduces the height of the index tree. However, the most important reason to use large block sizes is to enhance the performance of certain types of queries— more specifically, queries that require large scans of an index. For example, a select statement that utilizes a fast full scan of an index will perform much better with an index using a large block size than with an index that uses a smaller block size. However, most queries in an OLTP application, where index usage is highly critical, don't seek to retrieve large amounts of data. These queries are typically designed to retrieve a specific value or a range of values from an index. For these types of queries, a small block size is the right choice. A very large block size actually slows down the response time.

Compressing Indexes

You can avoid the duplication of keys in a non-unique index by specifying the compress option when creating an index. When using a composite index, you can specify the prefix length, as explained in Chapter 7. Here's an example that shows how to create a non-unique index on a composite index, where the first two columns have low cardinality and the third column (cust_id) has high cardinality:

```
SQL> create index cust_idx1
     on customer(sex,state, cust_id)
     compress 2;
```

Using Multiple Options Together

In the previous sections, you learned that specifying various options—such as parallel, nologging, and compress—can help you speed up index creation or reduce index storage. You can specify multiple options together, as shown in the following example:

```
SQL> create index a on x(y)
     nologging
     parallel 12
     compress 2;
```

Generating the DDL for Creating an Index

DBAs often need to re-create an index or create new indexes in a different environment, such as a pre-production database. There are actually a couple of ways you can do this (if you're not using a third-party tool such as TOAD or even Oracle's SQL Developer, which can get you the same information without having to run any script whatsoever).

Generating the DDL for a simple index might seem somewhat of a trivial task. However, if you consider the fact that many databases use partitioned indexes, and that the these indexes may have a large number of partitions and even subpartitions, it makes more sense as to why you'd want to extract the DDL using some kind of a tool or utility. In the following sections, let's review the ways that you can extract DDL for indexes.

Using the DBMS_METADATA Package

The easiest way to get the DDL for the creation of an existing index is to use the DBMS_METADATA package supplied by Oracle. You can employ the DBMS_METADATA package to extract the DDL for other objects besides indexes. The following is an example that shows how to get the DDL for creating an index named EMP_NAME_IDX that's part of the HR schema:

```
SQL> select dbms_metadata.get_ddl('INDEX','SALES_PROMO_BIX') from dual;

DBMS_METADATA.GET_DDL('INDEX','SALES_PROMO_BIX')
--------------------------------------------------------------------------------

  CREATE BITMAP INDEX "SYS"."SALES_PROMO_BIX" ON "SYS"."SALES" ("PROMO_ID")
  PCTFREE 10 INITRANS 2 MAXTRANS 255
  STORAGE(
  BUFFER_POOL DEFAULT FLASH_CACHE DEFAULT CELL_FLASH_CACHE DEFAULT) LOCAL
 (PARTITION "SALES_1995"
  PCTFREE 10 INITRANS 2 MAXTRANS 255
```

```
   STORAGE(INITIAL 65536 NEXT 1048576 MINEXTENTS 1 MAXEXTENTS 2147483645
   PCTINCREASE 0 FREELISTS 1 FREELIST GROUPS 1 BUFFER_POOL DEFAULT FLASH_CACHE DE

FAULT CELL_FLASH_CACHE DEFAULT)
   TABLESPACE "USERS" ,

 PARTITION "SALES_2016"
 PCTFREE 10 INITRANS 2 MAXTRANS 255
 STORAGE(INITIAL 65536 NEXT 1048576 MINEXTENTS 1 MAXEXTENTS 2147483645
 PCTINCREASE 0 FREELISTS 1 FREELIST GROUPS 1 BUFFER_POOL DEFAULT FLASH_CACHE DE

FAULT CELL_FLASH_CACHE DEFAULT)
   TABLESPACE "USERS" ,

 ...
SQL>
```

Once you get the DDL for an index, use that DDL to create your index.

```
SQL> CREATE INDEX "HR"."EMP_NAME_IX" ON "HR"."EMPLOYEES" ("LAST_NAME", "FIRST_NAME")
  2    PCTFREE 10 INITRANS 2 MAXTRANS 255 NOLOGGING COMPUTE STATISTICS
  3    STORAGE(INITIAL 65536 NEXT 1048576 MINEXTENTS 1 MAXEXTENTS 2147483645
  4    PCTINCREASE 0 FREELISTS 1 FREELIST GROUPS 1 BUFFER_POOL DEFAULT)
  5*   TABLESPACE "EXAMPLE"
SQL> /

Index created.

SQL>
```

The GET_DDL procedure of the DBMS_METADATA packages provides a quick way to generate the DDL for re-creating indexes and tables. If you want to generate the DDL for creating all the indexes in a schema, execute the DBMS_METADATA.GET_DDL procedure in the following way:

```
SQL> select dbms_metadata.get_ddl('INDEX', d.index_name)
  2   from dba_indexes d
  3* where owner='HR'
SQL>
```

One thing you want to do when executing the DBMS_METADATA package is to set the following SQL*Plus parameters to get nicely formatted (wrapped without inconvenient word breaks) output. If you're generating the DDL for creating all the indexes in a schema, you'll thank yourself!

```
set  linesize 80 (or some reasonable number)
column xyz format a100 word_wrapped
column x format a200 word_wrapped
```

A big advantage of using the DBMS_METADATA package is that just about anyone can execute the package through SQL*Plus. As shown in this example, you use the GET_DDL procedure to extract the DDL for an index. The DBMS_METADATA package contains several other procedures as well, and the following sections explain how to use two important procedures: SESSION_TRANSFORM and SET_FILTER.

Using the SESSION_TRANSFORM Procedure

You can use the SESSION_TRANSFORM procedure to modify or customize the output generated by the GET_DDL procedure. You can specify various controls, such as the following (note that some of the "transform parameters" are applicable to only certain object types):

- PRETTY formats output with indentation and line feeds.

- SQLTERMINATOR appends a SQL terminator to each DDL statement.

- STORAGE outputs the storage clause

- CONSTRAINTS outputs all non-referential constraints.

- BODY outputs the package body for a package.

Several of the transform parameters are set to the value of TRUE by default, but some, such as the value of the SQLTERMINATOR parameter, are set to FALSE. The following code chunk shows how to set various transform parameters before you run the GET_DDL procedure to generate the DDL for an index:

```
SQL> begin
  2  dbms_metadata.set_transform_param( DBMS_METADATA.SESSION_TRANSFORM,
'STORAGE', false );
  3  dbms_metadata.set_transform_param( DBMS_METADATA.SESSION_TRANSFORM,
'CONSTRAINTS', false );
  4  dbms_metadata.set_transform_param( DBMS_METADATA.SESSION_TRANSFORM,
'REF_CONSTRAINTS', false );
  5  dbms_metadata.set_transform_param( DBMS_METADATA.SESSION_TRANSFORM,
'SQLTERMINATOR', TRUE );
  6  end;
  7  /

PL/SQL procedure successfully completed.

SQL>
```

Using the SET_FILTER Procedure

The SET_FILTER procedure helps you restrict the objects to be retrieved by the DBMS_METADATA package. You can specify individual object names or restrict the objects by schema names. The SET_FILTER procedure comes in handy in various situations, such as when you're trying to extract the DDL for an index that you've created on an index-organized table (IOT). IOTs always include a primary key constraint, so when you invoke the GET_DEPENDENT_DDL procedure, it gets the index creation statements for both the primary key and the index that you created. The following example shows how to invoke the SET_FILTER procedure to get just the DDL for the index that you created:

```
SQL> set serveroutput on
SQL> declare
  2  l_myHandle number;
  3  l_transHandle number;
  4  l_ddl clob;
  5  begin
  6  l_myHandle := dbms_metadata.open('INDEX');
  7  dbms_metadata.set_filter(l_myHandle, 'SYSTEM_GENERATED', FALSE);
  8  dbms_metadata.set_filter(l_myHandle, 'BASE_OBJECT_SCHEMA',user);
```

207

```
 9    dbms_metadata.set_filter(l_myHandle, 'BASE_OBJECT_NAME', 'IOT_TAB_TST');
10    l_transHandle := dbms_metadata.add_transform(l_myHandle, 'DDL');
11     loop
13          l_ddl := dbms_metadata.fetch_clob(l_myHandle);
14          EXIT WHEN L_DDL IS NULL;
15          dbms_output.put_line( l_ddl);
16      end loop;
17    dbms_metadata.close(l_myHandle);
18*  end;
SQL> /


  CREATE INDEX "SYS"."IOT_IDX1" ON "SYS"."IOT_TAB_TST" ("B")
  PCTFREE 10 INITRANS
2 MAXTRANS 255 COMPUTE STATISTICS
  STORAGE(INITIAL 65536 NEXT 1048576
MINEXTENTS 1 MAXEXTENTS 2147483645
  PCTINCREASE 0 FREELISTS 1 FREELIST GROUPS 1
BUFFER_POOL DEFAULT FLASH_CACHE DEFAULT CELL_FLASH_CACHE DEFAULT)
  TABLESPACE
"USERS" ;

PL/SQL procedure successfully completed.

SQL>
```

Using Data Pump

You can also use the data pump utility to extract DDL for indexes and other database objects. Underneath, the data pump uses the DBMS_METADATA package to extract DDL for database objects. Generating DDL with the data pump is easy. Make sure that you use the following syntax to do so:

```
$ expdp content=metadata_only
```

When you specify the content=metadata_only option, Oracle doesn't export any data; it merely extracts the DDL for all database objects. If you are re-creating all the indexes in your test environment to your development environment, invoke the expdp utility first to get the dump file. You can then copy the dump file to the development environment and run the impdp utility, as shown here:

```
$ impdp sqlfile=myfile
```

The advantage to using the DBMS_METADATA package to extract the DDL for your objects is that you get to control the formatting of the output, making it much easier to run the index creation script. On the other hand, the data pump output has line size problems. In addition, running the data pump utility requires more privileges than executing procedures from the DBMS_METADATA package.

Dropping an Index

On occasion, you may find that you don't need an index because the index isn't providing any real performance gains or because your application doesn't use the index. You can drop an index by using the DROP INDEX command. You may also drop an index because the index is invalid and you want to rebuild it.

You'll also find that if an index is too fragmented, it is better to drop it and create a brand-new index than to rebuild it. As you'll recall, rebuilding an index requires twice the space of the index.

You execute the DROP INDEX command in the following manner:

```
SQL> drop index test_idx
SQL> /

Index dropped.
SQL>
```

You can drop any index that you have explicitly created through the DROP INDEX command. However, you can't drop any implicitly created index—such as those created by defining a key constraint on a table—with the DROP INDEX command. For example, you can only drop any index that the database has created to support a unique key or a primary key constraint by dropping (or disabling) the constraint itself. Here's what happens when you try to drop an index that supports a primary key constraint:

```
SQL> drop index test_pk1;
drop index test_pk1
            *
ERROR at line 1:
ORA-02429: cannot drop index used for enforcement of unique/primary key
SQL>
```

In order to drop a constraint, issue the drop constraint command, as shown here:

```
SQL> alter table test
  2  drop constraint test_pk1;

Table altered.
SQL>
```

If you drop a table, the database drops all indexes defined on that table as well.

Dropping an Index Online

Oracle Database 12c lets you drop an index online, which translates to fewer blocking issues in a busy database. Just add the ONLINE clause when dropping the index to take advantage of this enhancement,

The Hazards of Dropping an Index

Although the V$OBJECT_USAGE view tells you if an index has been used or not, be leery about dropping an index just because the INDEX_USAGE column shows a value of NO. There could very well be unexpected side effects from dropping or modifying a multicolumn composite index. Several writers have demonstrated that Oracle can potentially use an index for a sanity check, even if the index itself remains "unused"! Starting with Oracle Database 11g, Oracle uses certain index statistics, even when it doesn't use the index per se in retrieving a query's output. For example, if you create a composite index on two columns that are related, Oracle can potentially arrive at different results with and without the presence of the index, even if it doesn't use the index. There is some evidence that Oracle uses the DISTINCT_KEYS index statistic to determine the correct selectivity and the related cardinality estimates for a query. So, if you drop an index because your index monitoring shows that the index isn't being used, the optimizer could potentially lose vital information that it needs to estimate the selectivity and cardinality of the indexed columns.

Finally, as Chapter 5 explains, using Oracle's invisible indexes feature is quite often a smarter alternative to simply dropping an index.

Summary

This chapter explained some of the most common index maintenance operations. You learned how to collect statistics for indexes. In this connection, it's important to specify correct values for the METHOD_OPT parameter and this chapter explained how to do this. Rebuilding indexes is often a troublesome part of index maintenance due to the many arguments for and against regular index rebuilds. The chapter discusses both arguments and explains why an automatic rebuild of indexes may really be unnecessary. The chapter also explains shrinking and coalescing operations and offered guidelines as to when these operations are appropriate. The chapter explained when Oracle makes an index unusable and how to deal with it. You also learned how to render an index unusable and when to do this. Finally, the chapter explained how to use the DBMS_METADATA package to efficiently extract the DDL for creating indexes.

CHAPTER 9

■.■ ■

SQL Tuning Advisor

The SQL Tuning Advisor is a tool that analyzes one or more SQL statements and provides advice in the form of

- Creating indexes.

- Creating SQL profiles.

- Establishing plan baselines.

- Generating fresh statistics.

- Restructuring a query

To fully understand how the SQL Tuning Advisor tool works, we need to lay some groundwork and explain a few terms. Firstly, the Oracle query optimizer operates in two different modes: *normal* and *tuning*. When a SQL statement executes, the optimizer operates in normal mode and quickly identifies a reasonable execution plan. In this mode, the optimizer spends only a fraction of a second to determine the optimal plan.

When analyzing SQL statements, the SQL Tuning Advisor invokes the optimizer in tuning mode. When executing in this manner, the optimizer can take several minutes to analyze each step of a SQL statement's execution plan and generate a new plan that is potentially much more efficient than what is generated under normal mode.

■ **Tip**   The optimizer running in tuning mode is somewhat analogous to a computer chess game. When you allow the chess software to spend only a second or less on each move, it's easy to beat the game. However, if you allow the chess game to spend a minute or more on each move, the game makes much more optimal decisions.

The tuning mode of the optimizer is invoked whenever you execute the SQL Tuning Advisor. The SQL Tuning Advisor runs automatically but can also be manually invoked. The Automatic SQL tuning task is a preset background database job that by default runs the SQL Tuning Advisor every day. This task identifies high-resource-consuming statements in the Automatic Workload Repository (AWR) and then runs the optimizer in tuning mode and generates tuning advice (if any) for each statement analyzed. The output often contains advice regarding indexes, SQL profiles, restructuring the query, and so on.

You can also run the SQL Tuning Advisor manually and provide as input either a single SQL statement or several SQL statements. The SQL Tuning Advisor is manually invoked from the DBMS_SQLTUNE package, SQL Developer, or Enterprise Manager.

© Darl Kuhn, Sam R. Alapati and Bill Padfield 2016
D. Kuhn et al., *Expert Oracle Indexing and Access Paths*, DOI 10.1007/978-1-4842-1984-3_9

One key way to group SQL statements for input to the SQL Tuning Advisor is through a SQL tuning set. A SQL tuning set (STS) is a database object that contains one or more SQL statements *and* the associated execution statistics. You can populate a SQL tuning set from resource-intensive SQL recorded in the AWR or SQL currently in memory. Because SQL tuning sets are often used as inputs to Oracle tuning tools, we also cover the SQL tuning set feature in this chapter.

In the examples in this chapter, we focus on showing you how to use features via SQL and built-in PL/SQL packages. While we do show some screenshots from Enterprise Manager, we don't focus on the graphical tool usage. You should be able to use SQL and PL/SQL regardless of whether Enterprise Manager is installed. Furthermore, the manual approach allows you to understand each piece of the process and helps you to diagnose issues when problems arise.

The first section of this chapter deals with the Automatic SQL Tuning feature. You'll be shown how to determine if and when the automated job is running and how to modify its characteristics. The middle section of this chapter focuses on how to create and manage SQL tuning sets. Lastly, you'll learn how to manually run the SQL Tuning Advisor to generate indexing recommendations for SQL statements.

■ **Note**   The SQL Tuning Advisor is part of the Oracle Tuning Pack, which is an extra-cost option available with the Oracle Enterprise Edition.

Automatic SQL Tuning Job

When you create an Oracle database, an automatic SQL tuning job routinely runs the SQL Tuning Advisor for you and generates advice on how to improve performance. This advice can be in the form of creating indexes, restructuring SQL, creating a SQL profile, and so forth. This architecture is depicted in Figure 9-1.

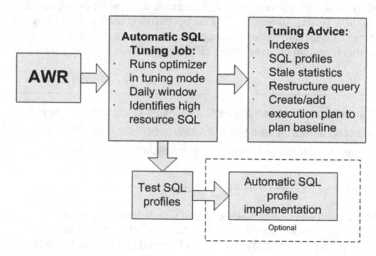

Figure 9-1. *Architecture of the automatic SQL tuning job*

Notice that the automatic SQL tuning job uses as its input the high-resource statements found in the AWR. Also, the job can be configured to automatically accept SQL profiles.

■ **Note** Use caution when implementing the automatic acceptance of SQL profiles in production environments. You should understand why a SQL profile is necessary and how it impacts performance before applying the profile in a production environment.

Verifying Automatic Jobs Running

You can check on the status of the automatic SQL tuning job via this query:

```
SELECT client_name, status, consumer_group
FROM dba_autotask_client
ORDER BY client_name;
```

Here is some sample output showing that there are three automatically configured jobs:

CLIENT_NAME	STATUS	CONSUMER_GROUP
auto optimizer stats collection	ENABLED	ORA$AUTOTASK
auto space advisor	ENABLED	ORA$AUTOTASK
sql tuning advisor	ENABLED	ORA$AUTOTASK

These tasks are automatically configured to run in regularly scheduled maintenance windows. A maintenance window is a specified time and duration for the task to run. You can view the maintenance window details with this query:

```
SELECT window_name,
TO_CHAR(window_next_time,'DD-MON-YY HH24:MI:SS') next_time,
sql_tune_advisor, optimizer_stats, segment_advisor
FROM dba_autotask_window_clients;
```

Here's a snippet of the output for this example:

WINDOW_NAME	NEXT_TIME	SQL_TUNE	OPTIMIZE	SEGMENT_
SUNDAY_WINDOW	14-FEB-16 06:00:00	ENABLED	ENABLED	ENABLED
THURSDAY_WINDOW	18-FEB-16 22:00:00	ENABLED	ENABLED	ENABLED
TUESDAY_WINDOW	16-FEB-16 22:00:00	ENABLED	ENABLED	ENABLED

Viewing Automatic SQL Tuning Job Advice

Now that you've established that the automatic SQL tuning job is running, you can view the advice it generates via SQL*Plus, as follows:

```
SET LINESIZE 80 PAGESIZE 0 LONG 100000
SELECT DBMS_AUTO_SQLTUNE.REPORT_AUTO_TUNING_TASK FROM DUAL;
```

Depending on the activity in your database, there may be a great deal of output. Here's a small sample of output from an active database:

```
SUMMARY SECTION
-------------------------------------------------------------------------------
                        Global SQL Tuning Result Statistics
-------------------------------------------------------------------------------
Number of SQLs Analyzed                      : 22
Number of SQLs in the Report                 : 6
Number of SQLs with Findings                 : 6
Number of SQLs with Statistic Findings       : 1
Number of SQLs with SQL profiles recommended : 3
Number of SQLs with Index Findings           : 1
```

Looking further down in the output, here is the specific advice in regards to creating an index:

```
Recommendation (estimated benefit: 99.39%)
------------------------------------------
- Consider running the Access Advisor to improve the physical schema design
  or creating the recommended index.
  create index MV_MAINT.IDX$$_00010001 on MV_MAINT.P("P");

- Consider running the Access Advisor to improve the physical schema design
  or creating the recommended index.
  create index MV_MAINT.IDX$$_00010002 on MV_MAINT.C("P","C");

Rationale
---------
  Creating the recommended indices significantly improves the execution plan
  of this statement. However, it might be preferable to run "Access Advisor"
  using a representative SQL workload as opposed to a single statement. This
  will allow to get comprehensive index recommendations which takes into
  account index maintenance overhead and additional space consumption.
```

This output provides a strong recommendation to create an index. Before following the advice, we recommend that you create the index in a test or development environment and verify that the benefit is worth the cost. Additionally, you should adjust the index creation script so that you follow your naming, storage, and tablespace placement standards.

AUTOMATICALLY E-MAILING TUNING ADVICE

On Linux/Unix systems, it's quite easy to automate the e-mailing of output from a SQL script. Here's a sample shell script that generates and sends automatic SQL tuning advice:

```
#!/bin/bash
# source oracle OS variables
export ORACLE_SID=O1212
export ORACLE_HOME=/u01/app/oracle/product/12.1.0.2/db_1
export PATH=$ORACLE_HOME/bin:$PATH
```

```
export LD_LIBRARY_PATH=/usr/lib:$ORACLE_HOME/lib
#
BOX=$(uname -a | awk '{print$2}')
OUTFILE=$HOME/sqladvice.txt
#
sqlplus -s <<EOF
/ as sysdba
SPO $OUTFILE
SET LINESIZE 80 PAGESIZE 0 LONG 100000
SELECT DBMS_AUTO_SQLTUNE.REPORT_AUTO_TUNING_TASK FROM DUAL;
EOF
cat $OUTFILE | mailx -s "SQL Advice: $BOX" dba@gmail.com
exit 0
```

You can run the shell script manually from the command line or from an automatic scheduling utility such as cron.

Depending on the activity and load on your database, the report may contain no suggestions, or it may provide a great deal of advice. You can adjust what is reported by the automatic SQL tuning job via parameters passed to the REPORT_AUTO_TUNING_TASK function. The parameters for the REPORT_AUTO_TUNING_TASK function are described in detail in Table 9-1. These parameters allow you a great deal of flexibility in customizing the advice output.

Table 9-1. Parameter Details for the REPORT_AUTO_TUNING_TASK Function

Parameter Name	Description	Default Value
BEGIN_EXEC	Name of beginning task execution. NULL means the most recent task is used.	NULL
END_EXEC	Name of ending task. NULL means the most recent task is used.	NULL
TYPE	Type of report to produce. TEXT specifies a text report.	TEXT
LEVEL	Level of detail. Valid values are BASIC, TYPICAL, and ALL.	TYPICAL
SECTION	Section of the report to include. Valid values are ALL, SUMMARY, FINDINGS, PLAN, INFORMATION, and ERROR.	ALL
OBJECT_ID	Used to report on a specific statement. NULL means all statements.	NULL
RESULT_LIMIT	Maximum number of SQL statements to include in report.	NULL

For example, if you want to generate a report with the greatest amount of detail, then set the LEVEL parameter to ALL.

```
set long 10000000
variable advice_out clob;
begin
 :advice_out := DBMS_AUTO_SQLTUNE.REPORT_AUTO_TUNING_TASK(LEVEL=>'ALL');
end;
/
print :advice_out
```

215

Generating a SQL Script to Implement Automatic Tuning Advice

Oracle provides the DBMS_SQLTUNE.SCRIPT_TUNING_TASK function that outputs only the SQL required to implement the advice generated by the automatic SQL tuning job. Before generating the SQL, first determine the name of the tuning task via this query:

```
select task_name, execution_start from dba_advisor_log
where task_name='SYS_AUTO_SQL_TUNING_TASK'
order by 2;
```

Here is some sample output:

```
TASK_NAME                          EXECUTION
------------------------------     ---------
SYS_AUTO_SQL_TUNING_TASK           13-FEB-16
```

Now use the DBMS_SQLTUNE.SCRIPT_TUNING_TASK function to generate the SQL statements to implement the advice of a tuning task. In this example, the name of the task is SYS_AUTO_SQL_TUNING_TASK.

```
SET LINESIZE 132 PAGESIZE 0 LONG 10000
SELECT DBMS_SQLTUNE.SCRIPT_TUNING_TASK('SYS_AUTO_SQL_TUNING_TASK')FROM dual;
```

For this database, the output is an index creation script.

```
create index MV_MAINT.IDX$$_00010001 on MV_MAINT.P("P");
create index MV_MAINT.IDX$$_00010002 on MV_MAINT.C("P","C");
```

If the tuning task doesn't have any advice to give, there won't be any SQL statements generated in the output. Before creating an index in a production environment, you should test whether or not an index actually increases performance and doesn't have any adverse impacts on the performance of other SQL statements. Also consider adjusting the index name, storage, and tablespace placement as per your standards.

Disabling and Enabling Automatic SQL Tuning

You might desire to disable the automatic SQL tuning job because you have a very active database and want to ensure that this job doesn't impact the overall performance of the database. The DBMS_AUTO_TASK_ADMIN. ENABLE/DISABLE procedures allow you to turn on and off the automatic SQL tuning job. These procedures take three parameters (see Table 9-2 for details). The behavior of the procedures varies depending on which parameters you specify.

Table 9-2. *Parameter Descriptions for DBMS_AUTO_TASK_ADMIN.ENABLE and DISABLE Procedures*

Parameter	Description
CLIENT_NAME	Name of client. Query DBA_AUTOTASK_CLIENT for details.
OPERATION	Name of operation. Query DBA_AUTOTASK_OPERATION for details.
WINDOW_NAME	Optional name of the window.

- If CLIENT_NAME is provided and both OPERATION and WINDOW_NAME are NULL, then the client is disabled.

- If OPERATION is provided, then the operation is disabled.

- If WINDOW_NAME is provided, and OPERATION is NULL, then the client is disabled in the provided window name.

These parameters allow you to control at a granular detail the schedule of the automatic task. Given the prior rules, you would disable the automatic SQL tuning job during the Tuesday maintenance window, as follows:

```
BEGIN
  dbms_auto_task_admin.disable(
  client_name => 'sql tuning advisor',
  operation => NULL,
  window_name => 'TUESDAY_WINDOW');
END;
/
```

You can verify that the window has been disabled via this query:

```
SELECT window_name,TO_CHAR(window_next_time,'DD-MON-YY HH24:MI:SS')
,sql_tune_advisor
FROM dba_autotask_window_clients;
```

Here is a snippet of the output:

```
WINDOW_NAME        TO_CHAR(WINDOW_NEXT_TIME,'D SQL_TUNE
---------------    -------------------------- --------
TUESDAY_WINDOW     16-FEB-16 22:00:00         DISABLED
```

To completely disable the automatic SQL tuning job, use the DBMS_AUTO_TASK_ADMIN.DISABLE procedure, like so:

```
BEGIN
  DBMS_AUTO_TASK_ADMIN.DISABLE(
  client_name => 'sql tuning advisor',
  operation => NULL,
  window_name => NULL);
END;
/
```

As mentioned, you can report on the status of the automatic tuning job by querying the STATUS column of DBA_AUTOTASK_CLIENT.

```
select client_name, status from dba_autotask_client;
```

Here is some sample output:

```
CLIENT_NAME                      STATUS
-------------------------------  --------------------
sql tuning advisor               DISABLED
auto optimizer stats collection  ENABLED
auto space advisor               ENABLED
```

To re-enable the job, use the ENABLE procedure, as shown:

```
BEGIN
  DBMS_AUTO_TASK_ADMIN.ENABLE(
  client_name => 'sql tuning advisor',
  operation => NULL,
  window_name => NULL);
END;
/
```

Managing SQL Tuning Sets

Before detailing how to manually run the SQL Tuning Advisor, let's first cover SQL tuning sets. As mentioned, SQL tuning sets are a grouping of SQL statements and associated execution metrics. SQL tuning sets are used as inputs to many of Oracle's tuning tools (such as the SQL Tuning Advisor and SQL Access Advisor). Therefore, it's critical that you understand how to create and manage SQL tuning sets. Figure 9-2 displays the SQL tuning set architecture.

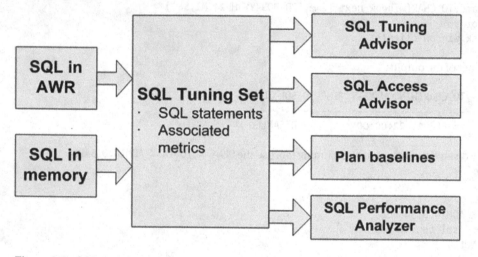

Figure 9-2. *SQL tuning set architecture*

To understand how a SQL tuning set is populated, it's instructional to manually run queries that retrieve high-resource SQL from the AWR and/or memory. The basic idea is that the result sets from these queries can be used as input to populate a SQL tuning set.

Viewing Resource-Intensive SQL in the AWR

The DBMS_SQLTUNE.SELECT_WORKLOAD_REPOSITORY function is used to extract resource-intensive SQL stored in the AWR. Before querying this function, first determine which snapshot IDs that you want to select from.

```
select snap_id from dba_hist_snapshot order by 1;
```

For example, this particular query selects queries in the AWR between snapshots 8200 and 8201 ordered by the top 10 in the disk reads usage category:

```
SELECT
 sql_id
,substr(sql_text,1,30) sql_text
,disk_reads
,cpu_time
,elapsed_time
FROM table(DBMS_SQLTUNE.SELECT_WORKLOAD_REPOSITORY(8200,8201,
            null, null, 'disk_reads',null, null, null, 10))
ORDER BY disk_reads DESC;
```

Here is a small snippet of the output:

```
SQL_ID          SQL_TEXT                        DISK_READS  CPU_TIME ELAPSED_TIME
-------------   -----------------------------   ----------  -------- ------------
cvn54b7yzOs8u   select /*+ index(idl_ub1$ i_id          74         0         6016
31dOw7aypfkw9   select count(*) from dba_regis          45     40002        34773
3un99aOzwp4vd   select owner#,name,namespace,r          43     12001        20457
39m4sx9k63ba2   select /*+ index(idl_ub2$ i_id          42      8001         4347
```

You have a great deal of flexibility in how you use the SELECT_WORKLOAD_REPOSITORY function (see Table 9-3 for descriptions of parameters). A few examples will help illustrate this. Let's say that you want to retrieve SQL from the AWR that was not parsed by the SYS user. Here is the SQL to do that:

```
SELECT sql_id, substr(sql_text,1,30) sql_text
,disk_reads, cpu_time, elapsed_time, parsing_schema_name
FROM table(
DBMS_SQLTUNE.SELECT_WORKLOAD_REPOSITORY(8200,8201,
'parsing_schema_name <> ''SYS''',
NULL, NULL,NULL,NULL, 1, NULL, 'ALL'));
```

Table 9-3. *Parameter Descriptions of the SELECT_WORKLOAD_REPOSITORY Function*

Parameter	Description
BEGIN_SNAP	Non-inclusive beginning snapshot ID.
END_SNAP	Inclusive ending snapshot ID.
BASELINE_NAME	Name of AWR baseline.
BASIC_FILTER	SQL predicate to filter SQL statements from workload; if not set, then only SELECT, INSERT, UPDATE, DELETE, MERGE, and CREATE TABLE statements are captured.
OBJECT_FILTER	Not currently used.
RANKING_MEASURE(n)	Order by clause on selected SQL statement(s), such as elapsed_time, cpu_time, buffer_gets, disk_reads, and so on. N can be 1, 2, or 3.
RESULT_PERCENTAGE	Filter for choosing top N% for ranking measure.
RESULT_LIMIT	Limit of the number of SQL statements returned in the result set.
ATTRIBUTE_LIST	List of SQL statement attributes (TYPICAL, BASIC, ALL, and so on).
RECURSIVE_SQL	Include/exclude recursive SQL (HAS_RECURSIVE_SQL or NO_RECURSIVE_SQL).

The following example retrieves the top 10 queries ranked by buffer gets for non-SYS users:

```
SELECT
 sql_id
,substr(sql_text,1,30) sql_text
,disk_reads
,cpu_time
,elapsed_time
,buffer_gets
,parsing_schema_name
FROM table(
DBMS_SQLTUNE.SELECT_WORKLOAD_REPOSITORY(
 begin_snap => 21730
,end_snap => 22900
,basic_filter => 'parsing_schema_name <> ''SYS'''
,ranking_measure1 => 'buffer_gets'
,result_limit => 10
));
```

In the prior queries, notice that the parameter is SYS in single quotes. In other words, the parameter is parsed as 'SYS' and not SYS.

Notice from the prior queries in this section that there are several ranking measures of resources consumed by SQL statements, such as CPU time, buffer gets, and so on. The resource-ranking measures and units of measurement are detailed in the following list:

- cpu_time: Number of seconds

- elapsed_time: Number of seconds

- disk_reads: Number of reads from disk

- buffer_gets: Number of reads from memory

- rows_processed: Average number of rows

- optimizer_cost: Calculated optimizer cost

- executions: Total execution count of SQL statement

These values allow you to retrieve SQL by the criteria that you're concerned with the most. They are valid for filtering SQL in the AWR and memory.

Viewing Resource-Intensive SQL in Memory

Similar to querying the AWR, you can also view the current high-resource usage SQL in memory. The DBMS_SQLTUNE.SELECT_CURSOR_CACHE function is used to view current high-resource-consuming SQL statements in memory. This query selects SQL statements in memory that have required more than a million disk reads:

```
SELECT
 sql_id
,substr(sql_text,1,30) sql_text
,disk_reads
,cpu_time
,elapsed_time
FROM table(DBMS_SQLTUNE.SELECT_CURSOR_CACHE('disk_reads > 1000000'))
ORDER BY sql_id;
```

Here is some sample output:

```
SQL_ID          SQL_TEXT                        DISK_READS   CPU_TIME  ELAPSED_TIME
-------------   ------------------------------  ----------  ---------- ------------
39m4sx9k63ba2 select /*+ index(idl_ub2$ i_id         1936     184012       1984907
6mcpb06rctk0x call dbms_space.auto_space_adv          1011  153029563    181196597
8jpxkhmbxsun1 /* SQL Analyze(1) */ select /*          1513     348020        635356
```

You have a great deal of flexibility in how you use this function (see Table 9-4 for a description of the SELECT_CURSOR_CACHE function parameters). Here's an example that selects SQL in memory, but excludes statements parsed by the SYS user and also returns statements with a total elapsed time greater than 100,000 seconds:

```
SELECT sql_id, substr(sql_text,1,30) sql_text
,disk_reads, cpu_time, elapsed_time
FROM table(DBMS_SQLTUNE.SELECT_CURSOR_CACHE('parsing_schema_name <> ''SYS''
                                  AND elapsed_time > 100000'))
ORDER BY sql_id;
```

Table 9-4. *Parameter Descriptions of the SELECT_CURSOR_CACHE Function*

Parameter	Description
BASIC_FILTER	SQL predicate to filter SQL in the cursor cache.
OBJECT_FILTER	Currently not used.
RANKING_MEASURE(n)	ORDER BY clause for the SQL returned.
RESULT_PERCENTAGE	Filter for the top N% queries for the ranking measure provided; invalid if more than one ranking measure provided.
RESULT_LIMIT	Top number of SQL statements filter.
ATTRIBUTE_LIST	List of SQL attributes to return in result set.
RECURSIVE_SQL	Include recursive SQL.

In the prior query, the SYS keyword is enclosed by single quotes (in other words, those aren't double quotes around SYS). Here is some sample output:

```
SQL_ID          SQL_TEXT                        DISK_READS   CPU_TIME  ELAPSED_TIME
-------------   ------------------------------  ----------  ---------- ------------
aw3h2x2dxynd6 select client_name, status fro          14    5392338       5465307
d9gtffrh94mch select * from p, c where p.p =           0    7304465      10201708
```

This next example selects the top 10 queries in memory in terms of CPU time for non-SYS users:

```
SELECT
 sql_id
,substr(sql_text,1,30) sql_text
,disk_reads
,cpu_time
,elapsed_time
```

```
,buffer_gets
,parsing_schema_name
FROM table(
DBMS_SQLTUNE.SELECT_CURSOR_CACHE(
 basic_filter => 'parsing_schema_name <> ''SYS'''
,ranking_measure1 => 'cpu_time'
,result_limit => 10
));
```

Once you have identified a SQL_ID for a resource-intensive SQL statement, you can view all of its execution details via this query:

```
SELECT * FROM table(DBMS_SQLTUNE.SELECT_CURSOR_CACHE('sql_id = ''d9gtffrh94mch'''));
```

Notice in the priory query that the parameter is d9gtffrh94mch in single quotes. In other words, the parameter is parsed as 'd9gtffrh94mch' and not d9gtffrh94mch.

Populating SQL Tuning Set from High-Resource SQL in AWR

As shown previously in this chapter, high-resource SQL statement information is stored in the AWR. You can use this as input when creating a SQL tuning set. Here are the steps:

1. Create a SQL tuning set object.

2. Determine begin and end AWR snapshot IDs.

3. Populate the SQL tuning set with high-resource SQL found in AWR.

These steps are detailed in the following subsections. Ensure that the user who runs these examples has the ADMINISTER SQL TUNING SET privilege granted, for instance:

```
grant administer sql tuning set to <user>;
```

Step 1: Create a SQL Tuning Set Object

This next bit of code creates a tuning set object named MY_TUNING_SET:

```
BEGIN
  dbms_sqltune.create_sqlset(
    sqlset_name => 'MY_TUNING_SET'
   ,description => 'STS from AWR');
END;
/
```

Step 2: Determine Begin and End AWR Snapshot IDs

If you're unsure of the available snapshots in your database, you can run an AWR report or select the SNAP_ID from DBA_HIST_SNAPSHOTS.

```
select snap_id, begin_interval_time
from dba_hist_snapshot order by 1;
```

Step 3: Populate the SQL Tuning Set with High-Resource SQL Found in AWR

Now the SQL tuning set is populated with the top 15 SQL statements ordered by disk reads. The begin and end AWR snapshot IDs are 29800 and 29802, respectively.

```
DECLARE
  base_cur dbms_sqltune.sqlset_cursor;
BEGIN
  OPEN base_cur FOR
    SELECT value(x)
    FROM table(dbms_sqltune.select_workload_repository(
      26800,26900, null, null,'disk_reads',
      null, null, null, 15)) x;
  --
  dbms_sqltune.load_sqlset(
    sqlset_name => 'MY_TUNING_SET',
    populate_cursor => base_cur);
END;
/
```

This code populates the top 15 SQL statements contained in the AWR ordered by disk reads. The DBMS_SQLTUNE.SELECT_WORKLOAD_REPOSITORY function is used to populate a PL/SQL cursor with AWR information based on a ranking criterion. Next, the DBMS_SQLTUNE.LOAD_SQLSET procedure is used to populate the SQL tuning set using the cursor as input.

The DBMS_SQLTUNE.SELECT_WORKLOAD_REPOSITORY function can be used in a variety of ways to populate a SQL tuning set using queries in the AWR. You can instruct it to load SQL statements by criteria such as disk reads, elapsed time, CPU time, buffer gets, and so on. (See Table 9-3 for descriptions for parameters of this function.)

Populating a SQL Tuning Set from High-Resource SQL in Memory

If you want to analyze a group of SQL statements currently in memory, use the DBMS_SQLTUNE.SELECT_CURSOR_CACHE function. The following example creates a tuning set named HIGH_DISK_READS and populates it with high-resource-consuming statements not belonging to the SYS schema and having more than one million disk reads:

```
-- Create the tuning set
EXEC DBMS_SQLTUNE.CREATE_SQLSET('HIGH_DISK_READS');
-- populate the tuning set from the cursor cache
DECLARE
  cur DBMS_SQLTUNE.SQLSET_CURSOR;
BEGIN
  OPEN cur FOR
  SELECT VALUE(x)
  FROM table(
  DBMS_SQLTUNE.SELECT_CURSOR_CACHE(
  'parsing_schema_name <> ''SYS'' AND disk_reads > 1000000',
  NULL, NULL, NULL, NULL, 1, NULL,'ALL')) x;
  --
  DBMS_SQLTUNE.LOAD_SQLSET(sqlset_name => 'HIGH_DISK_READS',
    populate_cursor => cur);
END;
/
```

In the prior code, notice that the SYS user is bookended by sets of two single quotes (not double quotes). The SELECT_CURSOR_CACHE function loads the SQL statements into a PL/SQL cursor, and the LOAD_SQLSET procedure populates the SQL tuning set with the SQL statements.

The DBMS_SQLTUNE.SELECT_CURSOR_CACHE function (see Table 9-4 for function parameter descriptions) allows you to extract from memory SQL statements and associated statistics into a SQL tuning set. The procedure allows you to filter SQL statements by various resource-consuming criteria, such as elapsed_time, cpu_time, buffer_gets, disk_reads, and so on. This allows you a great deal of flexibility with how to filter and populate the SQL tuning set.

Populating SQL Tuning Set with All SQL in Memory

If your requirement is to perform a tuning analysis on all SQL statements currently in memory, use the DBMS_SQLTUNE.CAPTURE_CURSOR_CACHE_SQLSET procedure. This example creates a SQL tuning set named PROD_WORKLOAD and then populates by sampling memory for 3,600 seconds (waiting 20 seconds between each polling event):

```
BEGIN
  -- Create the tuning set
  DBMS_SQLTUNE.CREATE_SQLSET(
    sqlset_name => 'PROD_WORKLOAD'
   ,description => 'Prod workload sample');
  --
  DBMS_SQLTUNE.CAPTURE_CURSOR_CACHE_SQLSET(
    sqlset_name     => 'PROD_WORKLOAD'
   ,time_limit      => 3600
   ,repeat_interval => 20);
END;
/
```

The DBMS_SQLTUNE.CAPTURE_CURSOR_CACHE_SQLSET procedure allows you to poll for queries and memory and to use any queries found to populate a SQL tuning set. This is a powerful technique that you can use when it's required to capture a sample set of all executing SQL statements.

You have a great deal of flexibility on instructing the DBMS_SQLTUNE.CAPTURE_CURSOR_CACHE_SQLSET to capture SQL statements in memory (see Table 9-5 for details on all parameters). For example, you can instruct the procedure to capture a cumulative set of statistics for each SQL statement by specifying a CAPTURE_MODE of DBMS_SQLTUNE.MODE_ACCUMULATE_STATS, like so:

```
BEGIN
  DBMS_SQLTUNE.CAPTURE_CURSOR_CACHE_SQLSET(
    sqlset_name     => 'PROD_WORKLOAD'
   ,time_limit      => 60
   ,repeat_interval => 10
   ,capture_mode    => DBMS_SQLTUNE.MODE_ACCUMULATE_STATS);
END;
/
```

Table 9-5. *CAPTURE_CURSOR_CACHE_SQLSET Parameter Descriptions*

Parameter	Description	Default Value
SQLSET_NAME	SQL tuning set name.	none
TIME_LIMIT	Total time in seconds to spend sampling.	1800
REPEAT_INTERVAL	While sampling, the amount of time to pause in seconds before polling memory again.	300
CAPTURE_OPTION	Either INSERT, UPDATE, or MERGE statements when new statements are detected.	MERGE
CAPTURE_MODE	When capture option is UPDATE or MERGE, either replace statistics or accumulate statistics. Possible values are MODE_REPLACE_OLD_STATS or MODE_ACCUMULATE_STATS.	MODE_REPLACE_OLD_STATS
BASIC_FILTER	Filter type of statements captured.	NULL
SQLSET_OWNER	SQL tuning set owner. NULL indicates the current user.	NULL
RECURSIVE_SQL	Include (or not) recursive SQL. Possible values are HAS_RECURSIVE_SQL, NO_RECURSIVE_SQL.	HAS_RECURSIVE_SQL

This is more resource-intensive than the default settings, but it produces more accurate statistics for each SQL statement.

Displaying the Contents of a SQL Tuning Set

Once you've created a SQL tuning set, you may want to manually view its contents. For example, you might want to know specifically which queries are in the set or you might want to verify various metrics associated with the queries. There are several methods for viewing SQL tuning set contents.

- Query DBA_SQLSET* data dictionary views (see Table 9-6 for a description of the applicable views).
- Query the DBMS_SQLTUNE.SELECT_SQLSET function.
- Use Enterprise Manager.

Table 9-6. *Views Containing SQL Tuning Set Information*

View Name	Description
DBA_SQLSET	Displays information regarding SQL tuning sets.
DBA_SQLSET_BINDS	Displays bind variable information associated with SQL tuning sets.
DBA_SQLSET_PLANS	Shows execution plan information for queries in a SQL tuning set.
DBA_SQLSET_STATEMENTS	Contains SQL text and associated statistics.
DBA_SQLSET_REFERENCES	Shows whether a SQL tuning set is active.

You can determine the name and number of SQL statements for SQL tuning sets in your database via this query:

```
SELECT name, created, statement_count FROM dba_sqlset;
```

Here is some sample output:

```
NAME                                         CREATED    STATEMENT_COUNT
-------------------------------------------- ---------- ----------------
MY_TUNING_SET                                13-FEB-16                15
HIGH_DISK_READS                              13-FEB-16                 0
PROD_WORKLOAD                                13-FEB-16               152
```

Recall that a SQL tuning set consists of one or more SQL statements and the corresponding execution statistics. You can use the following query to display the SQL text and associated statistical information for each query within the SQL tuning set:

```
SELECT sqlset_name, elapsed_time, cpu_time, buffer_gets, disk_reads, sql_text
FROM dba_sqlset_statements;
```

You can also use the DBMS_SQLTUNE.SELECT_SQLSET function to retrieve information about SQL tuning sets, like so:

```
SELECT sql_id, elapsed_time, cpu_time, buffer_gets, disk_reads, sql_text
FROM TABLE(DBMS_SQLTUNE.SELECT_SQLSET('PROD_WORKLOAD'));
```

Whether you use the DBMS_SQLTUNE.SELECT_SQLSET function or directly query the data dictionary views depends entirely on your personal preference or business requirement.

You can also manage SQL tuning sets from within Enterprise Manager. From the main page, navigate to Performance ➤ SQL ➤ SQL Tuning Sets. You should see a page similar to the one shown in Figure 9-3.

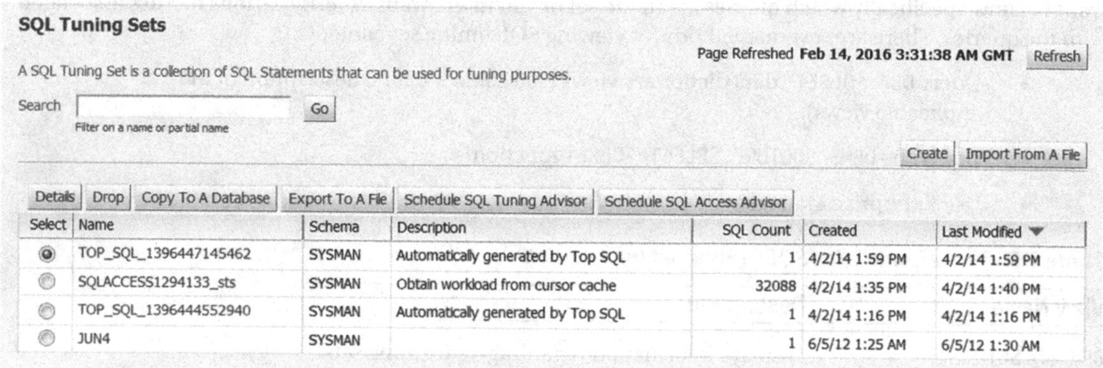

Figure 9-3. Managing SQL tuning sets

From this screen, you can create and manage SQL tuning sets. Clicking the SQL tuning set name displays all of the SQL within the tuning set and associated metrics.

Selectively Deleting Statements from a SQL Tuning Set

Once you've established a SQL tuning set, you may want to prune statements out of it. For example, suppose you want to prune from an STS any SQL statements that don't meet a performance measure, such as queries that have less than two million disk reads. First, view the existing SQL information associated with an STS, like so:

```
select sqlset_name, disk_reads, cpu_time, elapsed_time, buffer_gets
from dba_sqlset_statements;
```

Here is some sample output:

SQLSET_NAME	DISK_READS	CPU_TIME	ELAPSED_TIME	BUFFER_GETS
PROD_WORKLOAD	2	0	14033	15
PROD_WORKLOAD	0	4000	2102	10
PROD_WORKLOAD	0	8001	1832	10
PROD_WORKLOAD	2	0	6543	53
PROD_WORKLOAD	1984	184012	2156947	8893

Now use the DBMS_SQLTUNE.DELETE_SQLSET procedure to remove SQL statements from the STS based on the specified criterion. This example removes SQL statements that have less than 200 disk reads from the SQL tuning:

```
BEGIN
  DBMS_SQLTUNE.DELETE_SQLSET(
    sqlset_name  => 'PROD_WORKLOAD'
    ,basic_filter => 'disk_reads < 200');
END;
/
```

Because the metrics/statistics are part of the STS, you can remove SQL statements from a SQL tuning set based on characteristics of the associated metrics/statistics. You can use the DBMS_SQLTUNE.DELETE_SQLSET procedure to remove statements from the STS based on statistics such as elapsed_time, cpu_time, buffer_gets, disk_reads, and so on.

If you want to delete all SQL statements from a SQL tuning set, don't specify a filter.

```
exec  DBMS_SQLTUNE.DELETE_SQLSET(sqlset_name  => 'PROD_WORKLOAD');
```

■ **Tip**   You can also use Enterprise Manager to delete SQL statements. Navigate to the Performance tab, and then click SQL Tuning Sets. You should see a screen similar to Figure 9-3. Click the SQL tuning set of interest and selectively choose the SQL statements that you want to remove.

Adding Statements to an Existing SQL Tuning Set

You can add SQL statements to an existing SQL tuning set. To do this, use the MERGE option of the LOAD_
SQLSET procedure. The MERGE option instructs Oracle to insert any new SQL statements that are found, and if
a SQL statement already exists in the tuning set, to update the execution statistics. Here's an example:

```
DECLARE
  cur dbms_sqltune.sqlset_cursor;
BEGIN
  OPEN cur FOR
    SELECT value(x)
    FROM table(dbms_sqltune.select_workload_repository(
      26800,26900, null, null,'disk_reads',
      null, null, null, 15)) x;
  --
  dbms_sqltune.load_sqlset(
    sqlset_name => 'MY_TUNING_SET',
    populate_cursor => cur,
    load_option => 'MERGE');
END;
/
```

This technique allows you to add SQL statements to an existing SQL tuning set without having to drop
and re-create it.

Dropping a SQL Tuning Set

If you need to drop a SQL tuning set object, use the DBMS_SQLTUNE.DROP_SQLSET procedure to drop a tuning
set. The following example drops a tuning set named MY_TUNING_SET:

```
EXEC  DBMS_SQLTUNE.DROP_SQLSET(sqlset_name => 'PROD_WORKLOAD');
```

You can confirm the tuning set has been dropped by querying the DBA_SQLSET view.

Running the SQL Tuning Advisor

Figure 9-4 shows the SQL Tuning Advisor architecture. This tool takes as input any of the following:

- Single SQL statement

- SQL_ID from a statement in memory or the AWR

- Set of SQL statements contained in a SQL tuning set

This tool provides useful advice regarding the creation of indexes, restructuring the SQL statement,
stale statistics, and so on. You can manually execute the SQL Tuning Advisor from the DBMS_SQLTUNE PL/SQL
package, SQL Developer, or Enterprise Manager.

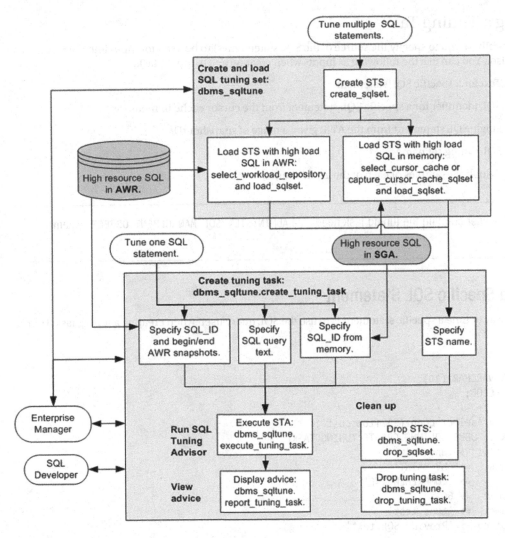

Figure 9-4. *The SQL Tuning Advisor architecture*

Let's focus first on running the SQL Tuning Advisor through the DBMS_SQLTUNE PL/SQL package. To execute the SQL Tuning Advisor from PL/SQL, follow these steps:

1. Create a tuning task.

2. Execute DBMS_SQLTUNE and view the advice.

These steps are explained in the following subsections.

Creating a Tuning Task

A tuning task allows you to specify the source of the SQL statement(s) to be used for input into the SQL Tuning Advisor. You can use the following as inputs when creating a SQL tuning task:

- Text for a specific SQL statement
- SQL identifier for a specific SQL statement from the cursor cache in memory
- Single SQL statement from the AWR given a range of snapshot IDs
- SQL tuning set name

Next, let's look at examples of each of these techniques.

■ **Note**   The user creating the tuning task needs the ADMINISTER SQL MANAGEMENT OBJECT system privilege.

Text for a Specific SQL Statement

One simple way to tune a specific statement is to use the SQL query itself when creating a tuning task. Here's an example:

```
DECLARE
  tune_task VARCHAR2(30);
  tune_sql  CLOB;
BEGIN
  tune_sql := 'select count(*) from cust';
  tune_task := DBMS_SQLTUNE.CREATE_TUNING_TASK(
    sql_text     => tune_sql
   ,user_name    => 'MV_MAINT'
   ,scope        => 'COMPREHENSIVE'
   ,time_limit   => 60
   ,task_name    => 'tune_test'
   ,description => 'Provide SQL text'
);
END;
/
```

SQL_ID for a Specific SQL Statement from the Cursor Cache

You can also use the SQL_ID of a statement in memory to identify the SQL statement that you wanted to tune. If you don't know which SQL_ID is associated with the query that you want to tune, then first query the V$SQL view, as follows:

```
SELECT sql_id, sql_text
FROM v$sql
where sql_text like '%&&mytext%';
```

Once you have the SQL_ID, you can provide it as input to DBMS_SQLTUNE.CREATE_TUNING_TASK, like so:

```
DECLARE
  tune_task VARCHAR2(30);
  tune_sql  CLOB;
BEGIN
  tune_task := DBMS_SQLTUNE.CREATE_TUNING_TASK(
    sql_id      => 'b62q7nc33gzwx'
   ,task_name   => 'tune_test2'
   ,description => 'Provide SQL ID'
);
END;
/
```

Single SQL Statement from the AWR Given a Range of Snapshot IDs

You can also use the SQL_ID of a statement stored in the AWR. If you're not sure which SQL_ID (and associated query) to use, run this query:

```
select sql_id, sql_text from dba_hist_sqltext;
```

If you're unaware of the available snapshot IDs, run this query:

```
select snap_id from dba_hist_snapshot order by 1;
```

Here's an example of creating a SQL tuning task by providing a SQL_ID and a range of AWR snapshot IDs:

```
DECLARE
  tune_task VARCHAR2(30);
  tune_sql  CLOB;

BEGIN
  tune_task := DBMS_SQLTUNE.CREATE_TUNING_TASK(
    sql_id      => '1tbu2jp7kv0pm'
   ,begin_snap  => 21690
   ,end_snap    => 21864
   ,task_name   => 'tune_test3'
);
END;
/
```

■ **Tip** By default, the AWR contains only high-resource-consuming queries. You can modify this behavior and ensure that a specific SQL statement is included in every snapshot (regardless of its resource consumption) by adding it to the AWR via the following code:

```
SQL> exec dbms_workload_repository.add_colored_sql('98u3gf0xzq03f');
```

SQL Tuning Set Name

If you have the requirement of running the SQL Tuning Advisor against multiple SQL queries, then a SQL tuning set is required. To create a tuning task using a SQL tuning set as input, do so as follows:

```
variable mytt varchar2(30);
exec :mytt := DBMS_SQLTUNE.CREATE_TUNING_TASK(sqlset_name => 'PROD_WORKLOAD');
print :mytt
```

Execute DBMS_SQLTUNE and View the Advice

After you've created a tuning task, you can generate and view advice by executing the EXECUTE_TUNING_TASK procedure and provide to it the name of your tuning task, like so:

```
exec dbms_sqltune.execute_tuning_task(task_name => 'tune_test');
```

Next, a report is generated that displays the tuning advice.

```
set long 10000 longchunksize 10000 linesize 132 pagesize 200
select dbms_sqltune.report_tuning_task('tune_test') from dual;
```

Here is a small snippet of the output:

```
GENERAL INFORMATION SECTION
-------------------------------------------------------------------------------
Tuning Task Name    : tune_test
Tuning Task Owner   : MV_MAINT
Workload Type       : Single SQL Statement
Scope               : COMPREHENSIVE
Time Limit(seconds): 60
Completion Status   : COMPLETED
```

Viewing and Dropping Tuning Tasks

The prior techniques provide a variety of ways to identify SQL statements to be analyzed by the SQL Tuning Advisor. Once you've created a tuning task, you can view its details via this query:

```
select owner, task_name, advisor_name, created
from dba_advisor_tasks
order by created;
```

You may want to drop a tuning task because you're re-running a test and want to use the same name, and/or you want to remove a task that isn't required any longer. If you need to drop the tuning task, you can do so as follows:

```
exec dbms_sqltune.drop_tuning_task(task_name => '&&task_name');
```

Running SQL Tuning Advisor from SQL Developer

If you have access to SQL Developer, it's very easy to run the SQL Tuning Advisor for a query. Follow these simple steps:

1. Open a SQL worksheet.

2. Enter a query.

3. Click the button associated with the SQL Tuning Advisor.

You will be presented with any findings and recommendations. If you have access to SQL Developer (it's a free download), this is the easiest way to run the SQL Tuning Advisor.

■ **Note** Before running SQL Tuning Advisor from SQL Developer, ensure that the user that you're connected to has the ADVISOR system privilege granted.

Running SQL Tuning Advisor from Enterprise Manager

You can also run the advisor from within Enterprise Manager. Log into Enterprise Manager and follow these steps:

1. Click the Performance tab and then Advisors Home.

2. Under the Advisors section, click the SQL Advisors link.

3. Click the SQL Tuning Advisor link.

You should be presented with a page similar to the one shown in Figure 9-5.

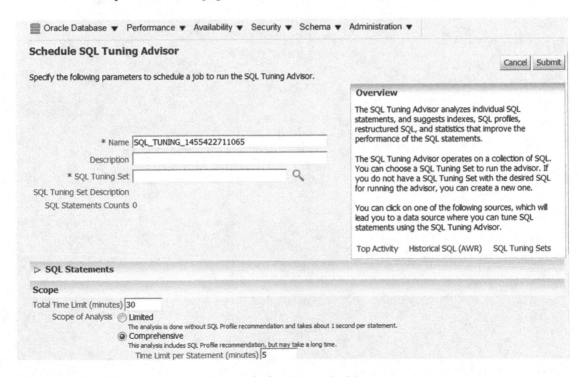

Figure 9-5. Scheduling SQL Tuning Advisor jobs from Enterprise Manager

From here, you can run a SQL Tuning Advisor tuning task on the top SQL statements or SQL in the AWR, or provide a SQL tuning set as input.

Summary

The SQL Tuning Advisor is a flexible tool that provides performance-tuning advice on indexes, SQL profiles, statistics, restructuring queries, and so on. Because this tool generates advice on indexes, we felt that it was appropriate to cover the use of the SQL Tuning Advisor in this book.

One key input to the SQL Tuning Advisor is through SQL tuning sets. Therefore, we also covered the management of SQL tuning sets in this chapter. Briefly, a SQL tuning set is a collection of one or more SQL statements and the associated execution metrics. You can populate a SQL tuning set either from high-resource SQL in the AWR or in memory.

The SQL Tuning Advisor can be invoked from the DBMS_SQLTUNE PL/SQL package, SQL Developer, or Enterprise Manager. Which tool you use depends on what you have installed in your environment and your comfort level with a manual approach vs. a graphical interface.

CHAPTER 10

■ ■ ■

In-Memory Column Store

When issuing a query to retrieve data from the database, the Oracle query optimizer quickly determines the most efficient way to return the requested information. The "path" to the data consists of accessing the table, or using an index, or a combination of tables and indexes. In this mode, the path entails Oracle reading table blocks from disk into memory in order to access the data. Within the blocks, rows of table data are stored. This method is tried and true and works well.

That said, Oracle is constantly improving its product. To this end, recent versions of Oracle have added new access paths to the data. One such access path to the data is the *in-memory (IM) column store* feature. Instead of storing information in row structures, Oracle organizes the data into column units in memory. This is an optional access path that is easily enabled and requires no changes to existing application code. To better understand the advantages of the IM column store access path, it's useful to first review the traditional row store format.

Traditional Row Store Format

Recall from earlier chapters that table data is stored in rows in blocks. Each block contains multiple rows of table data and a row is comprised of the columns in a table. Index blocks contain table column values and ROWIDs, which help quickly locate rows of data. When a query is issued, Oracle uses an index (if available) to identify which table blocks and rows contain the required data. Oracle reads into memory the table blocks required to satisfy the results of a query. Because the data in blocks is stored in rows, it is known as the *row store* format. To help visualize the row store format, consider a table created as follows:

```
create table sales
(cust_id    number,
 emp_id     number,
 store_id   number,
 amt        number,
 region     varchar2(10),
 sales_dtt  date);
```

With the row store format in mind, consider what happens when you run the following query:

```
select count(cust_id) from sales where amt > 3000;
```

Oracle reads into memory the blocks required to satisfy the results of this query. Each block that is identified is scanned for rows that contain the desired data. In this example, each row is examined to determine if the AMT column contains a value greater than 3,000. Since the AMT column isn't the first column in the table, Oracle uses an offset to determine where in the row the AMT column resides. Figure 10-1 displays a block stored in memory in the traditional row store format.

© Darl Kuhn, Sam R. Alapati and Bill Padfield 2016
D. Kuhn et al., *Expert Oracle Indexing and Access Paths*, DOI 10.1007/978-1-4842-1984-3_10

block of table data in memory

cust_id	emp_id	store_id	amt	region	sales_dtt
402	142	2	3488	E	12-MAY-11
185	158	6	4648	S	04-JUL-13
919	32	7	4433	N	01-JAN-12
202	36	7	959	E	22-NOV-14

many more rows here...

...	...	...	...	...	

Figure 10-1. *Row store format of a block of table data read into memory*

In this manner, even if you only need to access one column of data, Oracle still reads the entire blocks containing entire rows into memory. If the column of interest isn't the first column, Oracle must navigate to the column within the row to find the data. With that in mind, let's next discuss the new IM column store format.

Columnar Format

Starting with Oracle 12c, the IM column store architecture allows an alternate format for storing table data in memory. Instead of storing data in a row format, columns of data are stored. This new format is known as the *columnar format*.

■ **Note**   The IM column store feature is available with the Enterprise Edition of Oracle (starting with version 12.1.0.2). A license for the database in-memory option is required.

The IM column store is an optional static memory area that resides in the system global area (SGA). This memory area stores data in a columnar format. The IM column store can be configured to store all columns within a table or individual table columns. The IM column store can also be used with materialized views and table partitions. The IM column store does not replace the buffer cache, but rather it works seamlessly with the buffer cache. When enabled for a table, the optimizer determines if the IM column store is the most efficient way (lower cost) to retrieve the data.

To help visualize how the IM column store improves query efficiency, examine Figure 10-2.

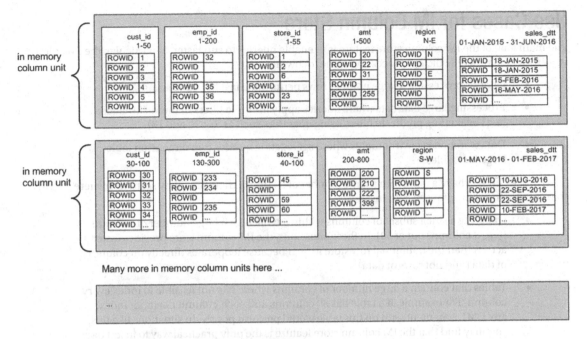

Figure 10-2. Data stored in memory in the columnar format

The columnar data is stored in in-memory compression units (IMCUs). Each IMCU contains a minimum and maximum value of column data stored within the unit. The big advantage of this format is that Oracle can access column data directly, without having the overhead of examining an entire row to retrieve the data. To that point, consider this query again:

```
select count(cust_id) from sales where amt > 3000;
```

In this situation, Oracle can directly examine the AMT column of data within the IMCU unit. The header of each column contains a minimum and maximum value for values within the IMCU. In this way, Oracle determines very quickly if a particular IMCU contains the column data of interest. Based on the minimum and maximum values stored in the header, Oracle prunes out and doesn't scan IMCUs that don't contain relevant data.

Furthermore, the data within the IMCU is compressed. At a high level, this means that it doesn't have to store each individual ROWID and column value. If there are duplicate column values, then multiple ROWIDs can be associated with one column value. There's no need to redundantly store column values. This saves on memory space and allows efficient processing of data.

___

■ **Note** Oracle uses SIMD (single instruction, multiple data) vector processing to rapidly scan IM column store data. This further adds to the efficiency of query processing.

___

Use Cases for IM Column Store

The main goal of the IM column store feature is to enable queries to run faster. In particular, the IM column store format allows the efficient processing of the following:

- Queries processing a large number rows performing fast full table scans

- Processing large data sets where queries apply multiple filters in the WHERE clause (e.g., evaluating predicate filters using operators such as =, <, >, and IN)

- Data warehouse environments where aggregating queries join dimension tables to large fact tables

Also, when you have a table with a large number of columns, there are many scenarios where the IM column format is advantageous; for instance:

- Querying a small subset of columns within a table with a large number of columns (e.g., 3 columns out of 50). In these situations, the IM column store provides faster access than the traditional row store format because it operates directly on columns of data (and not rows of data).

- Tables that contain a large number of columns where it is not feasible to index every column. For example, if a table has 50 columns and each column needs an index, any DML statements run on this table would perform poorly. In situations like this, you may find that the IM column store feature is the only practical way to insert data and efficiently query it.

The IM column store can be enabled without adversely impacting existing applications. Existing code continues to run as it always has. After the feature is turned on in the database, tables and columns can selectively be enabled to take advantage of the IM column store memory area. The Oracle query optimizer automatically takes advantage of the columnar format. The IM column store doesn't replace indexes in all situations; instead, it gives you an alternate access path that you can enable that is beneficial in many of the previously described scenarios.

■ **Tip** Applications taking advantage of the IM column store require fewer indexes, materialized views, and OLAP (online analytical processing) cubes. Fewer objects also mean that less disk space is required. On the other hand, applications using the IM column store require more SGA memory; therefore, the SGA needs to be sized accordingly.

Enabling a Database for the IM Column Store

The configuration of the IM column store is fairly simple. It is enabled by setting the INMEMORY_SIZE initialization parameter and stopping and starting the database instance. If you're using an SPFILE, you can do so as follows:

```
alter system set inmemory_size=300m scope=spfile;
```

Ensure that you set the INMEMORY_SIZE parameter to 100MB or larger. If you attempt to set the in-memory area to less than 100MB, you'll receive an error when starting your database:

```
ORA-64353: in-memory area size cannot be less than 100MB
```

Once the INMEMORY_SIZE is set, then stop and start the instance:

```
shutdown immediate;
startup;
```

■ **Note**   If you're not using an SPFILE, then manually edit the init.ora file with an OS text editor, and stop and restart your database instance.

When starting the instance, you should now see In-Memory Area in the output, which indicates that this feature is now enabled:

```
Total System Global Area 1073741824 bytes
Fixed Size                  2932632 bytes
Variable Size             448790632 bytes
Database Buffers          301989888 bytes
Redo Buffers                5455872 bytes
In-Memory Area            314572800 bytes
```

You can also verify the size of in-memory area with SHOW PARAMETER, as follows:

```
show parameter inmemory;
```

```
NAME                                     TYPE         VALUE
---------------------------------------- ------------ --------
inmemory_clause_default                  string
inmemory_force                           string       DEFAULT
inmemory_max_populate_servers            integer      2
inmemory_query                           string       ENABLE
inmemory_size                            big integer  300M
inmemory_trickle_repopulate_servers_     integer      1
percent
optimizer_inmemory_aware                 boolean      TRUE
```

Now that the in-memory area has been allocated in the SGA, you can now enable tables to take advantage of the in-memory column store feature.

The IM column store is an optional area within the system global area (SGA). It doesn't replace the buffer cache. It's a static memory area: once you enable it, it doesn't grow or shrink in size. Therefore, when setting the overall size of the SGA with MEMORY_TARGET or SGA_TARGET, these parameters must be sized to allow all memory components in SGA, plus the in-memory area. Figure 10-3 shows the SGA with the IM column store area enabled.

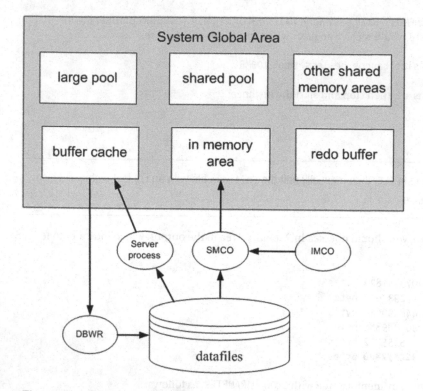

Figure 10-3. *IM column store area and associated background processes*

Two Oracle background process help manage the IM column store memory area: IMCO and SMCO. The IMCO (in-memory database) process schedules data to be populated and repopulated in the IM column store. The SMCO (space management coordinator) process populates the IM column store data in memory.

If you need to disable the IM column store, then set INMEMORY_SIZE to 0 and restart the instance:

```
alter system set inmemory_size=0 scope=spfile;
shutdown immediate;
startup;

Total System Global Area 1073741824 bytes
Fixed Size                  2932632 bytes
Variable Size             515899496 bytes
Database Buffers          549453824 bytes
Redo Buffers                5455872 bytes
```

Notice that the in-memory area is not present in the textual information displayed on startup.

Enabling a Table for IM Column Store

Once you've established a value for the INMEMORY_SIZE instance parameter, you can specify which tables and columns you want enabled to use the IM column store feature. Keep in mind that you, the DBA, must decide which columns are appropriate for this feature. If you make good choices, then you'll efficiently use memory and queries will run faster. If you choose poorly, you'll waste memory that could have been used by more appropriate columns.

You can enable the IM column store feature with any of the following objects:

- Table

- Column

- Table partition and subpartitions

- Materialized view

For example, when creating a table, specify the INMEMORY clause, as follows:

```
create table sales
(cust_id    number,
 emp_id     number,
 store_id   number,
 amt        number,
 region     varchar2(10),
 sales_dtt  date)
inmemory;
```

This enables all columns in a table to use the IM column store feature. If you have a table that already exists, you can alter it to enable IM column store, as shown:

```
alter table sales inmemory;
```

■ **Note**   The following cannot be enabled for IM column store: IOTs, hash clusters, out of line columns (LOBs > 4K, nested tables, and varrays).

You can verify at the table level if a table has been enabled for the IM column store—it's ENABLED or DISABLED:

```
select table_name, inmemory
from user_tables
where table_name='SALES';
```

Here is some sample output:

```
TABLE_NAME              INMEMORY
--------------------    --------
SALES                   ENABLED
```

If the table is partitioned, query the partition related views (e.g., USER_TAB_PARTITIONS or USER_TAB_SUBPARTITIONS) to determine which partitions are enabled for the IM column store feature. For example, say that you have a partitioned table created with one partition using the IM column store feature, like so:

```
create table sales
(cust_id    number,
 emp_id     number,
 store_id   number,
 amt        number,
 region     varchar2(10),
```

```
  sales_dtt date)
partition by range (region)
 (partition p1 values less than (50) inmemory,
  partition p2 values less than (maxvalue));
```

The following query displays which partitions are IM column store–enabled:

```
select table_name, partition_name, inmemory from user_tab_partitions;
```

Here is the output for this example:

```
TABLE_NAME            PARTITION_NAME        INMEMORY
-------------------   -------------------   --------
SALES                 P1                    ENABLED
SALES                 P2                    DISABLED
```

You can disable a table from using the IM column store with the NO INMEMORY clause; for instance:

```
alter table sales no inmemory;
```

Excluding Columns

If you determine that a column will not be used for filtering data (e.g., not used in a WHERE clause), then there's no need to have that column loaded into the IM column store memory area. It will potentially waste in-memory space. Therefore, if you want to exclude certain columns from using the IM column store, then you can do so by specifying NO INMEMORY for particular columns. Here's an example:

```
create table sales
(cust_id   number,
 emp_id    number,
 store_id  number,
 amt       number,
 region    varchar2(10),
 sales_dtt date)
inmemory
no inmemory (cust_id);
```

If the table is already created, you can selectively disable columns from the IM column store by specifying a comma-delimited list of columns to exclude, as follows:

```
alter table sales no inmemory(cust_id, store_id);
```

In this manner, you don't consume space in memory with columns that you predict will not benefit from using the IM column store feature.

Enabling New Tables to Automatically Use In-Memory

You may have situations where you're building or testing applications and you want to enable the IM column store by default when new tables are created. There are two methods to enable the IM column store for newly created tables:

- Tablespace default
- Instance default

You can create or alter a tablespace to enable tables for the IM column store. Once enabled at the tablespace level, any new tables created in the tablespace are automatically IM column store–enabled; for instance:

```
alter tablespace users default inmemory;
```

To disable the default feature for a tablespace, specify NO INMEMORY:

```
alter tablespace users default no inmemory;
```

Another technique for automatically enabling default use of the IM column store is to set the INMEMORY_ CLAUSE_DEFAULT initialization parameter. This can be enabled system wide or per session, as follows:

```
alter session set inmemory_clause_default='inmemory';
```

From this point on, all tables created in this session are by default IM column store–enabled. You would not ordinarily want to enable this system wide. The reasoning is that a DBA could be unaware that the feature is enabled and not understand why the IM column store area is filling up unexpectedly.

To disable this at the session level, do as follows:

```
alter session set inmemory_clause_default='no inmemory';
```

In this way, the INMEMORY_CLAUSE_DEFAULT parameter allows you to control the automatic enabling of newly created tables.

Determining if a Query Is Used in the IM Column Store

There are several ways to determine if a query is used in the IM column store in memory:

- Viewing the execution plan
- Displaying session-level statistics
- Querying the data dictionary views
- Observing performance differences

Each of the prior bullets is discussed in the following subsections.

Viewing the Execution Plan

You can tell if a query is using the IM column store feature by looking at the execution plan. To see this in action, let's create a table IM column store–enabled, insert some sample data, and generate statistics:

```
create table sales
(cust_id    number,
 emp_id     number,
 store_id   number,
 amt        number,
 region     varchar2(10),
 sales_dtt date)
inmemory;
```

Now let's insert some sample data:

```
begin
for i in 1..50 loop
insert into sales
select
  trunc(dbms_random.value(1,1000)) cust_id,
  trunc(dbms_random.value(1,200))  emp_id,
  trunc(dbms_random.value(1,10))   store_id,
  trunc(dbms_random.value(1,5000)) amt,
  decode(trunc(dbms_random.value(1,5)),1,'N',2,'E',3,'S',4,'W','X') region,
  sysdate + dbms_random.value(-2000,30) sales_dtt
from dual connect by level <= 500000;
commit;
end loop;
end;
/
```

Now generate statistics for the table:

```
exec dbms_stats.gather_table_stats( user, 'SALES');
```

Next, let's generate an execution plan for a query:

```
explain plan for select count(*) from sales where sales_dtt > sysdate - 10;
select * from table(dbms_xplan.display);
```

The INMEMORY FULL access path in the output indicates that the IM column store is being used to retrieve the result set:

```
---------------------------------------------------------------------------------
| Id  | Operation                   | Name  | Rows  | Bytes | Cost (%CPU)| Time     |
---------------------------------------------------------------------------------
|   0 | SELECT STATEMENT            |       |     1 |     8 |   989  (13)| 00:00:01 |
|   1 |   SORT AGGREGATE            |       |     1 |     8 |            |          |
|*  2 |    TABLE ACCESS INMEMORY FULL| SALES |  137K|  1077K|   989  (13)| 00:00:01 |
---------------------------------------------------------------------------------
```

To view that IM column store is not being used, you can disable the IM column store feature for this session and regenerate the execution plan:

```
alter session set inmemory_query=disable;
explain plan for select count(*) from sales where sales_dtt > sysdate - 10;
select * from table(dbms_xplan.display);
```

Notice that this execution plan shows that the access path doesn't include INMEMORY; instead, it shows the traditional TABLE ACCESS FULL path:

```
-----------------------------------------------------------------------------
| Id  | Operation         | Name  | Rows  | Bytes | Cost (%CPU)| Time     |
-----------------------------------------------------------------------------
|   0 | SELECT STATEMENT  |       |     1 |     8 |  8961   (2)| 00:00:01 |
|   1 |  SORT AGGREGATE   |       |     1 |     8 |            |          |
|*  2 |   TABLE ACCESS FULL| SALES |  137K|  1077K|  8961   (2)| 00:00:01 |
-----------------------------------------------------------------------------
```

■ **Tip**   You can use the INMEMORY and NO_INMEMORY hints to enable and disable the IM column store for a query.

Displaying Session-Level Statistics

Another way to determine IM column store usage is to examine session-level statistics. After running a query against a table with IM column store enabled, the session statistics show various metrics related to the IM store feature; for example:

```
select count(*) from sales where sales_dtt >
 sysdate - 10;
```

Now you can look in V$MYSTAT for various metrics beginning with the IM string:

```
select display_name, value
from v$mystat m,
     v$statname n
where m.statistic# = n.statistic#
and display_name in (
  'IM scan segments minmax eligible',
  'IM scan CUs pruned',
  'IM scan CUs optimized read',
  'IM scan CUs predicates optimized',
  'session logical reads - IM',
  'IM scan rows',
  'IM scan rows valid',
  'IM scan blocks cache',
  'IM scan CUs columns accessed');
```

Here is the output for this example:

```
DISPLAY_NAME                                                         VALUE
------------------------------------------------------------------ ----------
session logical reads - IM                                           30497
IM scan CUs columns accessed                                            17
IM scan rows                                                        7530341
IM scan rows valid                                                  7530341
IM scan blocks cache                                                     0
IM scan CUs predicates optimized                                         0
IM scan CUs optimized read                                               0
IM scan CUs pruned                                                       0
IM scan segments minmax eligible                                        17
```

The prior output clearly shows that the query is generating IM column store session statistics.

■ **Note**   When the IM column store feature is enabled, the IM column store statistics also appear in the AWR reports.

Querying the Data Dictionary

When you first create or alter a table to enable the IM column store feature, the table columns aren't loaded into memory immediately. For example, create a table as follows:

```
create table sales
(cust_id    number,
 emp_id     number,
 store_id   number,
 amt        number,
 region     varchar2(10),
 sales_dtt  date)
inmemory;
```

Before selecting from the table, you can query the V$IM_SEGMENTS data dictionary view and show that the IM column store has not yet been populated:

```
SELECT owner, segment_name, bytes, inmemory_size,
populate_status, inmemory_compression, inmemory_priority
FROM v$im_segments;

no rows selected
```

Next, let's query the table:

```
select count(*) from sales where sales_dtt > sysdate - 10;
```

After you query the table, then the column store object is loaded into memory:

```
SELECT owner, segment_name, bytes, inmemory_size,
populate_status, inmemory_compression, inmemory_priority
FROM v$im_segments;
```

Here is some sample output:

```
OWNER       SEGMENT_       BYTES INMEMORY_SIZE POPULATE_ INMEMORY_COMPRESS INMEMORY
---------- -------- ---------- -------------- --------- ----------------- --------
MV_MAINT    SALES    167772160      84606976 COMPLETED FOR QUERY LOW      NONE
```

Several of the prior columns in the output deserve additional explanation at this point.

- POPULATE_STATUS: The prior output indicates columns related to the SALES table are consuming space in memory. This is shown with the POPULATE_STATUS column with a COMPLETED status. The COMPLETED status indicates the IM column store has been populated in memory. You may see a status of STARTED indicating that the column is in the process of being populated in memory.

- BYTES: This column indicates the physical (on-disk) size of the table segment. In other words, the BYTES column in V$IM_SEGMENTS corresponds to the BYTES column in DBA_SEGMENTS.

- INMEMORY_SIZE: This column displays in bytes the amount of memory consumed in the IM column store memory area. This value allows you to determine what objects are in memory and how much memory is being consumed. This column helps you estimate your memory usage and overall memory requirements.

In addition to viewing objects using the IM column store, you can also view which columns are making use of the IM column store, via the following query:

```
select column_number, column_name
from v$im_col_cu  i,
     dba_objects  o,
     dba_tab_cols c
where i.objd = o.data_object_id
and   o.object_name = c.table_name
and   i.column_number = c.column_id
and   o.object_name = 'SALES';
```

Here is a small snippet of the output:

```
COLUMN_NUMBER COLUMN_NAME
------------- ------------------------------
            4 AMT
            4 AMT
            4 AMT
            5 REGION
            5 REGION
            6 SALES_DTT
```

Observing Performance Differences

You can also determine if a table is using the IM column store by observing differences in performance with the IM column store enabled and then disabled. Let's set SQL timing on and query the SALES table (created and populated earlier in the chapter). For this example, we'll observe the performance of a query that aggregates and applies multiple filters in the WHERE clause. First, let's observe how fast the query runs with IM column store enabled:

```
set timing on;

select sum(amt), min(amt), max(amt), cust_id, trunc(sales_dtt,'MON')
from sales
where amt between 100 and 2000
and cust_id in (1,2,4,21,32,66,93,200,402,643,823,931,993)
and store_id in (1,2,3,5,7,9)
and region in ('N','W','S')
and sales_dtt between sysdate-200 and sysdate-10
group by cust_id,trunc(sales_dtt,'MON')
order by cust_id, trunc(sales_dtt,'MON');
```

Here is the output for this example:

```
91 rows selected.
Elapsed: 00:00:00.19
```

Next, let's disable IM column store for the session:

```
alter session set inmemory_query=disable;
```

After rerunning the query, here are the results:

```
91 rows selected.
Elapsed: 00:00:02.13
```

From the output, you can see that the query ran more than ten times faster with IM column store enabled. Your results will vary depending on the hardware and the number of records. For this example, the table is populated with 50 million records.

Setting a Priority

When you enable a table for IM column store usage, by default the data is populated in the IM column store in memory when you first select from a table. You can modify this behavior via the PRIORITY clause. You may want to specify that some tables be loaded into the IM column store before other less critical tables. The following lists your options:

- NONE: Oracle controls when the data is loaded into the IM column store. This is the default value. In this mode, the columnar data is loaded into memory only after you first select a column from the table.

- LOW: This mode gives table data a higher priority to be loaded into memory than tables specified with NONE, but lower in priority than tables specified with MEDIUM, HIGH, or CRITICAL. Oracle does not wait for you to select from the table before it loads columnar data into memory.

- MEDIUM: Table data is stored into memory before tables specified with LOW or NONE, but after tables with HIGH or CRITCIAL priority. Oracle does not wait for you to select from the table before it loads columnar data into memory.

- HIGH: Table data is populated in the IM column store before data for database objects with NONE, LOW, or MEDIUM priority and after data for database objects with CRITICAL priority. Oracle does not wait for you to select from the table before it loads columnar data into memory.

- CRITICAL: Table data is populated in the IM column store before data for database objects with NONE, LOW, MEDIUM, or HIGH priority. Oracle does not wait for you to select from the table before it loads columnar data into memory.

Here's an example of modifying the priority:

```
alter table sales inmemory priority critical;
```

This way you can ensure that critical table data is populated in the IM column store based on the priority that you set.

Sizing the IM Column Store Memory Area

Now that you're familiar with enabling the IM column store and determining objects using memory and how much space is consumed, it's appropriate to discuss sizing the IM column store area. There are no hard-and-fast rules for sizing this area. The size is a function of how much physical memory is available and how many objects are enabled for the IM column store. Therefore, you'll need to consider these factors when determining an optimal size.

Keep in mind that once the IM column store becomes full, then no additional columnar objects will be read into memory. The IM column store memory is not flushed unless you stop and start your instance. Columnar objects are not swapped in and out; instead, once they're read into the IM column store, they remain in memory consuming space. If you have objects that you absolutely always want populated in the IM column store, then set the priority to a value such as CRITICAL or HIGH.

If you don't have enough memory available to read all tables enabled for the IM column store into the IM column store memory area, then ensure that you still have an indexing strategy in place to allow adequate performance. The optimizer determines whether a table column is available in the IM store and whether it's more efficient to use the IM column store over an index. If a table enabled for IM column store will not fit into memory (because the IM column store memory area is already full), then consider disabling IM column store on the table with NO INMEMORY.

Adjusting Compression

By default, IM column store data is compressed in a way that maximizes query performance. You can modify this behavior via the MEMCOMPRESS clause. The following options are available:

- MEMCOMPRESS FOR QUERY: This is the default, which maximizes query performance. This is the same as MEMCOMPRESS FOR QUERY LOW.

- NO MEMCOMPRESS: This mode instructs Oracle to not compress data.

- MEMCOMPRESS FOR QUERY HIGH: This mode compresses data more than MEMCOMPRESS FOR QUERY LOW, but less than MEMCOMPRESS FOR CAPACITY LOW.

- MEMCOMPRESS FOR DML: This option optimizes compression for DML, which results in a minimal amount of compress.

- MEMCOMPRESS FOR CAPACITY LOW: This setting compresses data more than MEMCOMPRESS FOR QUERY HIGH, buy still results in fast query performance.

- MEMCOMPRESS FOR CAPACITY HIGH: This mode provides the highest compression of data in the IM column store. It mode is used when you need to fit as much data in memory as possible. This mode uses more CPU but results in much higher compression. There's a trade-off between more CPU usage and more data being stored in the IM column store.

Here's an example of specifying compression:

```
alter table sales inmemory memcompress for query high;
```

Utilizing IM Column Store with RAC

A few IM column store features are specific to a RAC (Real Application Clusters) environment, namely:

- Distributing data across RAC instances

- Duplicating data across RAC instances

Recall that RAC environments have multiple instances associated with one physical database. Each RAC instance has its own memory area. Therefore, it's possible for the IM column store to be distributed across multiple RAC instances.

The default behavior is for the IM column store to be automatically distributed across multiple instances in a RAC cluster. You can alter this behavior via the DISTRIBUTE clause. For example, if you have a partitioned table, you can instruct Oracle to distribute partitions (and subpartitions) evenly across RAC instances:

```
alter table sales inmemory distribute by partition;
```

You can also specify BY ROWID RANGE. In this mode, Oracle will hash ranges of ROWIDs and distributes them evenly across multiple RAC instances:

```
alter table sales inmemory distribute by rowid range;
```

You can also modify the behavior of IM column store data for fault tolerance that mirrors copies of tables across multiple RAC instances. The idea is that if one RAC instance is unavailable, Oracle can read from a copy of the IM column store in another available RAC instance. This behavior is modified via the DUPLICATE clause. When you specify DUPLICATE, one copy of the IM column store is mirrored to another RAC instance, which means that you have two IM column stores with the same information:

```
alter table sales inmemory duplicate;
```

You can specify that the IM column be replicated across all RAC instances with the DUPLICATE ALL clause.

Summary

This chapter covered the IM column store feature. It is an optional feature that began in Oracle 12c. It provides an alternate access path to table data. The IM column store is assigned its own area within the SGA and is enabled via the `INMEMORY_SIZE` initialization parameter. This memory area stores data in a columnar fashion. The feature is ideal for queries that scan large amounts of data and aggregate data, and apply multiple filters in the `WHERE` clause.

The main purpose of the IM store is to enable faster query processing. Existing applications can continue to work exactly as they did before enabling the IM column store. Once the IM column store feature is enabled, then you can specify which tables and columns that you want to use this feature. The query optimizer is aware of the tables enabled for IM column store. The optimizer determines if the cost associated with using the IM column store is cheaper than accessing indexes and tables to retrieve the data. This feature provides you with an additional access path that you can use to achieve high query performance.

Index

Get the eBook for only $5!

Why limit yourself?

Now you can take the weightless companion with you wherever you go and access your content on your PC, phone, tablet, or reader.

Since you've purchased this print book, we're happy to offer you the eBook in all 3 formats for just $5.

Convenient and fully searchable, the PDF version enables you to easily find and copy code—or perform examples by quickly toggling between instructions and applications. The MOBI format is ideal for your Kindle, while the ePUB can be utilized on a variety of mobile devices.

To learn more, go to www.apress.com/companion or contact support@apress.com.

Printed in the United States
By Bookmasters